JUDGMENT IN MANAGERIAL DECISION MAKING

WILEY SERIES IN MANAGEMENT

JUDGMENT IN MANAGERIAL DECISION MAKING

MAX H. BAZERMAN
Northwestern University

John Wiley & Sons
New York   Chichester   Brisbane   Toronto   Singapore

Library of Congress Cataloging in Publication Data:

Bazerman, Max H.
  Judgment in managerial decision making.

  (Wiley series in management, ISSN 0271-6046)
  Bibliography: p.
  Includes indexes.
  1. Decision-making. 2. Management. I. Title.
II. Series.
HD30.23.B38   1986   658.4'03   85-32332
ISBN 0-471-89629-2

Printed in the United States of America

10 9 8 7 6 5 4 3

To My Parents

PREFACE

Between 1981 and 1983, I was on the faculty in the Organizational Behavior Department at Boston University. At the time, I was working with Maggie Neale on several laboratory studies on decision biases in negotiation. The faculty at Boston University included a number of excellent researchers—Lloyd Baird, Dave Brown, Marty Charns, Tim Hall, Kathy Kram, and Phil Mirvis—and through frequent lunchtime conversations with them, I was inspired to write this book. I had a personal interest in the study of judgment and thought it would be helpful in management training if linked to organizational behavior. Perceiving a general unawareness of recent developments in the study of judgment, I wanted to present this information to managers, students, and the organizational behavior community in an interesting manner that would improve the judgment capabilities of the readers and outline a junction between the judgment and organizational literatures.

Organizational behaviorists have had a history of interest in the process of decision making. However, they lost interest in the area of decision making just when behavioral decision theory was emerging as a field of its own during the 1970s and 1980s. Behavioral decision theory has developed considerably over the last 15 years and can provide many insights on decision making that are relevant for managers and organizational behavior researchers. These descriptions, however, focus primarily on the individual making a single or related set of judgments at a single point in time. Organizational behavior research emphasizes the context of decisions when, for example, multiple decisions are needed across a period of time, decisions are made by groups, and so forth. This book joins behavioral decision theory with organizational behavior research in order to develop our understanding of judgment in organizational contexts.

The first three chapters of the book attempt to present behavioral decision theory in an interesting and accessible form. No claim is made that the material in these chapters is new. These chapters are meant to provide background for those unfamiliar with behavioral decision theory and to set the stage for the conceptual linkages that follow between specific areas of organizational behavior and behavioral decision theory. Those familiar with behavioral decision theory should feel free to move quickly through these chapters. The last six chapters show the power of behavioral decision theory to enhance decision making topics that have been recognized in organizational behavior.

The primary audiences for this book are managers, students, and organizational behavior researchers. At certain points, I made the decision concerning what to include and exclude based on a consideration of what I felt would be most useful to these audiences. However, I would hope that other audiences would also find the book helpful. Behavioral decision theorists might be interested in the potential of their literature as it expands and is integrated with another area of conceptual development. Other applied areas (e.g., marketing or accounting) might be interested in how the behavioral decision theory literature can be used in a more applied field. Finally, I have made every effort to make all the information in this book accessible to the knowledgeable layperson.

I have had the opportunity to collaborate with many fine colleagues who have influenced my understanding of judgment decision making. These individuals include Bob Atkin, Joel Brockner, John Carroll, Ed Conlon, Pete Fader, Toni Giuliano, Paul Goodman, Tim Hall, Tom Kochan, Roy Lewicki, Leigh McAlister, Jeff Rubin, and David Schoorman. In addition, my research has been influenced substantially through interdisciplinary research with Bill Samuelson and Hank Farber. Many of the ideas in this book were developed in joint research with Margaret Neale. Many others have been very helpful in the development of this book. I mentioned earlier my colleagues at Boston University who inspired the book. From 1983 to 1985, I was a member of the faculty at MIT, where Harry Katz, Tom Kochan, and Bob McKersie were constant sources of intellectual inspiration.

My research has been strongly influenced by the intellectual atmospheres at both the Sloan School of Management at MIT and the Organizational Behavior Department at Boston University. Much of the research reported was supported by a National Science Foundation grant (BSN8107331). The work of Carole Ferguson has been central to limiting the delay of the book. Her typing, editing, and organizing skills are exceptional.

Four individuals read every page of this manuscript and provided helpful feedback and support during the three years of its creation. These four wonderful people are John Carroll, Marla Felcher, Tim Hall, and Roy Lewicki. Each served a different and complementary role and each helped improve the quality of the final manuscript. Any errors and lack of judgment that remain are my own.

Max Bazerman

CONTENTS

ONE
INTRODUCTION TO MANAGERIAL DECISION MAKING

Robert Davis, head of the legal staff of a Fortune 500 company, has delayed making one of the most critical recommendations in the organization's history. The company is faced with a class action suit from a hostile group of consumers. Although the organization feels that it is innocent, it realizes that a court may not have the same perspective. The organization is expected to lose $50 million if the suit is lost in court. Davis perceives a 50 percent chance of losing the case in court. The organization, however, has the option of settling out of court by paying $25 million to the "injured" parties. Davis' senior staff has been collecting information and organizing the case for more than six months. It is time for action. What should Davis recommend?

Decisions of this importance are common, yet we understand very little about how managers and professionals make judgments. We know a great deal about using computers to integrate data and make routine decisions, but computers cannot make judgments concerning decisions for which the individual or organization has not yet established values and risk preferences. Establishing values and risk preferences requires human judgment. Thus, even computer-aided decisions typically have a significant judgmental component in the formation and interpretation stages.

If a computer cannot help Mr. Davis, how can we help him? We cannot tell Robert Davis the degree to which he should take risks. This is a value judgment. It does not have a right or a wrong answer. We can, however, demonstrate a number of biases that are likely to affect his decision. The knowledge of these biases can be used to make more objective decisions, in accordance with the value judgments of Robert Davis and his organization. This book addresses the need to improve managerial judgment by identifying judgmental biases and suggesting strategies for overcoming these biases.

Let us return to Robert Davis' dilemma. Research evidence suggests that *at least* two types of biases are likely to affect his recommendation. First, it is very possible that Robert Davis' senior staff is biased in believing in the innocence

1

of the firm. This response is common among cohesive groups (see Chapter 8). They may fall victim to "groupthink," believing their side is invulnerable to attacks from the "opposition." If this is the case, Mr. Davis may underestimate the likelihood of actually losing the case in court.

The way in which the problem is presented, or "framed," represents a second potential bias. Robert Davis may identify his situation as follows: (Option 1) Settle out of court and accept a sure *loss* of $25 million; or (Option 2) Go to court expecting a 50 percent probability of *no loss* and a 50 percent probability of a $50 million *loss*. Research suggests that individuals tend to take risks concerning choices framed in terms of possible losses (see Chapter 3). However, Robert Davis instead identifies his situation as follows: (Option 1a) Settling out of court and saving $25 million (that could additionally be lost in court); or (Option 2a) Going to court with the expectation of a 50 percent probability of saving the entire $50 million. This time the problem is viewed from a positive perspective—the amount of money saved if Davis made alternative recommendations. Research has also shown that individuals tend to *avoid* risks concerning choices framed in terms of possible gains (see Chapter 3). Yet both sets of choices are the same! Although the objective choices are the same, most (80+ percent) MBA students select Option 2 in the first situation (framed in terms of losses), whereas most (80+ percent) select Option 1a in the second situation (framed in terms of savings). We will cover the psychological explanation of this counterintuitive effect in great detail in Chapter 3. For now, it is sufficient to say that decision makers are systematically affected by the way in which information is presented.

How can this brief analysis help Robert Davis? It does not tell him what to do. It does not guarantee him that his recommendation will turn out to be optimal. Can it help him to make a good decision? If he understands judgmental biases influencing his behavior, he can begin to change his decision processes to reduce these biases. Robert Davis' problem is complicated, yet many of the decision principles that help identify his biases are quite simple. This book can help Robert Davis (and you) by examining biases that typically affect judgment. The first step on the road to improved judgment is the identification of the biases affecting *your* behavior. Once we get to Chapter 6, we will discuss additional steps on the road to improved managerial judgment.

Although most managerial decisions are not concerned with $50 million, situations that require careful judgment arise continually in our daily lives. Such judgment is a major component of managerial work at all levels of the corporate world and constitutes a critical human resource in any organization. Although a variety of decision aids (computers, decision trees, and such) are available, most important managerial decisions require a final decision or recommendation based on human judgment (some people might loosely refer to this as intuition). Thus, human values and preferences are at the core of the decision-making processes in all organizations. Many managers accept judgment as innate; "some people have it and others do not." This attitude can waste a lot of potential human resources in organizations. Judgment may be partially innate, but training can have a significant effect on the quality of managers' judgments.

ANATOMY OF A DECISION

Some scholars define judgment as the evaluation of a single option and choice as the selection between two or more options. This book will use the term *judgment* to refer to the cognitive aspects of both evaluation and selection in the decision-making process. This section is concerned with diagnosing the different components of the decision-making process that require judgment. These components are generalizable to a large number of decisions. Consider the following decision situations:

- You are finishing your MBA with a "major" in finance at a well-known school. Your credentials are quite good, and you expect to obtain numerous job offers. How are you going to select your job?
- You are the director of the marketing division of a rapidly expanding high technology company. You need to hire a new product manager for a new "secret" product that the company plans on introducing to the market in 15 months. How are you going to hire the appropriate individual?
- You are the director of the new products division of a large organization in the automobile supply industry. You have a number of product development proposals that meet your preliminary considerations, but only a limited budget with which to fund new projects. Which projects will you fund?
- You are the corporate manufacturing coordinator for a national consumer products organization. You are going to expand your production facilities by creating a new, highly efficient plant. Where are you going to locate the plant?
- You are on the corporate acquisition staff of a large conglomerate that is interested in acquiring a small to moderate size firm in the oil industry. What firm, if any, are you going to recommend that the company should seek to acquire?

What do these situations have in common? Each situation proposes a problem. Each problem has a number of possible alternative solutions. In each situation a great deal of uncertainty is associated with determining the optimal choice. With these scenarios in mind, let us look at six steps that implicitly or explicitly occur during the process of decision making.

1. *Define the problem.* The problem has been fairly well specified in each of the five scenarios. However, many times managers act without an understanding of the problem to be solved. When this occurs, the manager may solve the wrong problem. It requires accurate judgment to identify properly the precise problem needing a decision. Huber (1980) suggests that managers often err by (a) "defining the problem in terms of a proposed solution," (b) "focus[ing] on narrow, lower order goals"—missing the big problem, and (c) "diagnos[ing] the problem in terms of its symptoms"—we want to solve the problem, not just eliminate the temporary symptoms.

2. *Criteria identification.* Most decisions require the decision maker to accomplish more than one objective. In buying a car, you may want to maximize fuel economy, minimize cost, maximize comfort, and so on. The rational decision maker will accurately identify all relevant criteria in the decision process.

3. *Criteria weighting.* The criteria identified are of varying importance to a decision maker. The rational decision maker will know the value he/she puts on each of the criteria identified (e.g., the relative importance of fuel economy, cost, and comfort).

4. *Alternative generation.* The fourth step in the decision-making process requires identification of possible courses of action. An inappropriate amount of search time in seeking alternatives is the most common barrier to effective decision making. An optimal search continues until the cost of search outweighs the value of the added information.

5. *Rating each alternative on each criteria.* How well will each of the alternative solutions perform on each of the defined criteria? This is often the most difficult part of the decision process, because this is the stage that typically requires forecasting events. Again, the rational decision maker will be able accurately to assess the consequences of selecting each of the alternative solutions on each of the identified criteria.

6. *Computing the optimal decision.* Ideally, after the first five steps have been completed, computing the optimal decision would consist of multiplying the expected effectiveness times the weighting of each criterion times the rating of each criterion for each alternative solution; the solution with the highest expected value would be chosen. Unfortunately, this represents a very simplistic view of the decision-making process.

The economist's model of the rational man views the decision maker as following these six logical steps with perfect judgment (Friedman, 1957):

1. Perfectly defining the problem
2. Knowing *all* relevant alternatives
3. Identifying *all* criteria
4. Accurately weighting all the criteria according to his/her goals.
5. Accurately assessing each alternative on each criterion
6. Accurately calculating and choosing the alternative with the highest value

The critical examination of the accuracy of the economist's description is central to the purpose of this book.

BOUNDED RATIONALITY

The economic model provides a critical and necessary set of assumptions fundamental to the existing field of economics. Simon (1957; March and Simon, 1958), however, has suggested that the economic model is not a very accurate view of the actual decision processes of individuals. In his Nobel prize work, Simon suggested that individual judgment is bounded in its rationality and that we can better understand decision making by explaining actual, rather than normative ("what should be done"), decision processes. The *bounded rationality* concept provides a framework for questioning the historical assumptions of the rational model of the individual, and it provides a foundation for the study of deviations from rational judgment.

The concept of bounded rationality suggests the following deficiencies in decision making:

* Decision makers may lack information on (a) the definition of the problem, (b) alternatives, (c) criteria, and (d) the impact of choosing varying alternatives on the various criteria.
* Decision makers often have time and cost constraints that inhibit the search for full information.
* Imperfections of the decision maker's perceptions in obtaining information may effectively limit the quality of decisions. What the individual "sees" is what he/she will act on.
* Human decision makers can retain only a relatively small amount of information in their usable memory.
* Limitations of human intelligence constrain the ability of decision makers to "calculate" the optimal choice accurately, given the information that is available to the individual.

These deficiencies provide a useful categorization of the various ways that a particular decision may deviate from the economic view of rationality.

Although the concept of bounded rationality is important in clarifying that judgment deviates from rationality, it does not tell us *how* judgment will be biased. Thus, this concept may help decision makers identify situations where they may be acting on limited information, but it does not help diagnose the specific systematic, directional biases that affect our judgment. Fifteen years after the publication of Simon's work, Kahneman and Tversky (1972, 1973, 1979; Tversky and Kahneman, 1971, 1973, 1974, 1981) continued what March and Simon had begun. They provided critical information about specific systematic biases that influence human judgment. Their work, and the work that followed, elucidated the modern understanding of human judgment. Kahneman and Tversky suggested that people rely on a number of *heuristic principles,* or rules of thumb, in making decisions. In general, heuristics are useful shortcuts that usually produce good outcomes, but sometimes lead to serious errors. Identification and illustration of these heuristics and resulting biases in a managerial setting form a central theme of this book. We will use examples of a wide variety of individual heuristics and biases to explain how individuals deviate from a fully rational decision process.

INTRODUCTION TO JUDGMENTAL HEURISTICS

One theme running through this book is that individuals develop simplifying strategies that help them to make decisions with limited information and limited cognitive skills. The use of such simplifying strategies, or heuristics, serves as a mechanism for coping with complex situations. Is the use of heuristics rational? Consider the following example:

> Sarah Edwards is the director of product marketing for XYZ, Inc., a consumer goods organization. She needs to hire a new MBA for a position as an assistant brand manager. The position is very important because the brand is critical to a new strategic thrust for the organization. Edwards has always followed the heuristic of limiting her search for new MBAs to the top six management schools. How would you evaluate that strategy?

If the criterion for good decisions is proceeding according to the economic model outlined earlier, Edwards' heuristic will be deficient. Her search will not be complete. Furthermore, this heuristic may eliminate the best possible candidate from consideration. However, the heuristic also has some benefits. It simplifies the search, saving time and effort. In addition, it is likely to produce more good decisions than bad decisions. Thus, although the heuristic could eliminate the best choice, the expected time savings may outweigh the expected difference between a full search and Edwards' heuristic strategy. In fact, economists would argue that individuals use heuristics because the benefit that they obtain through the time savings of the heuristic outweigh the costs of the reduction in the quality of the decision outcome.

The author takes the arguments in favor of the use of heuristics very seriously. It is critical to realize that they provide time-pressured managers and other professionals with a simple way of dealing with a complex world, producing correct or partially correct judgments more often than not. In addition, it may be inevitable that human beings will adopt some way of simplifying decisions. If, however, we can make managers aware of the potential adverse impacts of using heuristics, they can then decide whether or not to accept their use of heuristics, and if it is to their advantage to eliminate certain heuristics from their cognitive repertoire.

The thrust of this book is to illustrate that these heuristics often lead to biased decisions and sometimes result in serious, systematic errors. Managers function in a complex domain that often requires simplification. One way to simplify the domain is to adopt heuristics when making decisions. This reduces the time needed to make decisions. Individuals adopt these heuristics without being aware of them, yet they perpetually affect our judgment. The misapplication of such heuristics, unfortunately, leads people astray in many situations.

People use a variety of types of heuristics. The poker player follows the heuristic "Never play for an inside straight." The mortgage banker follows the heuristic "People can only afford 35 percent of their income for house payments." However, our concern in this book is with generalizable cognitive heuristics that virtually all individuals use without being aware of their use. Tversky and Kahneman (1974) have identified three specific heuristics that will show up repeatedly throughout the book. These three heuristics are described here:

The Availability Heuristic. Managers assess the frequency, probability, or likely causes of an event by the degree to which instances or occurrences are readily "available" in memory (Tversky and Kahneman, 1973). The subordinate in close proximity to the manager's office will receive a more critical performance evaluation in the year-end review because the manager is more aware of the closer subordinate's errors (Strickland, 1958). The product manager bases her assessment of the probability of a new product's success on her recollection of the successes and failures of similar products during the recent past. This judgmental heuristic can be a very useful managerial decision strategy because instances of more frequent events are generally revealed more easily than instances of less frequent events. Consequently, this heuristic will typically lead to accurate judgment. *This heuristic is fallible, however, because availability of information is systematically affected by other factors uncorrelated with the objective frequency of the judged event.* These normatively irrelevant factors can inappropriately influence an event's immediate perceptual salience, the vividness with which it is revealed, or the ease with which it is imagined. Tversky and Kahneman (1974) have identified numerous specific biases resulting from reliance on the availability heuristic that will be discussed in Chapter 2.

The Representativeness Heuristic. Managers assess the likelihood of an occurrence by the similarity of that occurrence to the stereotype of a set of occurrences. As Nisbett and Ross (1980, p. 7) note, "A botanist assigns a plant to one species rather than another by using this judgment strategy. The plant is categorized as belonging to the species that its principle features most clearly resemble." In this case, representativeness is the best information available to the botanist. Managers also use the representativeness heuristic. They predict a person's performance based on the category of persons that the focal individual represents. This process can lead to a variety of types of discrimination. They predict the success of a new product based on the similarity of that product to successful and unsuccessful products. In some cases the use of the heuristic is a good first-cut approximation. In other cases it leads to behavior that many of us find morally reprehensible. In either case, a clear problem is that individuals tend to rely on such strategies, even when this information is insufficient to make an accurate judgment. In Chapter 2, several biases that result from the representativeness heuristic will be specified.

Anchoring and Adjustment. Managers make assessments by starting from an initial value and adjusting this initial value to yield a final decision. For example, managers make salary decisions by adjusting an employee's last year's salary. The initial value, or starting point, may be suggested from historical precedent (as is the case in the salary example), the formulation of the problem (does the problem presentation suggest an anchor?), or random information. Regardless of the basis of the initial value, adjustments from the initial value tend to be insufficient (Slovic and Lichtenstein, 1971; Tversky and Kahneman, 1974). Thus, different initial values yield different decisions, which are biased toward the initial values.

Three central heuristics guide our decision processes. Chapter 2 will identify a number of biases that emanate from these heuristics. Each of these heuristics, like many other heuristics, offers us efficiency in our decision processes. However, after you examine the biases that result from these heuristics in Chapter 2, you can decide whether to accept the status quo or to consider alternative judgment-improvement strategies.

A DESCRIPTIVE APPROACH
TO IMPROVING JUDGMENT

The scholarly field of decision making includes the work of psychologists, political scientists, statisticians, economists, anthropologists, mathematicians, and others. The broad term *decision scientist* has been used to refer to anyone applying scientific (systematic) methods to the process of decision making (Huber, 1980). Given such a broad spectrum of research approaches, it is critical to define the specific domain of this book.

The distinction between descriptive and prescriptive models is an important dichotomy in the area of decision making. Descriptive decision scientists are concerned with the way decisions are actually made, including those aspects of the decision process that inhibit effective decision making. Thus, descriptive decision analysis is concerned not with rational behavior, but with actual behavior. Prescriptive decision scientists, in contrast, are concerned with prescribing optimal decision making—how decisions "should" be made. For example, they might suggest a mathematical model to determine optimal responses for a particular set of business decisions.

This book uses primarily a descriptive approach, by identifying how you (the reader) and all other decision makers deviate from rationality in making actual decisions. Although there is much disagreement concerning the definition of rationality, there is general agreement that any definition of rationality should include some basic requirements of consistency and coherence (Tversky and Kahneman, 1981). Rationality will be used in this book to refer to the decision process that is logically expected to lead to the optimal result, given the decision maker's values and risk preferences. The following chapters will identify specific biases that *describe* your present decision processes. However, we will use prescriptive models to define how actual decisions should be made, independent of the biases presented throughout this book.

Why bother with a descriptive approach when prescriptive methods lead to theoretically optimal decisions? Many managerial situations do not allow the time or search expense necessary to maximize the quality of a decision. Individuals should spend more resources (including time) for more information only when the marginal improvement in the quality of the decision justifies the added costs associated with the gathering of additional information. Typically, the cost of added information rises as additional information is collected. The value of additional information, however, usually decreases as additional information is collected. This is graphically shown in Figure 1.1.

Consider your search for the best deal on a Toyota Corolla in a large metropolitan area (you have already made a number of judgments to get to this point). The cost curve rises slowly because visits to local Toyota dealers have low cost. In addition, the first two or three trips are very valuable in providing added information about the car (and possible "extras"), as well as expected price differences after negotiating with several dealers. When your search leads you to other dealers outside the metropolitan area, the cost continually rises while the value of the additional information (and potential price improvements over the *best* existing choice) decreases. There comes a point when the value of the additional information is insufficient to cover the costs of the added search. In terms of Figure 1.1, you want to stop the search at the point that you *judge* to maximize the zone between the cost curve and the value curve.

This analysis suggests that complete information will not always be available to the decision maker at any given decision point. In addition, anecdotal information suggests that even at the point of stopping the search, most individuals

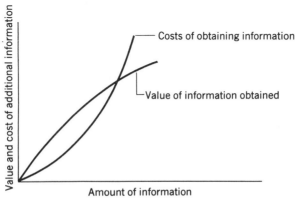

Figure 1.1 The value and cost of information obtained in search.

will *not* pull out a programmable calculator and follow a prescriptive method for buying a car. In fact, most significant decisions are eventually made by judgment, rather than by a defined prescriptive model. Even with the application of a prescriptive model, human judgment is necessary to define *and* provide relevant information to the decision process. Furthermore, many decisions do not fit into standard prescriptive frameworks. Many decisions are unique, the criterion for success is not known, and we lack sufficient ingredients for a full prescriptive analysis. Under these conditions, the manager is forced to rely on judgment. Because managerial *judgment* appears to be so critical, an attractive approach to improving decisions is to *describe* the biases that affect managers and to *prescribe* how these biases can be reduced.

This book further narrows its focus within descriptive approaches by addressing *judgment* in managerial decision making. A number of very good texts on managerial decision making include a significant treatment of descriptive issues (Harrison, 1981; Huber, 1980; Radford, 1981; Shull, Delbecq, and Cummings, 1970; Taylor, 1984, among others). However, these books cover the broad spectrum of the decision-making process (the environment of decisions, the sociology of decisions, when to use groups, implementing decisions, organizational decision making, and so on), giving limited attention to the topic of managerial judgment. Yet, because most managers do in fact spend a significant percentage of their efforts on making *judgments,* this book is an attempt to fill the gap left open.

GOALS OF THE BOOK

This book has a dual set of objectives. The first is to provide the reader with an integrated knowledge of literature that is relevant for describing managerial judgment. Early in the book, heavy emphasis will be placed on the behavioral decision theory literature. Later on, we will integrate the literatures on escalation of commitment to a previous course of action and creativity. Along with a discussion of improving decision making, this will provide a fairly comprehensive understanding on judgmental influences on individual decision making. The book will then extend this knowledge of individual judgment to managerial environments in which decisions must be made in the presence of cooperative/competitive others. Thus, this book attempts to integrate existing knowledge about judgment in individual, competitive, and group decision situations.

The second objective of this book is to improve the judgment of the reader. What can the book do to help improve Robert Davis's judgment? The first step for improving judgment is creating an awareness of what is wrong with intuitive judgment. We can make Davis aware of a number of biases that are likely to affect his decision. However, Lewin (1947) suggested that for a change in a system to occur and last over time, it is necessary to (1) get the system (e.g., a manager's decision processes) to "unfreeze" from existing processes, (2) change, and (3) create the conditions that allow the change to "refreeze," making the change part of the system's (manager's) standard repertoire. With-out unfreezing and refreezing, change is not expected to take place success-fully and last over time. Thus, any changes in Robert Davis's decision pro-cedures should be made in the context of Lewin's unfreeze–change–refreeze framework.

This book will attempt to unfreeze your present decision processes by dem-onstrating how *your* judgment deviates from rationality. Theory and demonstra-tions of biases will be provided to allow you to change your decision pro-cesses. The book is written in a style that the author hopes will motivate the reader to want to improve his/her judgment. The Lewinian change framework gives an initial structure within which judgmental improvement can be consid-ered. We will *not* make other specific suggestions for judgmental improvement in each chapter as the early chapters will only identify what is wrong with human intuition. Rather, Chapter 6 will provide an integrated discussion on how to use the information in the early chapters to improve managerial decision making.

AN OUTLINE OF THINGS TO COME

Nisbett and Ross (1980, pp. xi–xii) recently wrote

> One of philosophy's oldest paradoxes is the apparent contradiction between the greatest triumphs and the dramatic failures of the human mind. The same organism that routinely solves inferential problems too subtle and complex for the mightiest computers often makes errors in the simplest of judgments about everyday events. The errors, moreover, often seem traceable to violations of the same inferential rules that underlie people's most impressive successes. . . . How can any creature skilled enough to build and maintain complex organizations, or sophisticated enough to appreciate the nuances of social intercourse, be foolish enough to mouth racist cliches or spill its lifeblood in pointless wars?

Although Nisbett and Ross refer to the general population, the essence of their questions defines a fascinating issue for the field of managerial effectiveness. This book views managers as intelligent employees who have been generally successful, but whose decisions are biased in ways that seriously compromise their potential. My respect for managerial intuition should not inhibit attempts to eliminate biases when considerable room for improvement exists. The reader will see how habit has forced us into a set of hard-to-break heuristics, imposing constraints on our decision effectiveness.

Judgmental limitations can come from at least three sources: (1) emotions, (2) motivations, and (3) cognitions. Although all three areas are viable topics of inquiry, we are primarily concerned with cognitive judgmental errors. Given a motivated manager, unaffected by emotional limitations, what further con-straints limit decision effectiveness? With so many errors on the cognitive side,

Source: Nisbett and Ross, *Human Inferences: Strategies and Shortcomings of Social Judgment* (Prentice-Hall, 1980), pp. xi–xii.

we have plenty to do to cover this topic adequately. In addition, we are prejudiced in our belief that better cognitive decision making removes emotional and motivational barriers. That is, if one becomes a better cognitive decision maker, emotional barriers that inhibit decision making will break down as a result of the individual's increased confidence. Furthermore, motivation will increase because we tend to be more motivated when our ability allows for a high level of performance. Finally, the book will tangentially examine emotional and motivational limitations to the extent that they influence managerial cognition.

Before outlining the remainder of the book, it is critical to clarify its educational philosophy and role. I believe that before a manager's decision processes can be changed, that manager must be convinced that elements of his/her cognitive repertoire could use improvement (unfreezing). "Why should I change my existing decision processes when I have been so successful in my managerial career?" To respond to this very appropriate question, this book will include a number of experimential decision-making items to let the reader personally empathize with the biases discussed. Presenting this material to MBA and executive students in a classroom setting shows that many individuals are *initially* offended by being "tricked" by an "ivory-tower" academician. It might be helpful to clarify at the outset that the intent is not to insult, but to help identify and communicate biases that generally affect human judgment. Perhaps the reason for my personal interest in the material lies in my discomfort with the fact that such "evil" biases affect my own personal judgment. Consistent with this background, personally observed anecdotal evidence will be presented throughout.

Chapter 2. This chapter identifies and illustrates a number of biases that affect judgment. Quiz items and short scenarios demonstrate specific biases affecting the decision process and emphasize the prevalence of these biases. In this chapter we will look closely at the theoretical explanation for biases and apply it to managerial situations.

Chapter 3. Most management students are formally taught about the concept of risk in a microeconomics or statistics course. These courses typically treat risk from a normative perspective, by suggesting methods for making risky decisions. This chapter extends this normative perspective by examining the psychological factors that explain how managers deviate from "rationality" in dealing with risky decisions.

Chapter 4. There is much evidence suggesting that managerial decision makers who commit themselves to a particular course of action may make subsequent nonoptimal decisions to justify their previous commitment. This chapter will examine the research evidence and psychological explanation of this behavior. We will see how escalation has a significant effect in a variety of managerial domains, including new product development, bank loans, and performance appraisal.

Chapter 5. What is managerial creativity? Can you be more creative? These are central issues that are crucial to managerial success. This chapter identifies the components of managerial creativity and examines the role of earlier defined biases in limiting creativity. Specific recommendations are made for improving creativity.

Chapter 6. Although the entire book is concerned with improving managerial judgment, this chapter will clarify the steps necessary for the change in decision processes to be successful. Four alternative directions for improving judgment will be examined.

Chapter 7. The first six chapters deal strictly with individual judgment. This chapter also looks at the judgment of individuals, but within the context of two-party negotiation. That is, the focus will be on individual biases that occur when negotiating with at least one other decision maker. The resulting framework shows how consumers, managements, unions, salespersons, and society can simultaneously benefit from "debiasing" negotiators.

Chapter 8. This chapter looks at the judgment of individuals in multiparty organizational contexts. Specifically, this chapter examines the decision processes of individuals in the context of (1) third-party behavior in organizations, (2) coalition formation, (3) group decision making, and (4) competitive bidding. Although each of these domains has been explored by organizational researchers, past attention has ignored the critical role of judgment.

Chapter 9. The final chapter will briefly summarize some of the implications of the preceding chapters for the theoretical development of the literature on managerial decision making and the practical improvement of the decisions of managers. It is here that I will attempt to summarize the book's most important themes and emphases, as well as provide an indication of directions for future work.

TWO
BIASES

This chapter will use a number of quiz items to examine your judgments and to compare your judgment with others. The quiz items will be used to illustrate a number of ways in which judgment deviates from rationality. It is recommended that you now respond to the 13 items in Table 2.1, *before* reading the chapter. The presentation of items 3 through 13 will be repeated as the chapter is developed.

To begin the discussion of human judgment, examine your responses to quiz items 1 and 2. If your responses were "A" for each of the two problems, you may gain comfort in knowing that the majority of respondents also chose "A". If your responses were "B" for each of the two items, you are part of the minority. The minority, however, in this case, represents the more appropriate response. In the first problem, each of the corporations in Group B had greater sales volume in 1980 than any of the firms in Group A. In fact, the total sales for Group B is more than double the total sales for Group A. In the second problem, the student was actually a psychology major; but more important, selecting psychology as the student's major represents a more rational response based on the limited information provided.

The first problem illustrates the availability heuristic discussed in Chapter 1. In this problem, the first group contains consumer firms, whereas the second group consists of industrial firms and/or holding companies. Most of us have far greater experience with consumer firms; consequently, we can generate far more evidence about the size of these firms. If we were free from the availability heuristic, however, we would realize our differential exposure to this information and adjust our judgment accordingly.

By responding with the answer "Chinese studies" to the second question, the reader has fallen victim to the representativeness heuristic. Readers who responded "Chinese studies" most likely overlooked relevant *base-rate* information—the ratio of "Chinese studies" majors to "psychology" majors. Reconsider the problem realizing the probable ratio of "Chinese studies" versus "psychology" majors existing in the MBA student population. This reconsideration typically leads most individuals to change their response to "psychology" in view of the relative scarcity of "Chinese studies" majors seeking an MBA.

The purpose of quiz items 1 and 2 is to demonstrate that biased and faulty conclusions are often reached when decisions are made through the use of

Table 2.1 Chapter Quizzes

Respond to the following 13 quiz items before reading the chapter

Quiz Item 1: The following 10 corporations were ranked by *Fortune* magazine to be among the 500 largest U.S.-based firms according to sales volume for 1982:

Group A: American Motors, Wang Laboratories, Lever Brothers, Kellogg, Scott Paper
Group B: Coastal, Signal Companies, Dresser Industries, Agway, McDermott

Which group (A or B) had the largest total sales volume for the total of the five organizations listed?

Quiz Item 2: The best student in the author's introductory MBA class this past semester writes poetry, is rather shy, and is small in stature. What was the student's undergraduate major: (A) Chinese studies or (B) psychology?

Quiz Item 3: Which is riskier? (A) Driving a car on a 400-mile trip or (B) flying on a 400-mile commercial airline flight?

Quiz Item 4: Are there more words in the English language (A) that start with an "r" or (B) for which "r" is the third letter?

Quiz Item 5: Mark is finishing his MBA at a prestigious university. He is very interested in the arts and at one time considered a career as a musician. Is Mark more likely to take a job (A) in the management of the arts or (B) with a management consulting firm?

Quiz Item 6: Assume that two research groups sampled consumers on the driving performance of a 1986 Dodge Omni versus a 1986 Plymouth Horizon in a blind road test (the consumers did not know when they were driving the Omni or the Horizon). As you may know, these cars are identical; only the marketing varies. One research group (A) samples 66 consumers each day for 60 days (a large number of days to control for such factors as weather); the other research group (B) samples 22 consumers each for 50 days. Which consumer group would observe more days in which 60 percent or more of the consumers tested would prefer the Dodge Omni?

Quiz Item 7: You are about to hire a new central region sales director for the fifth time this year. You feel that the next director should work out reasonably well, because the last four were "lemons" and the odds favor hiring at least one good sales director in five tries. This thinking is (A) correct (B) incorrect.

Quiz Item 8: You are the sales forecaster for a department store chain with nine locations. The chain depends on you for quality projections of future sales in order to make decisions on staffing, advertising, information system developments, purchasing, renovation, and so on. All stores are similar in size and merchandise selection. The main difference in their sales occurs because of location and random fluctuations. Sales for 1985 were as follows:

Store	85	87
1	$12,000,000	_____
2	11,500,000	_____
3	11,000,000	_____
4	10,500,000	_____
5	10,000,000	_____

(*continued*)

Table 2.1 (*Continued*)

Store	85	87
6	9,500,000	_____
7	9,000,000	_____
8	8,500,000	_____
9	8,000,000	_____
TOTAL	90,000,000	99,000,000

Your economic forecasting service has convinced you that the best estimate of total sales increases between 1985 and 1987 is 10 percent (to 99,000,000). Your task is to predict 1987 sales for each store. Because your manager believes strongly in the economic forecasting service, it is imperative that your total sales are equal to $99,000,000.

Quiz Item 9: A newly hired engineer for a computer firm in the Boston metropolitan area has four years' experience and good all-around qualifications. When asked to estimate the starting salary for this employee, my secretary (knowing very little about the profession or the industry) guessed an annual salary of $17,000. What is your estimate?

Quiz Item 10: Which of the following appears most likely? Which appears second most likely?

A. Drawing a red marble from a bag containing 50 percent red marbles and 50 percent white marbles.

B. Drawing a red marble seven times in succession, with replacement (a selected marble is put back in the bag before the next marble is selected), from a bag containing 90 percent red marbles and 10 percent white marbles.

C. Drawing at least one red marble in seven tries, with replacement, from a bag containing 10 percent red marbles and 90 percent white marbles.

Quiz Item 11. Listed here are 10 uncertain quantities. Do not look up any information on these items. For each, write down your best estimate of the quantity. Next, put a lower and upper bound around your estimate, such that you are 98 percent confident that your range surrounds the actual quantity.

a. Mobil Oil's sales in 1980

b. IBM's assets in 1980

c. U.S. Steel's income in 1980

d. The number of U.S. industrial firms in 1980 with sales greater than Consolidated Papers

e. The U.S. gross national product in 1945

f. The amount of taxes collected by the U.S. Internal Revenue Service in 1970

g. The length (in feet) of the Chesapeake Bay Bridge–Tunnel

h. The area (in square miles) of Brazil

i. The size of the black population of San Francisco in 1970

j. The dollar value of Canadian exports of lumber in 1977

Table 2.1 (*Continued*)

Quiz Item 12: Linda is 31 years old, single, outspoken, and very bright. She majored in philosophy. As a student, she was deeply concerned with issues of discrimination and social justice and also participated in antinuclear demonstrations. Rank order the following seven descriptions in terms of the probability (likelihood) that they describe Linda:

A. Linda is a teacher in an elementary school.

B. Linda works in a bookstore and takes Yoga classes.

C. Linda is active in the feminist movement.

D. Linda is a psychiatric social worker.

E. Linda is a member of the League of Women Voters.

F. Linda is a bank teller.

G. Linda is an insurance salesperson.

H. Linda is a bank teller who is active in the feminist movement.

Quiz Item 13: It is claimed that when a particular analyst predicts a rise in the market, the market always rises. You are to check this claim. Examine the information available about the following four events (cards):

Card 1 Prediction: Favorable report	Card 2 Prediction: Unfavorable report	Card 3 Outcome: Rise in the market	Card 4 Outcome: Fall in the market

You currently see the predictions (cards 1 and 2) *or* outcomes (cards 3 and 4) associated with four events. You are seeing one side of a card. On the other side of cards 1 and 2 is the actual outcome, whereas on the other side of cards 3 and 4 is the prediction that the analyst made. Evidence about the claim is potentially available by turning over card(s). Which cards would you turn over for the *minimum* evidence that you need to check the analyst's claim? Circle the appropriate cards.

judgmental heuristics. This chapter uses such quiz items to develop an awareness of the impact of heuristics on your decisions and to develop an appreciation of the systematic errors emanating from overdependence on these judgmental heuristics. The biases examined in this chapter are all cognitive biases that are relevant to virtually all individuals. We do not focus on biases that are specific to special vocations or hobbies. The number of these remaining generalizable biases is large. Many of these biases are related to the three judgmental heuristics discussed in Chapter 1. This will be noted as we present the many biases. Finally, to help organize these biases, they are summarized in Table 2.2 at the end of the chapter.

To help you reduce the impact of such biases on your decisions, an attempt is made to "unfreeze" your decision-making patterns that employ these heuristics incorrectly. Unfreezing must occur in order to obtain the full benefit of understanding the limitations of judgmental heuristics. By working on numerous examples that demonstrate the failures of these heuristics, potential exists to reduce a number of biases in your decision making. In addition, for optimal effectiveness in improving your decision processes, it is suggested that you apply each of the defined biases to your own personal decisions. Finally, experience suggests that improvement in decision making occurs gradually through the practice of identifying biases in everyday life.

BIASES DUE TO THE RETRIEVABILITY OF INSTANCES (WHAT INFORMATION IS EASILY RECALLED?)

A buyer of women's wear for a leading department store is assessing the demand for footwear. She needs to choose between a proven best-selling brand of running shoes and a newer line of deck/boating shoes to fill the demand for casual wear shoes. The buyer recalls having seen a number of friends wearing the boating shoes at a party recently and concludes that the demand for the boating shoes has increased. She increases her order of the deck shoes and cuts back on the order size of the historically popular running shoes. Thus, she has biased her order based on limited data and the ease with which it came to mind.

Tversky and Kahneman (1974) argue that when the size of a class is judged by the *availability* of its instances, a class whose instances are easily retrieved will seem more numerous than a class of equal frequency whose instances are less retrievable. In this case, the demand for boat shoes is judged by the availability of the immediate recollection of friends wearing boating shoes at a recent party. She will be less likely to buy shoes worn by those of other subcultures with whom she tends not to socialize. Tversky and Kahneman note that individuals are, unfortunately, typically not aware of their biases.

Tversky and Kahneman cite experimental evidence of this bias, including one demonstration in which subjects were read a list of names of well-known personalities of both sexes and were asked to determine whether the list contained more names of men or women. Different lists were presented to two groups of subjects: one group received lists bearing names of women who were relatively more famous than men and the other group received lists bearing names of men who were relatively more famous than women. In each case, the subjects incorrectly judged the sex that had the more famous personalities to be the more numerous.

In the work setting, the availability heuristic is often employed to assess the probability or likelihood of an event occurring. A manager attempting to do a performance appraisal from memory often falls victim to the availability heuristic. Working from memory, the instances that are more easily retrievable from memory (either pro or con) will appear more numerous. General day-to-day performance that is less easily recalled is often insufficiently weighted in the performance appraisal process. Despite the personnel department's attempt to have managers assess the performance of employees in an unbiased manner throughout the year, managers continue to give more weight to performance during the three months prior to the evaluation than to the previous nine months of the evaluation period. The recentness of those three months biases the outcome of the performance appraisal system.

Quiz Item 3: Which is riskier: (A) Driving a car on a 400-mile trip or (B) flying on a 400-mile commercial airline flight?

Many people feel that flying in a commercial airplane is far riskier than driving a car. The safety record for flying, however, is far better than that for driving. This bias represents a special case of the influence of the retrievability of instances. This example demonstrates that a particularly *vivid* event will systematically influence the probability assigned to that event by an individual. This occurs because vivid events are more easily remembered and consequently more available when making a judgment. The sensationalism surrounding an airplane crash contributes to this perception. Excessive media attention enhances the salience of such events in memory. Similarly, this effect is observed when lottery enthusiasts flock to retail outlets where winning tickets recently have been sold. They believe that the likelihood of winning is greater because good fortune at this location is vivid in their recollection.

Extending this line of reasoning, Tversky and Kahneman (1974) suggest that by actually witnessing a burning house, the impact on one's subjective probability of such accidents is probably greater than the impact of reading about a fire in the local newspaper. The direct observation of such an event makes it more vivid to the decision maker. Similarly, Slovic, Lichtenstein, and Fischhoff (1979), in a paper covering the risks involved in the management of radioactive wastes, discuss the implications of the misuse of the availability heuristic on the perceived risks of nuclear power. They point out that any discussion of low-probability hazards, regardless of its content, will increase the memorability of those hazards and, hence, increase their perceived risks.

Many examples of this vividness bias can be observed in the decisions of managers in the workplace. The following came from the recent experience of an MBA student: To place an order, a purchasing agent must select only one of several possible suppliers. He chose the firm whose name is the most familiar to him. He later found that the salience of the name in his memory resulted from recent adverse publicity concerning the firm's extortion of funds from client companies!

Similarly, a corporate attorney has recently been involved in a product liability lawsuit that took many months of intense negotiation with government agencies, the plaintiff, and other outside interest groups before it was settled at a very high cost to the firm. That same attorney was hired by another firm for her expertise and has been asked by her new employer to assess the probability of product liability lawsuits being brought against the firm in the future. The attorney's deep involvement in the previous situation strongly biases her assessment of the probability of similar cases occurring in the future.

BIASES DUE TO THE EFFECTIVENESS OF A SEARCH SET (WHAT INFORMATION IS EASY TO FIND IN YOUR MEMORY?)

> ***Quiz Item 4:*** (From Tversky and Kahneman 1974) Are there more words in the English language (A) that start with an "r" or (B) for which "r" is the third letter?

If you responded "start with an 'r'," you have again joined the majority. Unfortunately, this is again the incorrect answer. Tversky and Kahneman explain that people typically resolve this question by first recalling words that begin with "r" (ran) and words that have an "r" as the third letter (bar). The difficulty of generating words in each of these two categories is then assessed. Because we tend to alphabetize words based on the first letter in the word, it is much easier to search for words that start with any particular letter than it is to generate words that have that letter in any other position in the word. Words that start with a particular letter are more available from memory. However, most consonants are more common in the third position than in the first (Tversky and Kahneman, 1973).

Just as our tendency to alphabetize affects our vocabulary search behavior, organizational modes affect information search behavior within our work lives. We structure organizations to provide order, but this same structure can lead to confusion if the presumed order is not always exactly as suggested. For example, many organizations have a Management Information Systems (MIS) division that has generalized expertise on computer applications. Assume you are a manager in a product division and need computer expertise. If that expertise exists within MIS, the organizational hierarchy will lead you to a solution. If they lack the expertise, yet it exists elsewhere in the organization, the existence of the hierarchy is likely to bias the effectiveness of your search set inappropriately. I am not arguing for the overthrow of organizational hierarchies. However, I am identifying the dysfunctional role of hierarchies in potentially biasing search behavior. If we are aware of the potential bias, we need not necessarily be affected by this limitation.

Consumers also may exhibit limited effectiveness in their search because of their expectations of the organizational world. Consider the J cars introduced by General Motors. These cars were compacts with a number of "extras." One of the divisions marketing J cars was Cadillac (Cimmaron). Cadillac has been the recognized General Motors premium dealer of very large cars. In addition, consumers do not normally think "Cadillac" when they think of compact cars, and they certainly do not think of a $15,000+ price tag when they think "compact car." One can only question whether part of the difficulty in marketing this car arose from the fact that Cadillac is not part of the search set of potential buyers of cars similar to the J car.

BIASES DUE TO ILLUSORY CORRELATION (WHEN WILL EVENTS BE FALSELY TIED TOGETHER IN OUR MINDS?)

Often, people fall victim to the availability bias in their assessment of the relationship between two items or events. Recently, a student recalling his high school basketball career cited the common belief among his white teammates that playing against a predominantly black team would mean sure defeat. Before going to a game against a black team, this team's main objective was to "psych themselves up to survive" the whole game, rather than win. In actuality, there was no relation between the race of the opposing players and the likelihood of winning.

Chapman and Chapman (1967) have noted that when the probability of two events co-occurring (e.g., playing a black team and losing) is judged by the availability of past co-occurring instances, the ability to generate former mutual occurrences is likely to result in an inappropriately high probability being assigned to the two events co-occurring in the future. Chapman and Chapman provided subjects with information concerning hypothetical mental patients. The information included a clinical diagnosis and a drawing of a person made by the patient. The subjects were asked to estimate the frequency with which each diagnosis (e.g., suspiciousness or paranoia) had been accompanied by various features of the drawing (e.g., peculiar eyes). The subjects markedly overestimated the frequency of co-occurrence of pairs commonly believed to exist by society, such as suspiciousness and peculiar eyes. Furthermore, conclusions based on illusory correlations have been found to be extremely resistant to change, even in the face of contradictory information. Chapman and Chapman found the effect to persist even when the actual correlation between symptom and diagnosis was negative. Finally, this effect also prevented the subjects from detecting relationships that were in fact present.

Consider the problem of determining whether marijuana use by teenagers is related to delinquency. Proper analysis would include four groups of observations: marijuana users who are delinquents, marijuana users who are not delinquents, delinquents that do not use marijuana, and nondelinquents who do not use marijuana. Most of the populace, however, would recall several delinquent marijuana users alone, the positive instance for the two events, inviting us into an illusion of correlation. Indeed, there are always at least four separate situations to be considered in assessing the association between two dichotomous events, but our everyday decision making commonly ignores this scientifically valid fact.

A lifetime of experience has led us to believe that, in general, instances of large classes of events are recalled better than instances of smaller classes. In addition, we have learned to believe that likely events will be easier to recall than unlikely events (Tversky and Kahneman, 1974). To respond to this learning, human beings have developed a procedure for estimating the likelihood of events (the availability heuristic). In many instances, this simplifying heuristic will lead to accurate, efficient judgments. It has been demonstrated, however, that the misuse of the availability heuristic can lead to systematic managerial judgment errors. This chapter has identified at least three categories of biases (retrievability of instances, effectiveness of the search set, and illusory correlation) that emanate from the use of the availability heuristic. I have attempted to alert you to common situations in which the misuse of this heuristic occurs.

INSENSITIVITY TO PRIOR PROBABILITY OF OUTCOMES

> *Quiz Item 5:* Mark is finishing his MBA at a prestigious university. He is very interested in the arts and at one time considered a career as a musician. Is Mark more likely to take a job (A) in the management of the arts or (B) with a management consulting firm?

How do people make this assessment? How did you decide on your answer? How should people make this assessment? According to the representativeness heuristic discussion in Chapter 1, people tend to analyze the degree to which Mark is representative of their image of individuals who take jobs in each of the two areas—and are likely to conclude "the management of the arts." In fact, most people respond "the management of the arts" to our specific quiz item.

What is wrong with this logic and response? By following the representativeness heuristic, you are overlooking or not fully incorporating relevant base-rate information. Reconsider the problem in light of the fact that a much larger number of MBAs take jobs in management consulting than in the management of the arts. This information should enter into any reasonable prediction of Mark's career path. When you combine the similarity information (between the description of Mark to prototypes of individuals taking each type of job) with the base-rate data, it is only reasonable to predict "management consulting," because far more management consultants are going to fit the specific description than are individuals in the management of the arts.

Judgmental biases of the type just illustrated may be due to the individuals cognitively asking the wrong question! Perhaps if you answered the "management of the arts," you were thinking in terms of the question "How likely is it that a person working in the management of the arts would have Mark's personal description?" when the actual question necessitates thinking about "How likely is it that someone fitting Mark's personal description will be in arts management?" Nisbett and Ross (1980) suggest that the representativeness heuristic incorrectly leads to a similar answer to both questions, because this heuristic leads individuals to compare the resemblance of the personal description and the career path. This judgmental distortion occurs as a result of the failure to consider base-rate data (i.e., the comparative probabilities of MBAs in management consulting versus arts management). These data are irrelevant to the first question given in this paragraph, but they are crucial to a reasonable prediction on the second question. Although a greater percentage of individuals in the management of arts may fit the personal description, there are undoubtedly a greater absolute number of management consultants fitting Mark's description—because of the relative preponderance of MBAs in management consulting.

An interesting aspect of the research done by Kahneman and Tversky (1972, 1973) is that subjects did use base-rate data correctly when no other information was provided. For example, in the absence of a personal description of Mark in Quiz Item 5, people will choose "management consulting" based on the past frequency of this career path for MBAs. Thus, people understand the relevance of base-rate information, but fail to use these data when similarity data are also available.

INSENSITIVITY TO SAMPLE SIZE

> ***Quiz Item 6:*** Assume that two research groups sampled consumers on the driving performance of a 1986 Dodge Omni versus a 1986 Plymouth Horizon in a blind road test (the consumers did not know when they were driving the Omni or the Horizon). As you may know, these cars are identical; only the marketing varies. One research group (A) samples 66 consumers each day for 60 days (a large number of days to control for such factors as weather); the other research group (B) samples 22 consumers each day for 50 days. Which consumer group would observe more days in which 60 percent or more of the consumers tested would prefer the Dodge Omni?

Most individuals expect consumer group A to find more evidence (days with a 60 percent preference) for the Dodge Omni, because of the larger number of sample days—there are 60 chances compared with 50. In contrast, simple statistics tells us that it is much more likely to observe a 60 percent preference on daily samples of 22 then on daily samples of 66, because a large sample is far less likely to stray from the expected preference for Dodge Omni (50 percent, because the cars are identical). Although this idea is fundamental in statistics, Tversky and Kahneman (1974, p. 1126) note that it "is evidently not part of the peoples' repertoire of intuitions." According to simple statistics, the reasonable answer to this quiz item is consumer group B (the interested reader can calculate this fact with the use of an introductory statistics book).

Why do most individuals use false logic and answer "consumer group A" to this quiz item? When responding to problems dealing with sampling, people often use the representativeness heuristic. They assess the likelihood of a possible result, for example, a 60 percent performance for the Dodge Omni, by the similarity of this result to the expected outcome (50 percent). This similarity measure does not depend on the size of the sample—which is critical to an accurate assessment of such problems. Without these relevant data, this quiz item reduces to the simple determination of which group tries more samples, which leads to an erroneous conclusion. This problem supports Tversky and Kahneman's (1974) initial demonstration that subjects fail to appreciate the role of sample size, even when such data were emphasized in the formulation of the problem. Their research asked:

> A certain town is served by two hospitals. In the larger hospital about 45 babies are born each day and in the smaller hospital about 15 babies are born each day. As you know, about 50 percent of all babies are boys. However, the exact percentage varies from day to day. Sometimes it may be higher than 50 percent sometimes lower.
>
> For a period of one year, each hospital recorded the days on which more than 60 percent of the babies born were boys. Which hospital do you think recorded more such days?
>
> The larger hospital (21)
> The smaller hospital (21)
> About the same (that is, within 5 percent of each other) (53)

The values in parentheses represent the number of individuals who chose each answer. As suggested earlier, sampling theory tells us that the expected number of days on which more than 60 percent of the babies are boys is much greater in the small hospital, because a large sample is less likely to stray from the mean. However, most subjects judged the probability to be the same in each hospital, effectively ignoring sample size.

Consider the implications of this bias for market research. People trained in market research recognize the need for a sizable sample. Nonetheless, they are often found to be victims of the representativeness bias. Given the characteristics of a population, they often expect that any subsample taken from the original sample population will accurately reflect the characteristics of the "parent" sample population. They ignore the size of the subsample.

Advertising agencies employ this bias to the advantage of their clients. "Four out of five dentists surveyed recommend sugarless gum for their patients who chew gum." There is no mention of the number of dentists involved in the survey; therefore the results of the survey are meaningless. If only 5 or 15 dentists were surveyed, the size of the sample might not generalize to the overall population of dentists.

MISCONCEPTIONS OF CHANCE

Quiz Item 7: You are about to hire a new central region sales director for the fifth time this year. You feel that the next director should work out reasonably well, because the last four were "lemons" and the odds favor hiring at least one good sales director in five tries. This thinking is (A) correct (B) incorrect.

Most people are comfortable with the logic presented here, or at least have been guilty of using similar logic in the past. However, the performance of the first four sales directors will not directly affect the performance of the fifth sales director—thus the logic is incorrect. Most individuals, however, rely on their intuition and the representativeness heuristic, which incorrectly tells us that a poor performance is unlikely because the probability of getting five "lemons" in a row is extremely low. Unfortunately, this logic ignores the fact that we have already witnessed four "lemons" (an unlikely occurrence) and that the performance of the fifth sales director is independent of the first four.

This question parallels Kahneman and Tversky's (1972) work in which they show that people expect that a sequence of random events will "look" random. They show that people believe the exact sequence of coin flips H–T–H–T–T–H to be more likely than H–H–H–T–T–T, which does not appear random, and also more likely than the sequence H–H–H–H–T–H, which does not represent the equal likelihood of heads and tails. Simple statistics, of course, tell us that each of these sequences is equally likely.

Kahneman and Tversky's (1972) work tells us about the independence of multiple random events. The "sales director" problem moves beyond dealing with random events in recognizing our inappropriate tendency to assume that random *and* nonrandom events will "balance out." Will the fifth sales director work out well? Maybe. You might spend more time and money on selection. The randomness of the hiring process may favor you this time. But your earlier failures on hiring sales directors will not directly affect the performance of the new sales director.

The logic concerning misconceptions of chance provides a process explanation of the gambler's fallacy. After holding bad cards on 10 hands of poker, the poker player believes that he/she is due for a good hand. After winning $1000 in the Pennsylvania State Lottery, an individual changes his regular number—after all, how likely is it that the same number would come up twice? Presumably, it is not representative of chance for the same number to occur twice. Tversky and Kahneman (1974) note that "Chance is commonly viewed as a self-correcting process in which a deviation in one direction induces a deviation in the opposite direction to restore the equilibrium. In fact, deviations are not corrected as a chance process unfolds, they are merely diluted."

Tversky and Kahneman's (1971) earlier work shows that misconceptions of chance are not limited to gamblers or laypersons. Research psychologists also fall victim to the "law of small numbers." They believe that small samples should be far more representative of the population from which they were drawn than simple statistics would dictate. The researchers put too much faith in the results of small samples and grossly overestimate the replicability of empirical findings. This suggests that the representativeness heuristic may be so well institutionalized in our decision processes that even scientific training with its emphasis on the proper use of statistics may not effectively eliminate its biasing influence.

REGRESSION TO THE MEAN (A LIMITATION IN PREDICTING THE FUTURE FROM THE PAST)

Quiz Item 8: You are the sales forecaster for a department store chain with nine locations. The chain depends on you for quality projections of future sales in order to make decisions on staffing, advertising, information system developments, purchasing, renovation, and so on. All stores are similar in size and merchandise selection. The main difference in their sales occurs because of location and random fluctuations. Sales for 1985 were as follows:

Store	85	87
1	$12,000,000	_____
2	11,500,000	_____
3	11,000,000	_____
4	10,500,000	_____
5	10,000,000	_____
6	9,500,000	_____
7	9,000,000	_____
8	8,500,000	_____
9	8,000,000	_____
TOTAL	90,000,000	99,000,000

Your economic forecasting service has convinced you that the best estimate of total sales increases between 1985 and 1987 is 10 percent (to 99,000,000). Your task is to predict 1987 sales for each store. Because your manager believes strongly in the economic forecasting service, it is imperative that your total sales are equal to $99,000,000.

Think about the processes involved in your decision. Consider the following logical pattern of thought: "The overall increase in sales is predicted to be 10 percent ($99,000,000 − $90,000,000)/($90,000,000). Lacking any other specific information on the stores, it makes sense simply to add 10 percent to each 1985 sales figure to predict 1987 sales. This means that I predict sales of $13,200,000 for store 1, sales of $12,650,000 for store 2, and so on. This logic, in fact, is the most common approach in responding to this task. Unfortunately, this logic is faulty.

Why is the logic faulty? Statistical analysis would dictate that we first assess the predicted relationship between 1985 and 1987 sales. This relationship, formally known as a correlation, can vary from total independence (1985 sales do not at all predict 1987 sales) to being perfectly correlated (1985 sales are a perfect predictor of 1987 sales). In the former case, the lack of a relationship between 1985 and 1987 sales would mean that knowing 1985 sales would provide absolutely no information about 1987 sales. Consequently, your best estimates of 1987 sales would be equal to total sales divided by the number of stores ($99,000,000 divided by 9 equals $11,000,000). However, in the latter case of perfect predictability between 1985 and 1987 sales, our initial logic of simply extrapolating 1985 performance by adding 10 percent to each store's performance would be completely accurate. Obviously, 1985 sales are most likely to be *partially predictive* of 1987 sales. Thus, the best prediction for store 1 should lie between $11,000,000 and $13,200,000, depending on how predictive you think 1985 sales will be in predicting 1987 sales. The key point is that in virtually all such predictions, you should expect the naive $13,200,000 estimate to regress toward the overall mean ($11,000,000).

Many effects regress to the mean. Brilliant students have somewhat disappointing siblings. Short parents tend to have somewhat taller children. Great rookies have mediocre second years (the "sophomore jinx"). Firms having outstanding profits in one year tend to have a somewhat disappointing subsequent year. In each case, individuals are commonly surprised by such predictable regression to the mean. Why is the regression to the mean concept (while statistically valid) counterintuitive? Kahneman and Tversky (1973) suggest that the representativeness heuristic accounts for this systematic bias in judgment. They argue that individuals typically violate the regression to the mean concept such that the prediction (e.g., 1987 sales) will be maximally representative of a predictor (e.g., 1985 sales)—this leads to the initially presented naive response.

In some unusual situations, individuals do intuitively expect a regression to the mean effect. In 1980, when George Brett batted .384, most people did not expect him to hit .384 the following year. When Wilt Chamberlain scored 100 points in a single game, most people did not expect him to score 100 points in his next game. When a historically 3.0 student got a 4.0 one semester, her friends did not expect a repeat performance the following semester. When a real estate agent sold five houses in one month (abnormally high), his co-agents did not expect similar performance in the following month. Why is regression to the mean not counterintuitive in these cases? In each of these cases, the performance is unusually extreme, and it appears that individuals expect unusual performance to regress. However, individuals generally do not recognize the regression effect in less extreme cases.

How do individuals respond when they do not follow the regression principle? Consider an employee with very high performance in one performance period. He (and his boss) may inappropriately expect similar performance in the next period. What happens when his performance regresses toward the mean? He (and his boss) begin to make excuses for not meeting expectations. Obviously, they are likely to develop false explanations and may inappropriately plan their future efforts.

Finally, consider Kahneman and Tversky's (1973) classic example where the misconceptions surrounding regression can lead to the overestimations of the effectiveness of punishment and the underestimation of the power of reward. In a discussion about flight training, experienced instructors noted that praise for an exceptionally smooth landing is typically followed by a poorer landing on the next try, whereas harsh criticism after a rough landing is usually followed by an improvement on the next try. The instructors concluded that verbal rewards are detrimental to learning, whereas verbal punishments are beneficial. Obviously, the tendency of performance to regress to the mean can account for the results. However, to the extent that the instructor is naive, he is likely to reach the false conclusion that using punishment is more effective in shaping behavior than is positive reinforcement.

This discussion concludes the examination of four biases (insensitivity to prior probability of outcomes, insensitivity to sample size, misconceptions of chance, and regression to the mean) that emanate from the use of the representativeness heuristic. Experience has taught us that the likelihood of an occurrence *is* related to the likelihood to the class of occurrences that the focal occurrence represents. Unfortunately, we tend to overuse this information in ways that impede our use of better information in making decisions. The biases identified show that the misuse of the representativeness heuristic can lead to significant errors in managerial decision making.

INSUFFICIENT ADJUSTMENT

> **Quiz Item 9:** A newly hired engineer for a computer firm in the Boston metropolitan area has four years' experience and good all-around qualifications. When asked to estimate the starting salary for this employee, my secretary (knowing very little about the profession or the industry) guessed an annual salary of $17,000. What is your estimate?

Was your answer affected by my secretary's response? Most people do not think that my secretary's response affected their response. However, reconsider how you would have responded if the question said that my secretary estimated $60,000. Individuals are affected by the fairly irrelevant information contained in my secretary's estimate. On average, individuals give higher salary estimates to the problem when the secretary's estimate is stated as $60,000, than when it is stated as $17,000. Why? People are found to make an estimate by starting from an initial (somewhat irrelevant) anchor that is provided and adjust it to yield a final answer. Slovic and Lichtenstein (1971) have provided conclusive evidence that such adjustments will typically be insufficient. Different starting points yield different answers, biased toward the initial anchoring. Tversky and Kahneman (1973) named this phenomenon *anchoring and adjustment.*

Salary negotiations represent a very common context for observing anchoring in the managerial world. It is very common for pay increases to come in the form of a percentage increase. For example, a firm may have an average increase of 8 percent, with increases for specific employees varying from 3 to 13 percent. Although society has led us to accept such systems as equitable, I argue that such a system falls victim to anchoring—which leads to substantial inequities. What happens if an employee has been *substantially* underpaid to begin with? The pay system described does not rectify past inequities, because a pay increase of 11 percent, for example, will probably keep that employee still underpaid. Rather, it accepts past inequities as an anchor, and makes inadequate adjustments from that point. Obviously, this would work in the employee's favor, had he/she been overpaid—inequity in the opposite direction. Similarly, it is common for an employer to ask a job applicant his/her current salary. Why? Does this figure tell the employer the true worth of the employee? We think not. Rather, the employer is searching for a value from which he/she can anchor an adjustment. If the employee is worth far more than his/her current salary, the anchoring and adjustment hypothesis would predict that the firm trying to hire the employee would make an offer below the employee's true value. For example, one large consumer goods organization is known to act in this way. Specifically, the personnel department is assigned the task of documenting the applicant's current salary. Then, as a company policy, any offer made to that employee is dictated to be 15 percent above his/her current salary.

There are numerous examples of the anchoring and adjustment phenomenon in everyday life.

- In education, children are tracked by a school system that may trap them into a certain level of performance at an early age. A child who is anchored in the "C" group may meet expectations of mediocre performance. Conversely, a child anchored in the "A" track may strive to meet expectations that will keep him/her in the "A" track.
- We all have fallen victim to the first-impression syndrome when meeting someone for the first time. Often, we place so much emphasis on that first impression that we do not adjust our opinion appropriately at a later date.
- Before 1973 to 1974, the speed limit on most interstate highways was 65 mph, with a normal cruising speed in the left-hand lane of 70 to 75 mph. This did not seem to be an extraordinarily unsafe speed to most people. After 1974, the speed limit was reduced to 55 mph. Currently, most people find a speed of 70 to 75 mph to be extremely unsafe—"something only crazy kids would do."

Tversky and Kahneman (1974) provide systematic, empirical evidence of the anchoring effect. For example, subjects estimated the percentage of African countries in the UN. For each subject, a *random* number (by an observed spin of a roulette wheel) was selected as a starting point. Subjects were asked to state whether the actual value of the quantity was higher or lower, and then to estimate that value of the quantity. Different groups were given different starting values (from the roulette wheel), and these *arbitrary* values had a substantial impact on estimates. For groups that received 10 countries and 65 countries as starting points, the median estimates were 25 and 45, respectively. Thus, even though the subjects were aware that the anchor was random and unrelated to the judgment task, the anchor had a dramatic effect on judgment. Interestingly, paying subjects for their accurancy did not reduce the magnitude of the anchoring effect.

Another example demonstrates the biased effect that a starting point, obtained from a partial calculation, has on a final estimate. Tversky and Kahneman (1974) asked high school students to estimate, within five seconds, a numerical expression written on the blackboard. One group was asked to estimate the product of $8 \times 7 \times 6 \times 5 \times 4 \times 3 \times 2 \times 1$, whereas the second group estimated the product of $1 \times 2 \times 3 \times 4 \times 5 \times 6 \times 7 \times 8$. To estimate quickly, a few steps of computation are performed and an estimate of the product is obtained through extrapolation or adjustment. Because adjustments are typically insufficient, this procedure should lead to underestimation. Because the result of the first few steps of multiplication is higher in the first expression, that expression should be judged greater than the second. These predictions were confirmed. The median estimate for the second sequence was 512, whereas the median for the first sequence was 2250. In fact, the correct answer is 40,320.

Joyce and Biddle (1981) have provided empirical support for the anchoring and adjustment effect on practicing auditors of the Big Eight accounting firms. Specifically, subjects in one condition were asked:

> It is well known that many cases of management fraud go undetected even when competent annual audits are performed. The reason, of course, is that Generally Accepted Auditing Standards are not designed specifically to detect executive-level management fraud. We are interested in obtaining an estimate from practicing auditors of the prevalence of executive-level management fraud as a first step in ascertaining the scope of the problem.
>
> **1.** Based on your audit experience, is the incidence of significant executive-level management fraud more than 10 in each 1000 firms (i.e., 1 percent) audited by Big Eight accounting firms?
>   **A.** Yes, more than 10 in each 1000 Big Eight clients have significant executive-level management fraud.
>   **B.** No, less than 10 in each 1000 Big Eight clients have significant executive-level management fraud.
> **2.** What is your estimate of the number of Big Eight clients per 1000 that have significant executive-level management fraud?
>   (Fill in the blank with the appropriate number.) _____ in each 1000 Big Eight clients have significant executive-level management fraud.

A second condition differed only in that subjects were asked whether the fraud incidence was more or less than 200 in each 1000 audited, rather than 10 in 1000. Subjects in the former condition on average estimated a fraud incidence of 16.52 per 1000 compared with an average estimated fraud incidence of 43.11 per 1000 in the second condition! Thus, auditors fell victim to the anchoring and adjustment as did Tversky and Kahneman's subjects.

Finally, Nisbett and Ross's (1980) work suggests that the anchoring and adjustment bias dictates that it will be very difficult to get *you* to change your decision strategies as a result of reading this book. They argue that each of the heuristics that we identify are currently serving as your cognitive anchors. They are central to your current judgmental processes. This means that any cognitive strategy that we suggest must be presented and understood in such a manner that you will break your existing cognitive anchors. Based on the evidence in this section, this should be a difficult challenge—but one that is important enough to be worth the effort!

CONJUNCTIVE AND DISJUNCTIVE EVENTS BIAS

Quiz Item 10: (Adapted from Bar-Hillel, 1973) Which of the following appears most likely? Which appears second most likely?

A. Drawing a red marble from a bag containing 50 percent red marbles and 50 percent white marbles.

B. Drawing a red marble seven times in succession, with replacement (a selected marble is put back in the bag before the next marble is selected), from a bag containing 90 percent red marbles and 10 percent white marbles.

C. Drawing at least one red marble in seven tries, with replacement, from a bag containing 10 percent red marbles and 90 percent white marbles.

The most common order of preferences is B–A–C. Interestingly, the correct order of likelihood is C (52 percent)–A (50 percent)–B (48 percent)—the exact opposite from the most common intuitive pattern! Why? This problem illustrates a general bias to overestimate the probability of conjunctive events and to underestimate the probability of disjunctive events (Tversky and Kahneman, 1974). Thus, when multiple events all need to occur (problem B), we overestimate the true likelihood, whereas if only one of many events needs to occur (problem C), we underestimate the true likelihood.

Tversky and Kahneman (1974) explain these effects in terms of anchoring. They argue that the probability of any one event (e.g., drawing one red marble) provides a natural anchor for the judgment of the total probability. Because adjustment from an anchor is typically insufficient, the perceived probability of choice B stays inappropriately close to .9, whereas the perceived probability of choice C stays inappropriately close to .1.

How is each of these biases manifested in an applied context? The overestimation of conjunctive events is a powerful explanation of the timing problems in multistage planning contexts. That is, many plans are of the type that for the plan to succeed every event in a sequence must occur. Consider the following:

- You are planning a construction project, which consists of five distinct components. Your schedule is tight, and every component must be on time in order to meet a contractual deadline. Will you meet this deadline?
- You are managing a consulting project that consists of six teams, each of which is analyzing a different alternative. The alternatives cannot be compared until all teams complete their portion. Will you meet a necessary deadline?
- After three years of study, doctoral students typically dramatically overestimate the likelihood of completing their dissertation within a year. At this stage, they typically can tell you how long each remaining component will take, with unshakable confidence. Why do they not finish in one year?

The underestimation of disjunctive events explains our surprise when an unlikely event occurs. As Tversky and Kahneman (1974) argue, "A complex system, such as a nuclear reactor or the human body, will malfunction if any of its essential components fails. Even when the likelihood of failure in each component is slight, the probability of an overall failure can be high if many components are involved." Tversky and Kahneman's discussion of complex systems is related to Perrow's (1984) arguments against nuclear reactors and DNA research. Perrow argues that we are significantly underestimating the likelihood of system failure because of our judgmental failure to realize the multitude of things that can go wrong in these incredibly complex and interactive systems.

The understanding of the underestimation of disjunctive events also has its positive side. Consider the following:

> It's Monday evening (10:00 P.M.). You get a phone call telling you that you must be at the Chicago office by 9:30 A.M. the next morning. You call all five airlines that have flights that get into Chicago by 9:00 A.M. Each has one flight, and all the flights are booked. When you ask for the probability of getting on each of the flights if you show up at the airport in the morning, you are disappointed to hear probabilities of 30, 25, 15, 20, and 25 percent. Consequently, you do not expect to get to Chicago in time.

In this case, the disjunctive bias leads you to expect the worst. In fact, if the probabilities given by the airlines are unbiased, there is a 73 percent chance of getting on one of the flights (assuming you can arrange to be at the right ticket counter at the right time)!

OVERCONFIDENCE

Quiz Item 11: Listed here are 10 uncertain quantities. Do not look up any information on these items. For each, write down your best estimate of the quantity. Next, put a lower and upper bound around your estimate, such that you are 98 percent confident that your range surrounds the actual quantity.

a. Mobil Oil's sales in 1980

b. IBM's assets in 1980

c. U.S. Steel's income in 1980

d. The number of U.S. industrial firms in 1980 with sales greater than Consolidated Papers

e. The U.S. gross national product in 1945

f. The amount of taxes collected by the U.S. Internal Revenue Service in 1970

g. The length (in feet) of the Chesapeake Bay Bridge–Tunnel

h. The area (in square miles) of Brazil

i. The size of the black population of San Francisco in 1970

j. The dollar value of Canadian exports of lumber in 1977

How many of your 10 ranges will actually surround the true quantities? If you set your ranges so that you were 98 percent confident, you should expect to surround approximately 9.8 (9 or 10) of the 10 quantities. Let us look at the correct answers: (a) $59,510,000,000; (b) $26,703,000,000; (c) $504,000,000; (d) 473; (e) $212,300,000,000; (f) $195,722,096,497; (g) 93,203; (h) 3,286,470; (i) 96,078; (j) $2,386,282,000. How many of your ranges actually surrounded the true quantities? If you surrounded 10 (or possibly 9), we can conclude that you were appropriately confident in your estimation ability. Most people, however, are overconfident and surround between 3 (30 percent) and 7 (70 percent), despite claiming a 98 percent confidence that each of the ranges will surround the true size of the quantity. Why? Most of us are inappropriately confident in our estimation abilities and do not accept the actual uncertainty that exists. In Alpert and Raiffa's (1969) initial demonstration, 42.6 percent of quantities fell outside ranges of 1000 observations (100 subjects on 10 items). Thus, substantial overconfidence is a common judgmental pattern. Furthermore, the format of questions in which the overconfidence bias has been demonstrated is varied and extensive.

The most well-established finding in the overconfidence literature is the tendency of people to be overconfident in answering questions of moderate to extreme difficulty (Fischhoff, Slovic, and Lichtenstein, 1977; Koriat, Lichtenstein, and Fischhoff, 1980; Lichtenstein and Fischhoff, 1977, 1980). Hazard and Peterson (1973) found the effect in the armed forces, whereas Cambridge and Shreckengost (1980) found extreme overconfidence in CIA agents. Finally, Fischhoff, Slovic, and Lichtenstein (1977) provide extreme evidence for the overconfident effect: Subjects who assigned odds of 1000:1 of being correct were correct only 81 to 88 percent of the times; for odds of 1,000,000:1, their answer were correct only 90 to 96 percent of the time!

Does overconfidence always exist? No, overconfidence is most common and extreme when subjects are more uncertain of the value of the quantity. That is, as the subject's knowledge of a question decreases, it does not suffi- ciently decrease their level of confidence (Nickerson and McGoldrick, 1965; Pitz, 1974). Subjects typically demonstrate no overconfidence, and often some underconfidence, to questions with which they are familiar. Thus, you should be most alert to overconfidence in areas outside your expertise.

Lichtenstein, Fischhoff, and Phillips (1982), in their review of the overconfi- dence literature, suggest two viable strategies for eliminating overconfidence. First, they suggest that giving people feedback about their overconfidence *based on their judgments* has demonstrated moderate success at reducing this bias. Second, Koriat, Lichtenstein, and Fischhoff (1980) found that getting people to think about why their answer might be wrong (or far off the mark) has the potential to decrease overconfidence by getting people to see contradic- tions in their judgment.

A large degree of controversy surrounds the social/cognitive explanation for why overconfidence exists (see Lichtenstein, Fischhoff, and Phillips, 1982, for an extensive discussion). Tversky and Kahneman (1974), however, explain overconfidence in terms of anchoring. Specifically, they argue that when indi- viduals set confidence ranges around their estimates, they adjust their esti- mate in each direction to achieve a certain level of confidence of capturing the actual value. According to a previous section, however, these adjustments will be insufficient. Thus, anchoring will result in an overly narrow confidence band.

Why should you eliminate your overconfidence? After all, it has given you the courage to attempt endeavors that stretched your abilities. Consider the following:

- You are a medical doctor and are considering performing a difficult opera- tion. The family of the patient needs to know the likelihood of the patient surviving the operation. You respond "95 percent." Are you guilty of mal- practice if you tend to be overconfident in your projections of survival?
- You work for the Nuclear Regulatory Commission and are 99.9 percent confi- dent that a reactor will not leak. Can we trust your confidence? If not, can we run the enormous risks of overconfidence in this domain?
- Your firm has been threatened with a multimillion dollar law suit. If you lose, your firm is out of business. You are 98 percent confident that the firm will not lose in court. Is this good enough to recommend rejecting an out-of-court settlement? Based on what you know now, are you still comfortable with your 98 percent estimate?
- You have developed a market plan for a new product. You are so confident in your plan that you have not developed any contingencies for early market failure. The plan of attack falls apart. Will your overconfidence wipe out any hope of expediting changes in the marketing strategy?

In each of these examples, the concluding question suggests a significant problem that results from the tendency to be overconfident. Thus, although confidence in your abilities is necessary for achievement in life, and perhaps to instill confidence in others, overconfidence may need to be monitored for effective decision making.

THE CONJUNCTION FALLACY

> ***Quiz Item 12:*** (Adapted from Tversky and Kahneman, 1983) Linda is 31 years old, single, outspoken, and very bright. She majored in philosophy. As a student she was deeply concerned with issues of discrimination and social justice and also participated in antinuclear demonstrations. Rank order the following seven descriptions in terms of the probability (likelihood) that they describe Linda:
>
> **A.** Linda is a teacher in an elementary school.
> **B.** Linda works in a bookstore and takes Yoga classes.
> **C.** Linda is active in the feminist movement.
> **D.** Linda is a psychiatric social worker.
> **E.** Linda is a member of the League of Women Voters.
> **F.** Linda is a bank teller.
> **G.** Linda is an insurance salesperson.
> **H.** Linda is a bank teller who is active in the feminist movement.

Examine your rank orderings of descriptions C, F, and H. Most people rank order C as more likely than H and H as more likely than F. The reason for this ordering is that C–H–F is the order of the degree to which the descriptions are *representative* of the short profile of Linda. The description of Linda was constructed by Tversky and Kahneman to be representative of an active feminist and unrepresentative of a bank teller. Recall that people make judgments according to the degree to which a description corresponds to a broader category. Linda's description is more representative of a feminist than of a feminist bank teller and is more representative of a feminist bank teller than of a bank teller. Thus, the representativeness heuristic accurately predicts that most individuals will rank order the items C–H–F.

Although the representativeness heuristic accurately predicts how individuals will respond, it also leads to another common, systematic distortion of human judgment—the *conjunction fallacy* (Tversky and Kahneman, 1983). This is illustrated by a reexamination of the potential descriptions of Linda. One of the simplest and most fundamental qualitative laws of probability is that a subset (e.g., being a bank teller and a feminist) cannot be more likely than a larger set that completely includes the subset (e.g., being a bank teller). That is, if Linda is a bank teller and a feminist, then Linda is a bank teller. In addition, there is some chance (although small) that Linda is a bank teller and is not a feminist. Based on this logic, a rational assessment of the likelihoods of Linda being depicted by the eight descriptions must include a more likely rank order for F than for H.

Although simple statistics can demonstrate that a conjunction (a combination of two or more descriptors) cannot be more probable than any one of its unique descriptors, the conjunction fallacy predicts and demonstrates that a conjunction will be judged intuitively to be more probable than a component descriptor when the conjunction is more representative than the component descriptor. The conjunction fallacy can also operate based on greater *availability* of the conjunction than one of the unique descriptors. For example, if the conjunction creates more intuitive matches with vivid events, acts, or people than does a component of the conjunction, then the conjunction is likely to be perceived falsely as more probable than the component.

Tversky and Kahneman (1983) have shown that the conjunction fallacy is likely to lead to deviations from rationality in the judgments of sporting events, criminal behavior, international relations, and medical judgments. The obvious concern (managerial or otherwise) is that if we make systematic deviations from rationality in the prediction of future outcomes, we will be less prepared for dealing with future events. For example, Tversky and Kahneman (1983) found experts (in July 1982) to evaluate the probability of

> a complete suspension of diplomatic relations between the USA and the Soviet Union, sometime in 1983.

as less likely than the probability of

> a Russian invasion of Poland, and a complete suspension of diplomatic relations between the USA and the Soviet Union, sometime in 1983.

As earlier demonstrated, *suspension* is necessarily more likely than *invasion and suspension*. However, a Russian invasion followed by a diplomatic crisis provides a more intuitively viable story than does (simply) a diplomatic crisis.

THE CONFIRMATION TRAP

Quiz Item 13: (Adapted from Einhorn and Hogarth, 1978) It is claimed that when a particular analyst predicts a rise in the market, the market always rises. You are to check this claim. Examine the information available about the following four events (cards):

Card 1	Card 2	Card 3	Card 4
Prediction:	Prediction:	Outcome:	Outcome:
Favorable report	Unfavorable report	Rise in the market	Fall in the market

You currently see the predictions (cards 1 and 2) *or* outcomes (cards 3 and 4) associated with four events. You are seeing one side of a card. On the other side of cards 1 and 2 is the actual outcome, whereas on the other side of cards 3 and 4 is the prediction that the analyst made. Evidence about the claim is potentially available by turning over card(s). Which cards would you turn over for the *minimum* evidence that you need to check the analyst's claim? Circle the appropriate cards.

Consider the following two (most) common responses: (1) "Card 1 (only)—that is the only card that I know has a favorable report and thus allows me to see if a favorable report is actually followed by a rise in the market" and (2) "Cards 1 and 3—card 1 serves as a direct test, whereas card 3 allows me to see if they made a favorable report when I know the market rose." Logical? Most people think that at least one of these two common responses is logical. Either strategy, however, demonstrates the tendency to search for confirming, rather than disconfirming, evidence. Einhorn and Hogarth (1978) argue that 1 and 4 is the correct answer to this quiz item. Why? Consider the following appropriate logic:

> Card 1 allows me to test the claim—a rise in the market will add confirming evidence, while a fall in the market will fully disconfirm the claim, since the claim is that the market will *always* rise following a favorable report. Card 2 has no relevant information, since the claim does not address unfavorable reports by the analyst. While Card 3 can add confirming evidence to Card 1, it provides no unique information since it cannot disconfirm the claim. That is, if an unfavorable report was made on Card 3, then the event is not addressed by the claim. Finally, Card 4 is critical. If it says favorable report on the other side, the claim is disconfirmed.

Card 4 allows potential disconfirmation of the hypothesis. Why do very few subjects select card 4? *Most of us seek confirmatory evidence and exclude the search for disconfirming information from our decision process.* This result was also observed by Einhorn and Hogarth (1978) on a sample of 23 statisticians. When that group responded to a problem very similar to the one just presented, 11 asked for card 1, 1 asked for card 1 or 3, 1 asked for any one card, 2 asked for either card 1 or 4, 3 asked for card 4 alone, and only 5 trained statisticians asked for cards 1 and 4.

Thus, this group tended to realize the worthlessness of card 3, but failed to realize the importance of card 4. The tendency to exclude disconfirming information in the search process is not eliminated by the formal scientific training that is expected of statisticians.

Although most of us seek only confirmatory evidence, it is typically not possible to know something to be true without checking for possible disconfirmation. If you chose cards 1 and 3, you may have obtained a wealth of confirmatory information, and thus were likely to fall into the confirmation trap and inappropriately accept the claim. However, if you searched for disconfirmation, you may find a favorable report under card 4 and completely reject the claim.

The initial demonstration of our tendency to ignore disconfirming information was provided in a series of projects by Wason (1960, 1968a,b). In the first study, Wason (1960) presented subjects with the three-number sequence 2–4–6. The subject's task was to discover the rule to which the three numbers conformed. To determine the rule, subjects were allowed to generate other sets of three numbers that the experimenter would classify as either conforming or not conforming to the rule. At any point, subjects could stop when they thought that they had discovered the rule. How would you approach this problem? Wason's rule was "any three ascending numbers." Solving the problem requires the accumulation of disconfirming rather than confirming evidence. For example, if you think the rule included "the difference between the first two numbers equaling the difference between the last two numbers" (a common expectation), you must try sequences that do *not* conform to this rule to find the actual rule. Trying the sequences 1–2–3, 10–15–20, 122–126–130, and so on will only lead you further into the confirmation trap. In Wason's (1960) experiment, only 6 out of 29 subjects found the correct rule the first time that they thought they knew the answer. Wason (1960, p. 139) concluded that obtaining the correct solution necessitates "a willingness to attempt to falsify hypotheses, and thus to test those intuitive ideas which so often carry the feeling of certitude."

It is easy to observe the confirmation trap in your decision processess. You make a tentative decision (e.g., to buy a new car, to hire a particular employee, to start research and development on a new product line). Do you search for data that supports your decision before making the final commitment? Most of us do. However, this section argues that the search for challenging, or disconfirming, evidence will provide the most useful insights. In confirming your decision to hire a particular employee, it is probably easy to find supporting positive information on the individual. In fact, the key issue may be the degree to which negative information on this individual as well as positive information on another potential applicant also exists.

HINDSIGHT

Consider the following scenarios:

- You are an avid football fan and you are watching a critical game in which your team is behind 35–31. With three seconds left, and the ball on the opponent's three-yard line, the quarterback *unsuccessfully* calls a pass play into the corner of the end zone. You immediately respond, "I knew that he shouldn't have called that play."

- You are riding in an unfamiliar area with your spouse driving. You approach an unmarked fork in the road, and your spouse decides to go to the right. Four miles and 15 minutes later, it is clear that you are lost. You blurt out, "I knew that you should have turned left at the fork."

- A manager that works for you hired a supervisor last year. You were well aware of the choices he had at the time and allowed him to choose the new employee. You have just received production data on every supervisor. The data on the recently hired supervisor are terrible. You call in the manager that did the hiring and claim, "There was plenty of evidence that he (the supervisor) was not the person for the job."
- As director of marketing in a consumer goods organization, you have just presented the results of an extensive six-month study on current consumer preferences for the products manufactured by your organization. After the conclusion of your presentation, a senior vice-president responds, "I don't know why we spend so much time and money to collect these data. I could have told you what the results were going to be."

Do you recognize yourself? Do you recognize someone else? Each scenario is representative of a phenomenon that has been named "the Monday morning quarterback syndrome" (Fischhoff, 1975b), "the knew-it-all-along effect" (Wood, 1978), "creeping determinism" (Fischhoff, 1975a,b, 1980), and "the hindsight bias" (Fischhoff, 1975a,b). This body of research demonstrates that people are typically not very good at recalling or reconstructing the way an uncertain situation appeared to a decision maker *before* finding out the results of a decision. What play would have you called? Did you really know that your spouse should have turned left? Was there really plenty of evidence that the selected supervisor was not the person for the job? Could the senior vice-president have predicted the results of the survey? Perhaps, but we tend to overestimate what we knew and distort our beliefs about what we knew beforehand by what we later found to be true. The phenomenon occurs when people look back on the judgment of others, as well as on their own.

Fischhoff has provided substantial evidence of the strength and prevalence of the hindsight effect (1975a,b, 1977; Fischhoff and Beyth, 1975; Slovic and Fischhoff, 1977). Fischhoff (1975a) examined the differences between hindsight and foresight in the context of judging historical instances. Subjects were assigned to one of five conditions: one without knowledge about the results to a set of questions (i.e., the foresight condition), and four who were told which of four alternative outcomes actually occurred (i.e., the hindsight subjects). For example, in one study, subjects were divided into five groups and asked to read a passage concerning the war between the British and Gurka forces in 1814. One group was not told the result of the war. The remaining four groups of subjects were told either that: (a) the British won; (b) the Gurkas won; (c) a military stalemate was reached with no peace settlement; or (d) a military stalemate was reached with a peace settlement. Obviously, only one group was told the truthful outcome—(a) in this case. Each subject was then asked what their subjective assessments of the probability of each of the outcomes would have been without the benefit of knowing the resulting outcome. Based on numerous and varied examples, the strong, consistent finding is that knowledge of an outcome increases an individual's belief about the degree to which they would have predicted that outcome without the benefit of outcome knowledge.

A number of explanations of the hindsight effect have been offered. Perhaps the most pervasive is to explain hindsight in terms of the heuristics earlier identified in this chapter (Tversky and Kahneman, 1974). Anchoring may occur because individuals interpret their apriori (initial) subjective probability of each event occurring in reference to the anchor of knowing whether or not that outcome actually occurred. For example, in the experiment described in the previous paragraph, if subjects that were told that "the British won" did not know how they would have assessed the probabilities without the benefit of outcome information, an alternative estimating procedure would be to assign the known probabilities (1.0 to "the British won," 0 to all other events) and then adjust according to their true lack of foresight knowledge of the event. Because adjustments are known to be typically inadequate, your hindsight knowledge can be expected to influence your perception of what you knew in foresight. Furthermore, to the extent that the various pieces of data on the event vary in terms of their support for the actual outcome, evidence that is consistent with the known outcome may become cognitively more salient and thus more *available* in memory (Slovic and Fischhoff, 1977). This will lead you to justify your claimed foresight in view "of the facts provided." Finally, the relevance of a particular piece of data may be judged important to the extent to which it is *representative* of the observed outcome.

Claiming that what has happened was predictable based on foresight knowledge puts us in a position of using hindsight to criticize another's foresight judgment. In the short run, hindsight has a number of advantages. It is very flattering to believe that your judgment is far better than it actually is! However, hindsight reduces our ability to learn from the past and to evaluate objectively the decisions of others. Leading researchers in performance evaluation (see Feldman, 1981) and decision theory (see Einhorn and Hogarth, 1981) have argued that, where possible, individuals should be rewarded based on the process and logic of their decisions, not the results. That is, if a decision maker makes a high-quality decision that does not work out, he/she should be rewarded, not punished. The rationale for this argument is that the results are affected by a variety of factors outside the direct control of the decision maker. However, to the extent that we use hindsight, we will inappropriately evaluate the logic used by the decision maker and will actually make our evaluations based on the outcomes that occurred.

INTEGRATION AND COMMENTARY

Heuristics, or rules of thumb, are the cognitive tools we use to simplify the decision-making process. The preceding pages have described the mental pitfalls or biases that result from using judgmental heuristics. Although the use of quiz items has emphasized the biases that result from heuristics, it should be vehemently stressed that the use of these heuristics results in far more adequate than inadequate decisions. For example, the representativeness heuristic will typically lead to the correct classification of an event or object. There exists a rationale for the categorization systems that we have developed. However, the representativeness heuristic may lead us to overlook data that should normatively affect judgment. Furthermore, people typically fail to distinguish between legitimate and illegitimate uses of these heuristics.

To emphasize the distinction between the legitimate and illegitimate uses of heuristics, reconsider quiz item 6. In that question, subjects tend to think Mark is more likely to take a job in the "management of the arts," despite the fact that the commonality of the two career paths overwhelmingly favors "management consulting." The representativeness heuristic, in this case, prevents us from appropriately incorporating the relevant base-rate data. If, however, the choice of "management consulting" was replaced with another uncommon career path for an MBA from a prestigious university (e.g., management in the steel industry), then the representativeness is likely to lead us to an accurate prediction. That is, when base-rate data are unavailable or irrelevant (the choices have the same base rate), the representativeness heuristic provides a reasonably good cognitive tool in matching Mark to a career path (management of the arts) that uses his special interests and skills. The key to improved judgment, therefore, may lie in identifying the inappropriate uses of heuristics. This chapter provides a start.

A second argument favoring the use of heuristics is that people develop them because the loss in quality of decisions is outweighed by the time saved by the decision maker. This argument is a strong one. It allows you to justify your past and future use of heuristics. Furthermore, there are undoubtedly many cases where this evaluation is accurate. However, this author strongly argues against the blanket acceptance of this explanation of the use of heuristics. First, there are many instances in which the loss in the quality of decisions far outweighs the time saved by the use of the heuristics. Second, the logic in this argument suggests that we have voluntarily accepted these heuristics. We have not—most of us have been unaware of their existence. When people are aware of the biases that affect them, they reject this "time-saved" argument and have a strong belief (coupled with high intrinsic motivation) that it is worth the effort to try to eliminate the biasing components of these heuristics.

This book's examination of biases and heuristics does not end here. In fact, we will continue to examine biases and heuristics in the areas of risk, the escalation of commitment, and creativity in the next three chapters. Toward the end of the book we will examine how heuristics affect negotiated resolutions and other multiparty contexts.

Table 2.2 Summary Descriptions of Biases Presented in Chapter 2

Bias	Description
1. Biases due to the retrievability of instances	Individuals judge instances that are more easily retrieved from memory to be more numerous than a class of equal frequency whose instances are less retrievable. Emanates from the availability heuristic.
2. Biases due to the effectiveness of a search set	Individuals are biased in their assessments of the frequency of events based on how the structure of memory (e.g., alphabetical) affects the search process. Emanates from the availability heuristic.
3. Biases due to illusory correlation	Individuals tend to overestimate the probability of two events co-occurring when they generate former mutual occurrence of the two events. Emanates from the availability heuristic.
4. Insensitivity to prior probability of outcomes	Individuals tend to ignore prior probabilities, or base rates, when any (even worthless) representative information is provided. Emanates from the representativeness heuristic.
5. Insensitivity to sample size	Individuals fail to appreciate the role of sample size in evaluating the accuracy of sample information. Emanates from the representativeness heuristic.
6. Misconceptions of chance	Individuals expect that a sequence of events generated from a random process will represent the essential characteristics of that process, even when the sequence is too short for that expectation to be valid statistically. Emanates from the representativeness heuristic.
7. Regression to the mean	Individuals fail to incorporate the statistical fact that extreme events tend to regress to the mean on subsequent trials. Emanates from the representativeness heuristic.
8. Insufficient adjustment	Individuals make estimates from an initial value (based on past events, random assignment, or whatever else is accessible) and make *insufficient* adjustments from that anchor.
9. Conjunctive and disjunctive events bias	Individuals tend to overestimate the probability of conjunctive events and to underestimate the probability of disjunctive events.
10. Overconfidence	Individuals tend to be overconfident in their fallible judgment when answering moderately to extremely difficult questions.

Table 2.2 (*Continued*)

Bias	Description
11. The conjunction fallacy	Individuals judge falsely that conjunctions are more probable than a more global category, of which the conjunction is a subset, when the conjunction is more representative or available than the more global category.
12. The confirmation trap	Individuals tend to seek confirmatory information for what they think is true and exclude disconfirming information from their search process.
13. Hindsight	After finding out whether or not an event occurred, individuals tend to overestimate the degree to which they would have predicted the event without the benefit of outcome knowledge.

THREE
JUDGMENT UNDER UNCERTAINTY

If you were to arrive at your desk next Monday morning and say to yourself, "I am going to be a better managerial risk taker," what would you mean? Would you take fewer risks? Would you take more risks? The answer to the last two questions for most people is "no." Yet, somehow you want to make better decisions when faced with risky situations. This chapter seeks to assist you in becoming a better decision maker by (1) helping you understand the nature of uncertainty[1] in the decision-making process; (2) demonstrating how judgment concerning risky decisions deviates from rationality; and (3) illustrating some simple normative tools for making decisions under uncertainty.

Many risky decisions are crucial, involving such issues as jobs, survival, safety, product viability, and organizational existence. This chapter will show how subtle aspects of the presentation and description of information can significantly affect decisions. Given the importance of risky decisions, it is critical to understand the limits that restrict the ways in which individuals formulate problems. Risk is treated as a separate topic in this book because of evidence that risk intuition deviates from rationality *and* that managers do not typically appreciate the nature of uncertainty.

Consider the following:

- A tough-minded executive has a reputation for rewarding "results." This sounds typical of corporate behavior and is commonly viewed as a positive managerial attribute.
- Edmund S. Muskie, a candidate in the 1972 presidential election, stated that what this country needed was a one-armed economist. When asked why, he responded that he was tired of economists who said "On the one hand . . . , but on the other hand . . . ."
- When budget crises hit an organization, a common response is to cut out

---

[1]Some scholars argue for a conceptual distinction between risk and uncertainty. For example, some argue that risks are associated with clear probabilities and uncertainty is associated with not knowing the probability of an event. Others argue that uncertainty does not eliminate the fact that we have a best estimate of the probability of an event. These scholars argue that risk and uncertainty are the same thing. This chapter treats the two terms as synonymous.

expenditures that are not expected to increase immediate productivity (e.g., organizational development). This administrative response reflects the belief that money should be allocated only to expenses that are sure to lead to increased short-term profit and productivity.

What is the common element in these scenarios? In each case, the decision maker(s) is grasping for certainty in an uncertain world. They want to know what *will* happen, not what may happen. Unfortunately, many problems cannot be answered with certainty. Managers are constantly faced with decisions concerning uncertain outcomes. When a manager makes an excellent decision (based on an objective analysis of the data available), and it does not work out, should the manager be rewarded or punished? The tough-minded executive would punish the manager. I disagree with the executive! When an economist provides an excellent forecast, specifying the factors that will influence GNP (gross national product), should she be rewarded for incorporating the uncertainties affecting GNP or punished for not providing a single GNP forecast? Muskie, displeased with "two-armed economists," would be displeased with her report. I disagree with Muskie! When a manager develops an excellent long-run plan for responding to a budget crisis, should the plan be abandoned because the manager admits that there is a very real possibility of failure? It seems that the administration would favor abandonment. Again, I disagree! Virtually any plan will have a great deal of uncertainty, regardless of whether the planner admits the risk.

Most of us fail to accept the fact that many decisions must be made in the face of uncertainty. This means that even the best of decisions (in terms of process) may turn out poorly (in terms of outcome). This chapter seeks to provide managers with an understanding of risk that will enhance their ability to make and evaluate decisions. Perhaps if one understands the nature of a risky decision, one is more likely to evaluate based on the quality of the decision process rather than on the uncertain consequences.

This chapter starts by presenting a normative overview of risk taking. The second part and core of this chapter identifies the systematic ways in which risky judgment is biased. This section introduces *prospect theory,* which is the most comprehensive descriptive theory of how we make risky decisions. The remainder of the chapter briefly examines individual variation in risk taking, risk taking in organizations, and the determination of an "acceptable" risk level.

A NORMATIVE BACKGROUND TO RISK

Although this book is primarily descriptive, it is important to consider some basic normative concepts for two reasons. First, a normative framework will provide some order with which to organize risky decisions. We know that individuals are typically neither rational nor consistent in making judgments under conditions of uncertainty. It is for this reason that it is useful to outline the rational structuring of risky problems. Also, a normative framework provides a background for the illustration of systematic deviations from rationality as the chapter progresses. Readers with some background in statistics and economics may find this section trivial, whereas others will find it necessary for understanding the material that follows.

Going back to Chapter 1, you will recall that a rational decision process includes: (1) specifying the problem, (2) identifying all criteria, (3) weighting criteria, (4) identifying all alternatives, (5) rating alternatives on each criterion, and (6) choosing the optimal alternative. Up until this point, however, the rational model has not told us how to rate alternatives when the outcome on a particular factor is uncertain. Also, it has not yet provided rules for determining the optimal alternative under uncertainty. These are central topics in a normative theory of risk preference. To present a normative background to risk, we need to begin by introducing two concepts: probability and expected value.

Probability The probability concept conveys the likelihood that any particular outcome will occur in a statistical sense. For example, assume that you flipped four quarters (A, B, C, D). The possible combinations of *equally likely* outcomes can be represented by the following 16 events:

Event	A	B	C	D	Event	A	B	C	D
1.	T	T	T	T	9.	T	H	H	T
2.	T	T	T	H	10.	H	T	H	T
3.	T	T	H	T	11.	H	H	T	T
4.	T	H	T	T	12.	H	H	H	T
5.	H	T	T	T	13.	H	H	T	H
6.	T	T	H	H	14.	H	T	H	H
7.	T	H	T	H	15.	T	H	H	H
8.	H	T	T	H	16.	H	H	H	H

Based on the specification of all possible outcomes, it is possible to observe the probability of various events. For example, the probability of "two or more heads" appearing would be equal to (all events 6 through 16) 11/16. Or the probability of getting "exactly two heads" would be equal to (all events 6 through 11) 6/16.

This presentation treats probability in a very simple way. In contrast, probability can be very complex, both mathematically and psychologically. For example, it is very difficult to assess the probability of the prime rate falling below 10 percent by the end of 1990. Why? We are now forecasting the future, without being able to specify the likelihood of all possible outcomes. Unfortunately, most real decisions (excluding the worlds of gambling, cards, games, and such) take this more complex form.

Expected Value The expected value of an alternative weights all possible outcomes of that alternative by the probability of the associated outcome. For example, if we were going to calculate the expected value of the number of heads occurring from four flips of a coin (the answer is obviously two), we would weight all possible number of heads of their likelihood of occurrence (see the combinations given earlier):

Expected value = (1/16)(0) + (4/16)(1) + (6/16)(2) + (4/16)(3) + (1/16)(4) = 2.

Again, the actual calculation of expected value becomes more complicated when we cannot specify the objective likelihood of all possible outcomes. For example, in assessing the subjective expected value of your salary 18 months from now, you will have to assess the likelihood of holding various positions and assess the expected pay for each of the possible positions. As problems become more complex, this assessment can become very demanding and biased.

One simple rule for making decisions is to always select the alternative with the highest expected value. The argument for an expected value decision rule is that in the long run decisions made according to this rule will, in the aggregate, be optimal: good and bad random errors will cancel out over time. Sounds rational! However, consider the following scenarios:

- You can (A) have $10 million for sure (expected value = $10 million) or (B) flip an honest coin where you get $22 million if a heads occurs, but get nothing if a tails occurs (expected value = $11 million). An expected value decision rule would pick B. What would you do?
- You are being sued for $5000 and estimate a 50 percent chance of losing the case (expected value = − $2500). The other side, however, is willing to accept an out-of-court settlement of $2400 (expected value = − $2400). Ignoring attorney fees, court costs, aggravation, and such, would you (A) fight the case or (B) settle out of court? An expected value decision rule would lead you to settle out of court.

Most people would take A in both cases. This suggests that a number of situations exist in which people do not follow an expected value rule. To understand when and how people deviate from expected value brings the concept of risk into the problem.

The final prerequisite to the discussion of risk is the concept of *certainty equivalent*. A certainty equivalent establishes the certain value that would make a decision maker indifferent when deciding between an uncertain event and that certain value. For example, if you had an opportunity to accept a 50 percent chance of obtaining $1 million, what would be the certain amount that would make you indifferent between the 50 percent chance of $1 million and that amount? $100,000? $300,000? This is your certainty equivalent to a 50 percent chance of $1 million. For most people, this amount is far less than the expected value of $500,000. Returning to Robert Davis's dilemma in Chapter 1, before engaging in any negotiation concerning the amount of an out-of-court settlement, he may want to assess the amount that would make him indifferent between that payment and a 50 percent chance of paying the $50 million. That amount is defined as his certainty equivalent.

An individual who has a certainty equivalent for an uncertain event that is equal to the expected value of the uncertain payoff is *risk-neutral* with regards to that decision. For example, if your certainty equivalent in the preceding paragraph was $500,000, you would be risk-neutral concerning that choice. Thus, risk-neutrality is synonymous with using an expected value decision rule. An individual with a certainty equivalent for an uncertain event that is less than the expected value of that uncertain payoff is *risk-averse* with regards to that decision. That is, if your certainty equivalent in the problem was $400,000, you are risk-averse, because you are willing to take an expected value reduction of $100,000 to avoid the risk associated with the uncertain event.

Although unlikely in this context, an individual with a certainty equivalent for an uncertain event that is more than the expected value for that uncertain payoff is *risk-seeking* with regards to that decision. That is, if your certainty equivalent was $550,000, you are risk-seeking, because you are demanding an extra expected value of $50,000 to forgo the risk—you seek risk, holding expected value constant.

When decision makers are risk-averse or risk-seeking, they may make decisions that exclude maximizing expected value. To explain departures from an expected value decision rule, Daniel Bernoulli first suggested replacing the criteria of expected monetary value with the criteria of expected utility in 1738. Expected utility theory suggests that each level of an outcome is associated with a degree of pleasure (utility). The utility of an uncertain choice is the weighted sum of the utilities of its outcomes, each multiplied by its probability (Kahneman and Tversky, 1982). Although an expected value approach to decision making would treat $1 million as being worth twice as much as $500,000, a gain of $1 million does *not* necessarily create twice as much utility as a gain of $500,000. That is, most individuals would not obtain as much benefit from the second $500,000 as they did from the first $500,000. Under expected utility theory, the decision maker is predicted to select the option with the highest expected utility, regardless of whether that choice has the highest expected value.

According to expected utility theory, individuals identify outcomes in terms of the overall amount of assets (wealth state) they will have as a result of the choice. That is, we are posited to evaluate a choice between two (or more) options in terms of the subjective expected utility of our total wealth state as a result of making each of the two (or more) possible choices. As we will see in the next section, Kahneman and Tversky's (1979) prospect theory refutes this aspect of expected utility theory.

Researchers have identified a number of descriptive generalizations concerning when risk-neutrality, risk-aversion, and risk-seeking are most likely to be observed:

1. *Individuals typically approximate risk-neutrality for "small" gambles* (Holloway, 1979). For example, small purchase decisions are usually made in terms of expected value. Although defining "small" is a difficult task, its definition is clearly dependent on the wealth of the decision maker.

2. *Individuals are typically risk-averse concerning "large" gambles associated with gains* (Tversky and Kahneman, 1981). For example, most people would take $500,000 over a 50 percent chance of obtaining $1 million.

3. *Individuals tend toward risk-seeking behavior concerning large gambles associated with losses.* That is, most people would risk a 50 percent chance of losing $10,000, rather than accepting a sure loss of $5,000. Holloway (1979) argues that people reason, "If I can break even, I will get back to the status quo, which is important to me." Furthermore, many individuals may be risk-seeking regarding losses in order to avoid being labeled a loser.

4. *Risk-seeking behavior is observed where a desired level of wealth necessitates taking a risk to achieve that level* (Friedman and Savage, 1948; Siegal, 1957). This is explained in terms of the threshold leading to a new "way of life," such as a new career or a new home. This explanation of risk-seeking explains the health of the lottery industry, which provides gambles that "rational" analysts view to not be in the best interest of the consumer. Anything short of this threshold does not create a significant life change. Thus, if taking the "sure thing" allows you to reach your threshold, risk-averse behavior would be predicted. You will not want to take a risk and possibly fall below the threshold level (e.g., losing your house).

5. *Individuals are risk-averse in avoiding catastrophic losses.* That is, individuals are willing to pay a premium to avoid the downside risk of a loss that would cause them to dramatically change their lifestyle.

6. *In the aggregate, risk-aversion is the dominant attitude toward risk.* Holloway (1979) points to the enormous size of the insurance industry as evidence of our risk-aversion—buying insurance is risk-avoiding behavior.

This section is not a thorough overview of normative risk theory; rather, we have simply reviewed some concepts that are needed for the material that follows. First, however, a few additional comments are in order. We have objectively defined risk-taking preference. We have *not* put any value statement on various risk strategies. In fact, we would strongly argue that there is no correct risk-taking strategy. However, this chapter will discuss some inconsistent risk-taking strategies. Finally, although individual differences in risk taking exist, it is important to mention that individuals cannot be accurately described by a summary of their risk preference (e.g., risk-seeking). Rather, risk-taking behavior depends greatly on the situation. Research will be presented later in this chapter that demonstrates that all of us are risk-seeking in some situations and risk-averse in others.

THE FRAMING OF RISKY PROBLEMS

Consider the following problem (adapted from Bazerman, 1983):

Quiz Item 1: A large car manufacturer has recently been hit with a number of economic difficulties, and it appears as if three plants need to be closed and 6000 employees laid off. The vice-president of production has been exploring alternative ways to avoid this crisis. She has developed two plans:

Plan A: This plan will save one of the three plants and 2000 jobs.

Plan B: This plan has a one-third probability of saving all three plants and all 6000 jobs, but it has a two-thirds probability of saving no plants and no jobs.

Which plan would you select?

There are a number of things that we might consider in evaluating these options. For example, what will be the impact of each action on the union? What will be the impact of each plan on the motivation and morale of retained employees? How do the values of the vice-president of production differ from those of the larger corporation? Although all these questions are important and have been addressed in the organizational behavior literature, a more fundamental question underlies the subjective situation and the resulting decision. Reconsider this problem, replacing the choices provided with the following choices:

Plan C: This plan will result in the loss of two of the three plants and 4000 jobs.

Plan D: This plan has a two-thirds probability of resulting in the loss of all three plants and all 6000 jobs but has a one-third probability of losing no plants and no jobs. Which plan would you select?

Close examination of the two sets of alternative plans finds them to be *objectively* the same. For example, saving one of three plants and 2000 of 6000 jobs (Plan A) is the same objective outcome as losing two of three plants and 4000 of 6000 jobs (Plan C). In addition, Plans B and D are objectively identical. Informal empirical investigation, however, demonstrates that *most* individuals (80+ percent) choose Plan A (objectively the same as Plan C) in the first set, whereas *most* individuals (80+ percent) choose Plan D (objectively the same as Plan B) in the second set. Although the two sets of choices are objectively identical, changing the description of the outcome states from jobs and plants saved (gains) to jobs and plants lost (losses) was sufficient to shift prototypic choice from risk-averse (take the sure thing) to risk-seeking. Why do individuals demonstrate this apparent contradiction in their risky judgment?

This shift is consistent with a growing body of literature (Kahneman and Tversky, 1979, 1982; Tversky and Kahneman, 1981; Thaler, 1980) that shows that individuals treat risks concerning perceived gains (e.g., saving jobs and plants—see plans A and B) differently from risks concerning perceived losses (e.g., losing jobs and plants—see plans C and D). In an attempt to explain these common and systematic deviations from rationality, Kahneman and Tversky (1979) developed *prospect theory.* This theory suggests that (1) rewards and losses are evaluated relative to a neutral reference point; (2) potential outcomes are expressed as gains (e.g., jobs and plants saved) or losses (e.g., jobs and plants lost) relative to this fixed, neutral reference point; and (3) the resultant change in the asset position is assessed by an S-shaped value function (see Figure 3.1).

As demonstrated in Figure 3.1, decision makers tend to avoid risk concerning gains and seek risk concerning losses. On this graph, the x axis represents the nominal units gained or lost and the y axis represents the value units associated with varying levels of gain or loss. For example, this curve suggests that most individuals would choose a $10 million gain for sure over a 50 percent chance of getting a $20 million gain, because the value placed on $20 million is *not* twice as great as the value placed on $10 million. In addition, this curve suggests that most individuals would choose a 50 percent chance of a $20 million loss over a sure loss of $10 million, because the negative value

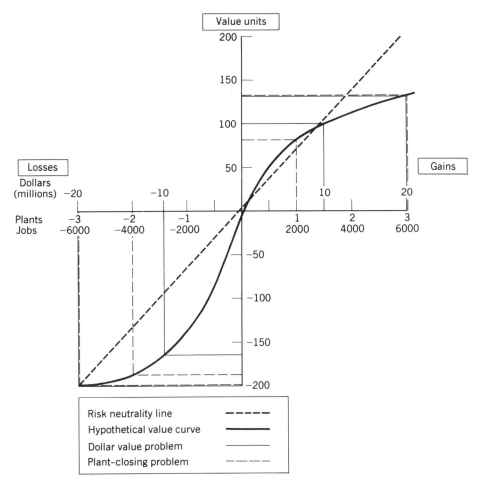

Figure 3.1 Hypothetical value function accounting for framing. *Source:* Adapted from Kahneman and Tversky (1979). Reprinted by permission of the Econometric Society.

placed on $20 million is *not* twice as great as the negative value placed on $10 million.

Furthermore, the way in which the problem is framed, or presented, can dramatically change the perceived neutral point of the question. Thus, in this example, if the problem is framed in terms of losing jobs and plants, the current position is neutral, the choices are evaluated on the loss part of the curve, and risk-seeking behavior results. That is, if we think in terms of *losing* jobs, the negative value placed on the loss of three plants and 6000 jobs is viewed (by most individuals) as not being three times as negative as losing one plant and 2000 jobs (see Figure 3.1). However, if the problem is framed in terms of saving jobs and plants, the potential disaster (losing everything) becomes the neutral point, the choices are evaluated on the gain part of the curve, and risk-averse behavior results. Within this alternative frame, Figure 3.1 clarifies that the gain placed on saving three plants and 6000 jobs is viewed (by most individuals) as not being three times as great as saving one plant and 2000 jobs. Kahneman and Tversky (1979) have identified a *systematic* pattern of how the framing of the problem will affect subsequent decisions that deviate from expected utility theory. Expected utility theory would posit that the rational decision maker would be immune from the format of the choices.

A second characteristic of our decision processes identified by prospect theory is that our response to loss is more extreme than our response to gain. The pain associated with losing x dollars is generally greater than the pleasure associated with winning the same amount. Tversky and Kahneman (1981) cite "people's reluctance to accept fair bets on a toss of a coin" as evidence of this effect.

Prospect theory identifies a third way in which our decision processes deviate from expected utility theory. This concerns our treatment of probabilities. As stated earlier, expected utility theory weights a risky option by its probability. In contrast, Kahneman and Tversky (1979) incorporate systematic deviations from rationality in probability assessment into their decision model. Prospect theory states that we tend to overweight the probability of low probability events and underweight the probability of moderate and high probability events. Furthermore, underweighting is strongest for high probability events.

The preceding paragraphs have presented the logic of prospect theory and the ways in which it departs from the normative tenets of expected utility theory. The excitement that prospect theory is causing in the fields of decision theory, psychology, and economics, however, is further developed by answers to the following seven questions: How are your decisions affected by the framing of acts? How are your decisions affected by the framing of outcomes? How are your decisions affected by the pseudocertainty and certainty of choices? How do you differentially respond to paying premiums versus accepting sure losses? How do you evaluate the quality of a transaction? How are your decisions affected by summing gains and losses? How does the frame of the problem affect how much your time is worth? The answers to these questions build on one another and are not meant to provide a taxonomy of framing effects. Rather, these questions organize much of what is known about the framing of risky decisions and outline the core of the rest of this section on the framing of risky problems. These seven questions and the description of how individual behavior typically responds to these questions are summarized in Table 3.2 at the end of the chapter. A detailed discussion of each question follows.

1. How are Your Decisions Affected by the Framing of Acts?   Tversky and Kahneman (1981) asked 150 subjects the following questions:

> *Quiz Item 2:* Imagine that you face the following pair of concurrent decisions. First examine both decisions, then indicate the options you prefer.

Decision (i). Choose between:

A. A sure gain of $240

B. 25 percent chance to gain $1000 and 75 percent chance to gain nothing

Decision (ii). Choose between:

C. A sure loss of $750

D. 75 percent chance to lose $1000 and 25 percent chance to lose nothing

In decison (i), 84 percent of the subjects chose A, whereas only 16 percent chose B. In decision (ii), 87 percent of the subjects chose D, whereas only 13 percent chose C. The majority chose "a sure gain of $240" in decision (i) because of our tendency to be risk-averse to gains and positively framed questions. In contrast, the majority chose "75 percent chance to lose $1000" in decision (ii) because of our tendency to be risk-seeking to losses and negatively framed questions. In terms of Figure 3.1, the value associated with a gain of $240 is greater than 24 percent of the value associated with a gain of $1000, whereas the negative value associated with a loss of $750 is less than 75 percent of the negative value associated with a loss of $1000. Combining the responses to the two problems, 73 percent of the respondents chose A and D; only 3 percent chose B and C.

Now consider the following problems presented by Tversky and Kahneman (1981) to 86 subjects (who had not been previously exposed to quiz item 2):

Chose between:

E. 25 percent chance to win $240 and 75 percent chance to lose $760

F. 25 percent chance to win $250 and 75 percent chance to lose $750

Not surprisingly, all 86 subjects took F over E. In fact, F dominates E in all respects. Why is this problem even interesting? When you combine A and D (the preferred choices) in quiz item 2, E results, whereas when you combine choices B and C (the choices not preferred), F results:

Adding Choices A and D

$$+ \$240 + \begin{array}{c} (75\%)(-\$1000) \\ \& \\ (25\%)(0) \end{array} = \begin{array}{c} (75\%)(-\$760) \\ \& \\ (25\%)(+\$240) \end{array}$$

Adding Choices B and C

$$\begin{array}{c} (25\%)(+\$1000) \\ \& \\ (75\%)(0) \end{array} + (-\$750) = \begin{array}{c} (25\%)(+\$250) \\ \& \\ (75\%)(-\$750) \end{array}$$

The sum of the undesirable choice *dominates* the sum of the desirable choices! Thus, the framing of the combined problem in two parts results in a clear reversal of preference.

Prospect theory's suggested preference curve (Figure 3.1) accounts for this finding. That does not, however, imply that the choices are rational. In fact, this inconsistency violates the fundamental requirements for rational decision making: consistency and coherence. Many interconnected decisions in the real world, such as portfolio selection, budgeting, and funding for new projects, can be framed as separate or joint decisions. Furthermore, the subdivision of risky decision making throughout an organization is likely to enhance the possibility of inconsistency and nonrational choice. Sales departments are encouraged to think in terms of the acquisition of corporate gains, whereas the credit office is encouraged to frame their decisions in terms of avoiding corporate losses. The disparity between different frames is likely to lead to the inconsistent risk taking exhibited in quiz item 2. Individuals and organizations need to develop procedures for identifying and integrating risky decisions in order to arrive at a coherent strategy for making judgments under uncertainty.

2. How Are Your Decisions Affected by the Framing of Outcomes?   As previously suggested, outcomes are evaluated relative to a "neutral" reference point. Consequently, the location of the reference point may be critical to whether the decision is positively or negatively framed, and it may also affect the resulting risk preference of the decision maker. The plant closing problem (quiz item 1) illustrates the importance of the reference point. In the positively framed case, the question is: How many plants (and jobs) can be saved? Saved from what? Saved from the possible loss of three plants. Thus, the loss of three plants is used as a *neutral* reference point. In contrast, in the negatively framed case, the question is: How many plants (and jobs) will be lost? Lost from what? Lost from the existing (all plants open) condition. The existing condition is used as a *neutral* reference point. By shifting the reference point, we are able to move most individuals from evaluating the choice on the upper part of the curve (Figure 3.1) to the lower part.

For other examples of the importance of this reference point shift, consider the following scenarios:

Quiz Item 3: You were given 100 shares of stock in XYZ corporation two years ago, when the value of the stock was $20 per share. Unfortunately, the stock has dropped to $10 per share during the two years that you have held the asset. The corporation is currently drilling for oil in an area that may turn out to be a big "hit." On the other hand, they may find nothing. Geological analysis suggests that if they hit, the stock is expected to go back up to $20 per share. However, if the well is dry, the value of the stock will fall to $0 per share. Do you want to sell your stock now for $10 per share?

Quiz Item 4: (Adapted from Tversky and Kahneman, 1981) You are spending the afternoon at the race track. You have lost $90 and are considering a $10 bet on a 10:1 long shot in the last race. Are you going to bet on the long shot?

In quiz item 3, what is your reference point? Is it the amount that you can gain (the amount that you receive for the stock above $0 per share), or is it the amount that you can lose (the amount that the stock has fallen from $20 per share when you sell the stock)? Figure 3.1 suggests that if you cognitively adopt $0 per share as your reference point, you will be risk-averse and will take the sure "gain" by selling the stock now. If your reference point is $20 per share, however, you will be risk-seeking and will hold onto the stock rather than accept a sure "loss."

In quiz item 4, as you consider the tenth race, what is your reference point? Are you considering the race independent of the first nine races, or are you thinking about this race from the perspective of "$90 in the hole." Prospect theory predicts that the latter frame will lead to more risk-seeking behavior. Interestingly, if people do not adjust their reference point as they lose, they may take risks that they would ordinarily find unacceptable (Tversky and Kahneman, 1981). Tversky and Kahneman (1981) argue that this analysis is supported by the popularity of long shots on the last race of the day.

What should you do about your decisions in light of the impact of the reference point? Identify your reference point when making risky decisions, and find out if other reference points are just as reasonable? If the answer is yes, think about your decision from multiple perspectives and see if there is a contradiction. At this point you will be prepared to respond to the problem with a full awareness of the alternative frames in which the problem could have been presented.

3. How are Your Decisions Affected by the Pseudocertainty and Certainty of Choices? Prospect theory suggests that people underweight high probability events, but appropriately weight events that are certain. That is, if an event has a probability of 1.0, we tend to incorporate or weight the event's probability accurately. However, if the event has a probability of .99, we tend to respond as the expected utility framework would expect us to respond if there was a probability less than .99. Slovic, Lichtenstein, and Fischhoff (1982, p. 24) note that "any protective action that reduces the probability of harm from, say, .01 to zero will be valued more highly than an action that reduces the probability of the same harm from .02 to .01."

Interestingly, the *perception* of certainty can be easily manipulated. Slovic, Lichtenstein, and Fischhoff (1982) provide an example concerning an insurance policy that covers fire but not flood. This insurance can be accurately advertised either as full protection against fire or as a reduction in the overall probability of loss. The logic of prospect theory presented in the preceding paragraph predicts that the policy will be more attractive to potential buyers with the "full protection" advertisement. The perceived certainty that results through this form of advertisement, or problem frame, has been labeled *pseudocertainty* (Tversky and Kahneman, 1981; Slovic, Lichtenstein, and Fischhoff, 1982). Obviously, the insurance is the same in both cases.

Slovic, Lichtenstein, and Fischhoff (1982) provide empirical evidence of the strength of the pseudocertainty effect in the context of disease vaccination. Two forms of a questionnaire were created. Form 1 described a disease that was expected to afflict 20 percent of the population. Subjects in this condition were asked if they would receive a vaccine that protected half the individuals vaccinated. Form 2 described two mutually exclusive and equiprobable strains of the disease, each of which was expected to afflict 10 percent of the population. Vaccination, in the latter case, was said to give complete protection (certainty) against one strain and no protection against the other. Would you take the vaccine described in Form 1? What about the vaccine described in Form 2? In either case, the vaccine would objectively reduce one's overall risk from 20 to 10 percent. Slovic, Lichtenstein, and Fischhoff (1982), however, predicted that Form 2 (pseudocertainty) would be more appealing than Form 1 (probabilistic). They found that 57 percent of subjects who were given Form 2 said that they would get the vaccination, compared with only 40 percent of the subjects who received Form 1.

Tversky and Kahneman (1981) simultaneously investigated the impact of certainty and pseudocertainty on judgmental choice. Consider the following problems (taken directly from Tversky and Kahneman, 1981):

Quiz Item 5: Which of the following options do you prefer?

A. A sure win of $30

B. 80 percent chance to win $45

Quiz Item 6: Consider the following two-stage game. In the first stage, there is a 75 percent chance to end the game without winning anything and a 25 percent chance to move into the second stage. If you reach the second stage, you have a choice between:

C. A sure win of $30

D. 80 percent chance to win $45

Your choice must be made before the game starts, that is, before the outcome of the first stage is known. Please indicate the option you prefer (C or D).

Quiz Item 7: Which of the following options do you prefer?

E. 25 percent chance to win $30
F. 20 percent chance to win $45

Tversky and Kahneman (1981) presented each of these problems to a different groups of subjects. In quiz item 5, 78 percent of the subjects chose A, 22 percent chose B. In quiz item 6, 74 percent of the subjects chose C, 26 percent chose D. In quiz item 7, 42 percent of the subjects chose E, 58 percent chose F.

Some interesting contrasts result. Consider quiz item 6: By combining the first and second parts of the problem, it becomes evident that C offers a .25 chance to win $30 and D offers a .25 × .80 = .20 chance to win $45. The same choice offered in quiz item 7! Yet the modal choice has shifted. Quiz item 6 differs from quiz item 5 only in the existence of the initial stage in quiz item 6. In quiz item 6, if you lose in the first stage, it does not matter what choice you made. If you win in the first stage, quiz item 6 reduces to quiz item 5. Consequently, there seems to be no reason to respond differently to quiz items 5 and 6. Because quiz item 6 is equivalent to quiz item 5 and Quiz Item 7, it can also be inferred that quiz items 5 and 7 should also be treated similarly. In contrast, subjects responded similarly to quiz items 5 and 6, but differently to quiz item 7. Why this discrepency in response to quiz item 7?

The difference between quiz items 5 and 7 illustrates a phenomenon labeled by Tversky and Kahneman (1981, p. 455) as the *certainty effect:* "A reduction of the probability of an outcome has more importance when the outcome was initially certain than when it was merely probable." The discrepancy, in response to objectively identical quiz items 6 and 7, illustrates a pseudocertainty effect (Tversky and Kahneman, 1981; Slovic, Lichtenstein, and Fischhoff, 1982). The prospect of winning $30 is more attractive in quiz item 6 than in quiz item 7. This occurs because of the *perceived* certainty ("a sure win") associated with choice C. This "certainty," however, is contingent on reaching the second stage of the game (making the outcome uncertain).

The certainty effect leads to judgmental inconsistencies. The pseudocertainty effect highlights a clear deviation from the rational treatment of risky decisions. Any constant reduction of (the same) risk should have the same value. Reducing the risk of cancer from 20 to 10 percent should have the same value as a reduction from 10 to 0 percent. Prospect theory, in contrast, tells us that perceived certainty has a special value to most people. Manipulations of perceived certainty have important implications for the design of communications concerning medical treatments, personal insurance, corporate liability protection, and a variety of other forms of protection. The data presented suggest that individuals may buy insurance not only to protect against risk but also to eliminate the worry caused by *any* amount of uncertainty (Tversky and Kahneman, 1981).

4. How Do You Differentially Respond To Paying Premiums Versus Accepting Sure Losses?   What is an insurance premium? It is the certain loss that you accept (the premium) in exchange for the reduction of a small probability of a large loss. However, Slovic, Lichtenstein, and Fischhoff (1982) have found that certain losses are more attractive when *framed* as insurance premiums, rather than as monetary losses. In one situation, Slovic asked people to choose between a .001 chance of losing $5000 and a certain loss of $5. In another situation, subjects were asked to choose between a .25 chance of losing $200 and a certain loss of $50. In addition, each problem was *framed* by refering to the certain loss either as a premium or as a certain loss. Each subject responded to only one of the two situations. The results of Table 3.1 demonstrate that the certain loss was more likely to be selected in the insurance context, for both of the gambles. Schoemaker and associates (Schoemaker and Kunreuther, 1979; Hershey and Schoemaker, 1980) have obtained similar results on a variety of problems.

This framing effect can be explained in a number of ways. Prospect theory would suggest that the "preference" condition leads people to use their status quo as a reference point. In contrast, in the insurance condition, the reference point is the loss of the premium (Slovic, Lichtenstein, and Fischhoff, 1982). It is easy to use Figure 3.1 to determine how these reference points lead to differing decisions.

Kahneman and Tversky (1979) and Hershey and Schoemaker (1980) also argue that "insurance" triggers social norms. "How can you not carry insurance?" "All good citizens carry insurance." Buying insurance is an activity that most of us do without considering an alternative strategy. When was the last time you considered dropping your car insurance (assuming that you live in a state where it is legal to be uninsured)?

Table 3.1   Proportions of Subjects Choosing the Certain Loss in Insurance and Preference Contexts

	Probability of Loss	
Context	.001	.25
Insurance	37/56	26/40
	66%	65%
Preference	28/72	8/40
	39%	20%

Source: From Slovic, Fischhoff, and Lichtenstein (1982, p. 27).

Regardless of the cause of this framing effect, it is critical to realize the implications of the framing of decisions concerning insurance (accepting certain losses). Empirical data suggest that people are more likely to accept a certain loss if it is viewed as insurance, rather than a preference for a sure monetary loss (Slovic, Lichtenstein, and Fischhoff, 1982; Kunreuther *et al.*, 1978).

5. How Do You Evaluate the Quality of a Transaction?   The term *transactional utility* was recently introduced by Thaler (1985) and can be best seen in terms of his scenario: (Read this scenario twice, first with the words in parentheses and excluding the words in brackets, then with the words in brackets and excluding the words in parentheses.)

> You are lying on the beach on a hot day. All you have to drink is ice water. For the last hour you have been thinking about how much you would enjoy a nice cold bottle of your favorite brand of beer. A companion gets up to go make a phone call and offers to bring back a beer from the only nearby place where beer is sold (a fancy resort hotel) [a small run-down grocery store]. He says that the beer might be expensive and so asks how much you are willing to pay for the beer. He says that he will buy the beer if it costs as much as or less than the price you state. But if it costs more than the price you state, he will not buy it. You trust your friend, and there is no possibility of bargaining with the (bartender) [store owner]. What price do you tell him?

Notice some of the features of this dual problem. First, in both the hotel and the grocery store versions, you get the same product. Second, there is no possible negotiation on price. And third, there will be no advantage to resort hotel "atmosphere," because you are going to drink the beer on the beach. According to expected utility theory, people should be willing to pay the same amount in both versions of the scenario. In fact, Thaler (1985) found participants in an executive development program were willing to pay significantly more if the beer was purchased from the "fancy resort hotel" (medians: $2.65 and $1.50). Why does this occur?

Thaler (1985) suggests that the reason for this contradiction is that whereas "paying $2.50 for a beer at a fancy hotel would be an expected annoyance, paying $2.50 at a grocery store would be an outrageous 'rip-off.'" This leads to the conclusion that something else matters besides the value you place on the commodity acquired. Thaler (1985) explains this by suggesting that purchases are affected by both *acquisition utility* and *transactional utility*. Acquisition utility is associated with the value you place on the commodity (e.g., the beer). Transactional utility refers to the quality of the deal that you receive, evaluated in reference to "what the item should cost." Obviously, paying $2.50 for a beer at a grocery store leads to a greater negative transactional utility than paying $2.50 at the fancy resort hotel. One can argue that the inclusion of transactional utility in decision making is not rational, but it does describe our behavior. Did you ever buy something because it was "too good a deal to pass up," despite the fact that you had no need for the commodity? Or, consider the following interaction: "Why did you buy bananas?" "They were only 14 cents a pound." "But nobody in the family eats bananas!"

6. How are Your Decisions Affected By Summing Gains and Losses?

Would you rather receive two checks in the mail (on different days) for $100 each, or a single check for $200? Would you rather be forced to pay two investment losses of $250 each or a single loss of $500? You are probably thinking that it obviously makes no difference. This subsection will attempt to show that most people would say that the choices are the same, yet behave in a manner that suggests that perceived differences exist. The argument for perceived differences follows logically from the S-shaped curve (Figure 3.1) identified by prospect theory. Prospect theory argues that we value initial gains from a reference point more highly than we value subsequent gains. Thus, the first $100 gained is valued more than one-half of the value associated with a $200 gain. When you receive $100 on each of two different days, you are likely to evaluate each in reference to the neutral reference point of neither gaining nor losing anything. Prospect theory also argues that we value initial losses more negatively than subsequent losses, as evaluated in terms of a reference point. Thus, an initial loss of $250 causes more than 50 percent of the loss in value caused by the $500 loss. Of course, if choices were presented as described at the beginning of this paragraph, you would realize that the choices were identical. This subsection, however, identifies situations in which we will be less aware of the impact of the framing of the summation of gains and losses.

In giving presents, should you give all the presents to one person at once? Prospect theory suggests that the recipient's comparatively strong weighting associated with initial gain would lead to giving gifts independently—thus each gift will be evaluated separately, maximizing the *value* received. In recruiting a key executive, should you display all the benefits of the company at once, or let them be seen and evaluated one at a time? In negotiating with another party, should you give in on a number of issues at once, or let the opposition feel each "victory" independently? Should the company give the work force a lot of "fringes" (bonus, parties, and such) at Christmas or spread them out throughout the year? Thaler (1985) concludes that the received value can be maximized by not wrapping "all the Christmas presents in one box."

Prospect theory also suggests that we lose less value by one large loss than by an identical loss suffered in multiple parts. Thaler (1985) suggests that one of the many desirable properties of credit cards is that they pool many small losses (debts) into one larger loss. Financial agencies also use this preference to their advantage by "allowing" you to pay off "all your debt and owe just one payment every month." Often, this transaction increases your overall debt, yet it is very attractive to many consumers.

The positive perceived impact of summing losses can also be seen in the context of summing probabilistic losses. In Slovic, Fischhoff, and Lichtenstein's (1978) analysis of seat belt use, it is argued that the resistence to seat belts is largely due to the extremely small probability of an accident on a single trip. A fatal accident occurs only once in every 3 million person trips and a disabling injury only once in every 100,000 person trips (Slovic, Fischhoff, and Lichtenstein, 1978). Based on the rarity of these events, it is easy to argue that refusing to buckle seems reasonable. Slovic, Fischhoff, and Lichtenstein (1978) point out, however, that the risks of not using seat belts can be framed very differently—by summing across multiple probabilistic losses. They summed the probabilities of fatality and disabling injury across a 50-year lifetime of driving—on average, 40,000+ trips. Using this summation analysis, Slovic, Fischhoff, and Lichtenstein (1978) concluded as follows: "The probability that one of these trips will end in a fatality is .01, and the probability of experiencing at least one disabling injury during this period is .33. It is as appropriate to consider these cumulative probabilities of death or disability as it is to consider the odds on a single trip."

Slovic, Fischhoff, and Lichtenstein (1978) investigated this framing contradiction empirically by inducing subjects to adapt either a lifetime or a trip-by-trip perspective. Ten percent of the subjects exposed to single-trip risk statistics claimed that they would increase their use of seat belts, whereas 39 percent of those exposed to lifetime statistics said that they would increase their usage. Furthermore, 54 percent of the subjects exposed to single-trip statistics favored mandatory protection, whereas 78 percent of those exposed to lifetime statistics favored such a law. Thus, by summing probabilistic losses, significant changes in preference and intended behavior were observed.

7. How Does the Frame of the Problem Affect How Much Your Time Is Worth? (Answer in dollars per hour)   Before reading further, answer that question. Now consider the following items:

> *Quiz Item 8:* Assume that you are planning on cleaning your home or residence next Saturday morning for four hours. What is the *most* that you would pay someone to do the same amount of cleaning for you—so that you could relax for those four hours? (Assume quality of cleaning will be the same, security is not a problem, and so on.)

> *Quiz Item 9:* Assume that you were planning on relaxing next Saturday morning. What is the *least* amount that you would accept to clean a house or residence the size of yours for four hours?

Each of these questions should identify the value that you place on your relaxation time (in comparison to cleaning). Most people, however, would demand far more to clean (quiz item 9) than they would be willing to pay to avoid cleaning (quiz item 8). It is common for individuals to demand 5 to 20 times as much in quiz item 9 than they were willing to pay in quiz item 8. Why?

Economic and other normative frameworks would suggest that your responses should be identical to these two quiz items. Through the use of prospect theory, however, Thaler (1980) explains the empirical difference concerning the two quiz items by arguing that a certain degree of inertia exists in the consumer process, such that goods (and free time) that you possess will be more highly valued than goods (and free time) that you do not possess. That is, you will demand more for giving up your free time than you would pay for receiving additional free time.

The following quiz items adapted from Tversky and Kahneman (1981) further illustrate contradictions in the way people value their time:

> **Quiz Item 10:** Imagine that you are about to purchase a calculator for $50. The calculator salesperson informs you that the caclulator that you wish to buy is on sale at the other branch of the store, located a 20-minute drive away. What is the *highest* price that the calculator could cost at the other store such that you would be willing to travel there for the discount?

> **Quiz Item 11:** Imagine that you are about to purchase a color television for $500. The television salesperson informs you that this television is on sale at the other branch of the store, located a 20-minute drive from where you are now. What is the *highest* price that you would be willing to pay at the other store to make the "discount" worth the trip?

How much is 20 minutes of your time plus the cost of travel worth? The answer to this comparison in relation to the amount saved by traveling should determine whether or not you will make the trip. Most people, however, would demand a greater discount (in dollars) to make the television trip than to make the calculator trip. Why? The issue of transactional utility enters into your evaluation of the worth of your time. You are only willing to travel the 20 minutes to get a "very good deal." A $25 dollar savings is not a big discount on the television (saving 5 percent), but it is an outstanding deal on the calculator (saving 50 percent). Normatively, however, the difference in percentage reduction is irrelevant to considering these problems. Rather, one should simply compare the savings obtained versus the cost incurred.

Integration of Various Framing Effects

The previous subsections have attempted to demonstrate the critical importance of the frame in which we make decisions. Each of the ideas has been illustrated and, I hope, you can identify situations in which you currently adopt a particular frame to the exclusion of other perspectives. Prospect theory represents the most critical advance in our understanding of our decision processes in the last 20 years. If you can understand and apply the knowledge explained in the preceding sections, it is expected that the consistency and quality of your decisions can be greatly improved.

Finally, consider how these effects can be applied in a variety of organizational contexts. The concept of framing has enormous potential for expanding our understanding of applied managerial problems. For illustration purposes, consider the area of job choice:

> An employee with five years of experience since his MBA has a reasonable job, security, and an average salary for someone with his background. He now has the

option of abandoning his current, safe position and committing himself to a high-risk, high-opportunity start-up firm. Will he make the job change?

According to the careers literature, common considerations include his family situation, his current salary, promotion potential, and his life-style. Prospect theory suggests, however, that the reference point from which he evaluates the options will be a critical factor. A low reference point (where he thinks he should be at this point in his career) will lead to an evaluation on the gain part of the utility curve (see Figure 3.1) and a risk-averse choice (not switching jobs). A high reference point, however, will lead to an evaluation on the loss part of the curve and a risk-seeking choice (switching jobs). This analysis is critical in identifying the inappropriate impact that false career expectations can have on employees. Graduate schools and employers frequently create unrealistic career expectations as part of their marketing strategy. This type of analysis is not unique to issues of job choice, rather it is intended to highlight the potential of the framing concept to clarify applied managerial situations.

SOME ADDITIONAL COMMENTS ON RISK

Individual Variation in Risk Taking

When most people think about risk, it is common to attempt to identify whether they are risk-averse or risk-seeking. Some people put value judgments on varying risk-taking levels. "You will never get very far in life if you don't take risks." We all know of people that we categorize as risk-seekers and others that we would categorize as risk-averse. Fischhoff, Slovic, and Lichtenstein (1981) have argued that risk taking is one of the first dimensions to come to mind in describing someone's personality. Are you risk-seeking or risk-averse? Interestingly, most people have trouble answering this question, because they can identify contexts in which they are typically risk-averse and other contexts in which the are risk-seeking. In fact, Slovic (1972) compared the scores of 82 people on nine different measures (dimensions) of risk taking. He found strong evidence against the belief that a generalizable risk-taking trait exists. The correlations between the nine dimensions ranged from $-.35$ to $.34$, with a mean of $+.006$. This provides evidence for the view that people who are aggressive in one situation may be conservative in another. The person who gambles with money for a living may be conservative in caring for her health or making rules for her children. The conservative financial analyst may let "all hell break loose" on weekends.

Is risk taking related to intelligence? It has been found that intelligence is not related to a general risk-taking level (Slovic, 1972). However, Slovic (1972) did find intelligence to be related to variability in risk-taking strategy. Individuals with higher intelligence tend to develop a consistent risk-taking approach, whereas less intelligent people were found to be very random in their risk-taking behavior—without any discernable strategy. Recall from earlier sections that inconsistencies in risk taking can lead to definably irrational choices (see quiz item 2).

Slovic's research suggests that we should try to be more aware of how much risk we prefer across a variety of settings. We should understand why we take risk in one context and not in another. This will allow for understanding the importance of the context in our risky judgments and allow for the critical evaluation of the appropriateness of our risk-taking strategies.

Individual Risk Taking in Organizations

This chapter has focused entirely on risk taking by individuals. Organizations have an even more difficult task. How can an organization get employees to follow a selected risk-taking strategy? For example, earlier we mentioned the sales department that tried to make risky decisions, whereas the credit department was trying to make conservative decisions. There is probably a strategy somewhere in between that more closely resembles the preferred strategy of the organization (i.e., the stockholders). The stockholders should prefer to have all divisions following a more *consistent* overall approach, similar to their risk preferences.

Swalm (1966) has suggested that division and lower level managers are typically more risk-averse than are the top managers of their organization. Further, Swalm (1966) has found managers to readily admit that they make many decisions using a risk strategy that responds to their own best career interests, rather than the best interests of their organization. Why do departments have different risk strategies? Why do managers use risk strategies that are different from their organization's risk strategy? Two factors contribute to such inconsistency in managerial risk taking: communication and rewards.

One reason that managers may not make decisions consistent with an organization's overall risk strategy is that they may not know the organization's risk strategy. If an organization does not address the degree of risk allowed in providing customer credit, for example, fighting between the sales and credit department is predictable. The organization must develop and *communicate* the company's overall perspective concerning risk.

In addition, managers may not make decisions consistent with the organization's overall risk strategy because the organization provides rewards that go *against* its best interests. This is manifested in at least two ways. First, organizations tend to reward results—"If your decision turns out disastrously, then you made a terrible decision." As we argued earlier, this should not be the case. Most decisions are probabilistic, and even the best decisions may not work out well. To the extent that the organization rewards results, however, some managers will behave conservatively to avoid making the "mistake" that leads to dismissal, whereas others will make unusually risky decisions in the hope that an unexpected success will lead to a promotion. How can the organization change such behavior? By rewarding the quality of the decisions rather than the results of the decisions. A second strategy to get managers to make decisions in the best interests of the organization is to reward based on the organization's, rather than the individual's, success. This is a primary tenet of organizationwide incentive systems. These plans link the individual's rewards to the success of the organization. The individual is no longer rewarded or punished based on personal success (which leads to differing risk strategies). The goals of the individual and the organization no longer conflict.

Acceptable Risk

Determining an acceptable level of risk when considering hazards concerns everyone. How risky would it be to build one more nuclear power plant? How risky is it to expose assembly-line employees to the chemicals necessary to make animal flea collars? What level of risk is acceptable? One tempting response to the last question is to claim that *no* risk is acceptable. However, throughout our lives, we must all choose between risks. To never expose yourself to common risks would risk limiting the benefits that you obtain in life. Fischhoff, Lichtenstein, Slovic, Derby, and Keeney (1981) have produced an outstanding book that thoroughly examines issues concerning acceptable risks to society. This section reviews a few points to consider when identifying acceptable risk levels.

How much is safety worth? Some would immediately answer "any price." Yet that would imply that we should devote *all* our efforts to highway improvement, cures for cancer, and such, to the exclusion of productivity. To the extent that we do not directly answer this question, or only respond in an artificial manner, some unfortunate inconsistencies occur. For example, Fischhoff, Lichtenstein, *et al.* (1981) note

> Our legal statutes are less tolerant of carcinogens in our food than in our drinking water or our air. In the United Kingdom, 2,500 times more money per life saved is spent on safety measures in the pharmaceutical industry than in agriculture (Sinclair, Marstand, & Newick, 1972). According to some calculations, U.S. society spends about $140,000 in highway construction to save one life and $5 million to save a person from death due to radiation exposure (R. A. Howard, Matheson, and Owen, 1978, pg. 2).

The key point is that risk reduction has costs. Sometimes these costs are in the form of insurance. In the power plant dilemma, the cost may be a greater dependence on foreign energy. Unfortunately, we know that risk perceptions are typically faulty (Fischhoff, Slovic, and Lichtenstein, 1981). To the extent that risk perceptions are faulty, risk reduction efforts by societal and organization decision makers are likely to be misdirected. We may be saving fewer lives at greater costs. Protection from such errors can only be obtained through the improvement of decision makers' judgment.

CONCLUSION

This chapter has attempted to provide an analytical framework that increases your understanding of risky decisions, identifies systematic ways in which your risky judgment deviates from rationality, and puts this information into a context that will allow you to generalize the material presented. In addition, a key purpose of the chapter has been to create an awareness (that is currently missing in many individuals) of the probabilistic nature of decisions. This is critical for the development of the managerial ability necessary to evaluate effectively the decisions of others.

Table 3.2 Summary Descriptions of Seven Effects of Framing Presented in the Chapter 3

Organizing Question	Description of How Most People Are Affected
1. How are your decisions affected by the framing of acts?	Individuals tend to be risk-averse to positively framed choices and risk-seeking to negatively framed choices.
2. How are your decisions affected by the framing of outcomes?	After individuals gain or lose some commodity, future decisions (in the short term) are evaluated in terms of Figure 3.1, in reference to the current sure loss or gain position.
3. How are your decisions affected by the pseudocertainty and certainty of choices?	Individuals value the reduction of uncertainty more when it creates perceived certainty than when it merely reduces the level of uncertainty.
4. How do you differentially respond to paying premiums versus accepting sure losses?	Certain losses are more attractive when *framed* as insurance premiums than when *framed* as monetary losses.
5. How do you evaluate the quality of a transaction?	Individual purchasing behavior is affected by acquisition utility and transactional utility. Acquisition utility is associated with the value the individual places on the commodity. Transactional utility refers to the quality of the deal, in reference to "what the item should cost."
6. How are your decisions affected by summing gains and losses?	Individuals value a series of small gains more than a single gain of the same summed amount. In addition, individuals lose less value by one large loss than by an identical loss suffered in multiple smaller parts.
7. How does the frame of the problem affect how much your time is worth?	Individuals value their time at extremely different rates depending on social norms, transactional utility, anchor points based on market values, and expectations of how much "work" they should do in a given time period.

FOUR
THE NONRATIONAL ESCALATION OF COMMITMENT

If at first you don't succeed, try, try again. Then quit. No use being a damn fool about it.

W. C. Fields

In the examples in the previous chapters, we examined single decisions made at a single time. In contrast, many critical managerial decisions concern a series of choices, rather than an isolated decision. Consider the following examples:

> You personally decided to hire a new middle-level manager to work for you. Although you expected excellent performance, early reports suggest that she is not performing as expected. Should you fire her? Perhaps you really cannot afford her current level of performance. On the other hand, you have invested a fair amount in her training. Furthermore, she may just be in the process of learning the ropes. So you decide to invest in her a bit longer and provide additional resources so that she can succeed. Again, she does not perform as expected. Although you have more reason to "cut your losses," you now have even more invested in this employee. When do you give up on your "investment"?

> You take a position for a well-known firm with an excellent reputation, thinking that it is a career opportunity that you can be happy with, and a firm that you can grow with. After two years, you are not progressing as rapidly as you had expected. You decide to invest large amounts of unpaid overtime in demonstrating your contribution to the company. You still do not get the recognition that you expect. By now, you have been with the organization for several years and would lose numerous benefits including a vested interest in the company's pension plan if you decide to leave. You are in your late thirties and feel that you have invested your best years with this company. Do you quit?

> You are a bank loan officer. A seemingly good credit risk comes to you and asks for $50,000 business start-up loan. After a careful review of the application, you personally made the decision to grant the loan. Six months later, the same applicant shows up in your office and says: "I have bad news, and I have good news. The bad news is that the company is having problems. In fact, without additional help, we are going under and you are losing the $50,000. The good news is that I am quite confident that if you lend us an additional $50,000, we can turn the whole thing around." Do you

lend him an additional $50,000? (This scenario was inspired by an excellent study of bank loan decision making by Lewicki, [1980]).

You have spent the last three years working on a doctorate in a field with very poor job prospects (e.g., Victorian history). You chose to invest more time to finish the degree, rather than quitting the program and shifting fields. After all, you had a lot invested in your doctoral program. You stick with it, and two years later, you have your degree. You take a job as a part-time instructor at a low-quality institution—it is the best job available in your field. Furthermore, you are dissatisfied with the way the school treats part-timers, and quite frankly, you think you deserve more recognition than you are receiving. You can stick with this position for a long time, but the prospects for improvement are low. When do you shift to a different field?

Although each of these decision problems represents a very different situation, they share a number of common elements. In each case, you have a decision to make as a result of a previous decision. You hired the employee. You took the job. You made the loan. You decided to pursue a doctorate in a field with poor job prospects. In each case, you invested a great deal of time, effort, and/or resources in your selected course of action. In each case, things are not working out in an optimal way. Nevertheless, inertia causes you to continue on the previously selected course of action. After all, you are likely to feel that you have "too much invested to quit." We are frequently faced with similar decisions of less importance. Do you put more money into that old wreck you call a car? You call the airline and are put on hold. How long do you stay on hold? If you think about your own career and life, you will probably come to the conclusion that traps of the type exemplified here are common. Is continuing the course of action irrational? Why? How do you know when to quit? If continuing the course of action is irrational, why is such behavior so common? These are the central questions of this chapter.

A variety of authors from different fields have presented ideas related to the problems identified, and a number of different terms (e.g., escalation, entrapment, persistence) have been used to describe this commitment to a previously selected course of action. Without presenting the diversity of definitions used in the literature, this chapter defines *nonrational escalation* as the degree to which an individual escalates commitment to a previously selected course of action to a point beyond that which a rational model of decision making would prescribe.

Accountants and economists provide insight into the scenarios presented. Experts from these areas would tell us that in each of these situations we need to recognize that the time and/or expenses already invested are "sunk costs." That is, these costs are historical costs that are *not* recoverable and should *not* be considered in any future course of action. Rather, we should consider all alternative courses of action (e.g., keeping versus firing the employee) by evaluating only the *future* costs and benefits associated with each course of action. That is, it does not matter whether it took you six months or four years to get to a particular point in the doctoral program; the key decision involves the future costs versus the future benefits of continuing. This strategy would lead to an "optimal" decision.

Accountants teach their students to recognize sunk costs in an accounting context. And their students learn to follow their prescriptions in textbook problems. However, the decisions of managers trained in accounting suggests that it is difficult to translate this textbook training to real-world problems. A key deficiency in their training is a descriptive identification of why individuals intuitively tend to include sunk costs in their calculations. Why is it that it is so hard for the accountants to convey the sunk-cost concept? The answer lies in a psychological explanation of the tendency to escalate. To eliminate escalatory behavior—beyond the accounting textbook problem—we need to identify the existing nonrational behavior, unfreeze that behavior, then prepare for change.

Psychologists bring a perspective to the escalation problem that is very different from that of accountants and economists. Psychologists begin by describing what decision makers actually do, rather than prescribing what they should do. In general, psychologists (Brockner and Rubin, 1985; Staw, 1976, 1981; Teger, 1980) have demonstrated that decision makers who commit themselves to a particular course of action have a tendency to make decisions that commit added resources in a nonoptimal way in order to justify the previous commitment—the hiring decision, the job choice decision, the loan decision, the professional field decision. Why does this tendency to escalate occur? Northcraft and Wolf (1984, p. 3) offer the following:

> The decision-maker may, in the face of negative feedback [about the consequences of his/her decision], feel the need to reaffirm the wisdom of time and money already sunk in the project. Further commitment of resources somehow 'justifies' the initial decision (Staw, 1976), or at least provides further opportunities for it to be proven correct. The decision-maker may also treat the negative feedback as simply a learning experience—a cue to redirect efforts within a project, rather than abandon it (Connelly, 1978). Or perhaps the decision-maker will rationalize away the negative feedback as a whim of the environment—a storm to be weathered, rather than a message to be heeded.

This description provides a number of psychological explanations of why individuals fail to follow the accountant's prescription. The decision maker feels the need to reaffirm the wisdom of the initial decision and to justify why he/she made the initial decision. The individual attempts to rationalize away the negative information. These are some of the reasons why we nonrationally escalate commitment to a previous chosen course of action. We will return to the question of why escalation occurs later in the chapter.

The remainder of this chapter will review several research paradigms that address the tendency to escalate and develop a taxonomy of alternative explanations of the psychological tendency to escalate. Throughout, the chapter will use a number of specific applications. These applications will be used as an alternative to the quiz format of previous chapters to illustrate concepts. We will return to the quiz format in Chapter 5. In terms of improving your decision processes, it is recommended that you translate the applications presented to parallel situations in which you have escalated your investment to a previously selected course of action.

THE UNILATERAL ESCALATION PARADIGM

To introduce this paradigm, reconsider your problem as the bank loan officer specified earlier. The way the escalation problem has been described probably biased your impression toward assuming that "it is bad" to escalate your commitment to the loan. However, it might be economically rational to continue. After all, we are not always expected to quit at the first sign of failure. In fact, many would argue that such behavior would be a serious sign of a psychological abnormality. Furthermore, children are taught from an early age to "try, try, again." Then how do you separate out the rational from the nonrational tendency to escalate? You should be *trying* to determine the rational course of action, excluding the fact that you personally made the initial loan commitment.

A number of studies have attempted to separate the rational from the nonrational components of escalation by trying to pull out the effect of being the person who made the initial commitment. These studies investigated the difference between how decision makers in two different conditions would make a second decision that followed an initial failure—where decision makers in one condition made the initial decision, and decision makers in the other condition inherited the initial decision.

In Staw's (1976) initial study of escalation, one group of subjects (high responsibility) was asked to allocate research and development funds to one of two operating divisions of an organization. The subjects were then told that after three years the investment had either proved successful or unsuccessful and that they were faced with a second allocation decision concerning the division to which they had previously given funds. A second group (low responsibility) was told that another financial officer of the firm made a decision that had been either successful or unsuccessful (the same content information as provided to the previous group of subjects) and that they were to make a second allocation of funds concerning that division.

When the outcome of the previous decision was negative (an unsuccessful investment), high-responsibility subjects allocated significantly more funds to the original division in the second allocation than did low-responsibility subjects. In contrast, for successful initial decisions, the amount of money allocated in the second decision was not related to responsibility. Given that the escalation of commitment occurred only for high-responsibility subjects who had made a previously unsuccessful decision, Staw (1976) concluded that the mechanism underlying escalation is a cognitive dissonance (Festinger, 1957) or a self-justification (Aronson, 1968) process. That is, when the individual makes the initial decision to a course of action, receiving failure information is dissonant with having made the initial decision. One way to eliminate this dissonance is by escalating commitment to the initial action and believing that eventual success in that course of action will be obtained. This explanation of escalation parallels Festinger's argument that once a person commits him/herself to a course of action, there will be "less emphasis on objectivity . . . and more partiality and bias in the way in which the person views and evaluates the alternatives."

An important conclusion from Staw's (1976) study is that the responsibility felt by the decision maker for the initial decision significantly biased his/her subsequent decision. Although responsibility for the initial decision emerged as a key variable, the results demonstrated that individuals vary substantially in how they respond to the escalation trap. Other studies have identified additional factors that predict whether or not escalatory behavior is observed. For example, Staw and Ross (1978) showed that the tendency to escalate commitment by high-responsibility subjects was particularly pronounced where there was some way to develop an explanation for the initial failure that was unpredictable and unrelated to the decision maker's action (e.g., the economy suffered a severe setback). Bazerman, Giuliano, and Appelman (1984) found escalation to occur when the decision was made by groups as well as by individuals. That is, using the Staw (1976) methodology, groups that made an initial collective decision that proved unsuccessful allocated significantly more funds to the initially chosen division than did groups that inherited the initial decision. In addition, Bazerman, Giuliano, and Appelman (1984) found the level of escalation to be related to the degree to which individuals and groups experienced dissonance as a result of the feedback from the initial decision. Bazerman, Schoorman, and Goodman (1980) found that the tendency to escalate was significantly affected by the degree of disappointment felt by the decision maker when the negative feedback from the initial decision was provided, the perceived importance of the decisions, and the perceived relationship between the two decisions.

Bazerman, Beekun, and Schoorman (1982) found that the tendency to escalate generalized from the financial context (used in all previous studies) to the performance appraisal domain. Specifically, they found that individuals who made an initial decision to hire an employee subsequently evaluated that employee more favorably, provided larger rewards, and made more optimistic projections of future performance than did evaluators who did not make the initial decision to hire the employee. Thus, in the performance appraisal dilemma that was presented at the beginning of the chapter, the evaluator is not only likely to escalate his/her commitment to keep the employee nonrationally, but his/her performance reviews, salary reviews, and expectations of future performance are likely to be distorted.

The thrust of the evidence presented suggests an "experimenting" approach to management (Campbell, 1969). That is, managers should make a decision, try it out, but be open to dropping the commitment and shifting to another course of action if the first plan is not working out. You should view your decisions as experiments—some will work and others will not. You should be constantly reassessing the rationality of future commitment. A primary managerial task is to identify the failures early. Staw and Ross (1980), however, have suggested that a false belief may exist in society that administrators who are consistent in their actions are better leaders than those who switch from one line of behavior to another. They offer the following excerpts from the public press evaluation of Jimmy Carter as support for their position:

> Carter has exacerbated many of the difficulties he has faced. His most damaging weakness in his first two years has been a frequent indecisiveness . . . ("The State of Jimmy Carter," 1979).

> A President must, plainly, show himself to be a man made confident by the courage of his clear convictions . . . The American people find it easy to forgive a leader's great mistakes, but not long meanderings (Hughes, 1978).

Indecisiveness also was cited as the second most common reason for dissatisfaction with Carter in the Gallup poll collected after Carter's first year in office (Staw, 1981). Thus, although decisiveness, commitment, and escalation may decrease the quality of an individual's decisions, quitting will reduce the person's *perceived* effectiveness. This is a central conclusion in the experimental work of Staw and Ross (1980). From an organizational standpoint, this suggests that we need to create reward systems that do not encourage escalation. Otherwise, the bank loan officer who made the initial loan has the incentive to escalate commitment (to be a consistent decision maker) in comparison with a loan officer that did not make the initial decision. We will return to the topic of how to create the environment that reduces the nonrational escalation of commitment later in the chapter.

In the unilateral escalation paradigm that emanates from Staw's (1976) initial experiment, all the justification forces that lead to nonrational escalation lie within the individual. The individual escalates because of *his/her* previous commitment. As we shift discussion to the competitive escalation paradigm, this will not be the only reason for escalation. Although individuals will escalate in competitive situations to justify a previous commitment, there are also competitive forces that feed the escalatory process. We will examine both justification and competitive processes as we examine escalation in competitive situations.

THE COMPETITIVE ESCALATION PARADIGM

Imagine yourself in a room with 30 other individuals and the person at the front of the room takes out a dollar bill from his/her pocket and announces the following:

> I am about to auction off this dollar. You are free to participate or just watch the bidding of others. People will be invited to call out bids in multiples of 5 cents until no further bidding occurs, at which point the highest bidder will pay the amount bid and win the dollar. The only feature that distinguishes this auction from traditional auc-

tions is a rule that the second highest bidder must also pay the amount bid, although he/she will obviously not win the dollar. For example, if Bill bid 35 cents and Jane bid 40 cents, and bidding stopped, I would pay Jane 60 cents ($1.00 − .40) and Bill, the second highest bidder, would pay me 35 cents.

Would you be willing to bid 15 cents to start the auction? Most people would. Make this decision before reading further. Assuming you said yes, after someone else bid 20 cents, would you bid higher? What would you do if no one else entered the auction?

I have run this auction with undergraduate students, graduate students, and executives. The pattern is always the same. The bidding starts out fast and furious until the bidding reaches the 50 to 75-cent range. At that point, everyone except the two highest bidders drops out of the auction. The two bidders then begin to feel the trap. One bidder has bid 80 cents and the other 85 cents. The 80 cent bidder must either bid 90 cents or suffer an 80-cent loss. The uncertain situation (that might even produce a gain if the other guy quits) seems more attractive than the sure loss. He/she bids 90 cents. This continues until there are bids of 95 cents and a dollar. Surprisingly, the decision to bid $1.05 is very similar to all previous decisions. You can accept a 95 cent loss or continue and reduce your loss if the other guy quits. Of course, the rest of the group roars with laughter when the bidding goes over a dollar—which it virtually always does. The skeptical reader should try out the auction. It is very common to have final bids in the $3 to $7 range. Obviously, the bidders are acting irrationally. But which were the irrational bids?

The dollar auction paradigm was first introduced by Shubik (1971), an economist and game theorist. More recently, Teger (1980) has used the paradigm extensively for the experimental investigation of why individuals escalate their commitment to a previously selected course of action. Teger (1980) argues that subjects naively enter the auction with very few expecting the bidding to exceed $1.00—"after all, who would bid more than a dollar for a dollar?" The potential gain, coupled with the possibility of "winning" the auction are enough reason to enter the auction. Once the subject is in the auction, it takes only a few extra cents to stay in the auction rather than to accept a sure loss. This "reasoning," along with a strong need to justify why the bidder entered the auction, are enough to keep most bidders bidding for an extended period of time.

Thoughtful examination of the dollar auction game suggests that individuals who bid develop a real problem for themselves. It is true that one more bid may get the other guy to quit. However, if both bidders feel this way, the result can be catastrophic. Yet, without knowing the expected bidding patterns of the opponent, we cannot conclude that continued bidding is clearly wrong. So where is the bidder's solution? Successful decision makers must learn to identify traps. Thus, the key to the problem lies in identifying the auction as a trap and never making even a very small bid. One cognitive strategy for identifying competitive traps is to try to consider the decision from the perspective of the other decision maker(s). In the dollar auction, this strategy would quickly tell you that the auction would look naively attractive to other bidders. With this knowledge, you can begin accurately to predict what will occur, giving you enough information to stay out of the auction.

We can find similar traps in business, war, and our personal lives. Teger concludes that the Vietnam War was a clear application of the dollar auction paradigm. Two gasoline stations staging a price war can also result in the dollar auction trap. The price of gasoline is $1.20/gallon. Your competitor decides to drive you out of business. You would also like to drive her out of business. She drops the price to $1.13/gallon. You drop the price to $1.10/gallon—your breakeven point. She drops her price to $1.07/gallon. What is your next move? Both parties may suffer tremendous losses in an effort to win the price war, and, like the dollar auction, neither side is likely to actually win the competition.

The dollar auction paradigm has much in common with the Staw paradigm. In both cases the decision maker makes an initial decision that he/she feels a need to justify through future decisions. In both cases the decision maker feels that he/she has "too much invested to quit." In both situations we empirically observe that decision makers nonrationally commit too much to the previously chosen course of action. However, there is one major difference between the two paradigms. In the dollar auction paradigm, the competition with the other party, the desire to "win," serves as an added motivation to escalate commitment. We will return to a comparison between the two paradigms when we examine the psychological explanations of escalation.

ADDITIONAL FACTORS AFFECTING THE TENDENCY TO ESCALATE

The unilateral and competitive escalation paradigms illustrate different types of entrapping situations. Rubin and Brockner (1975; Brockner et al., 1982, 1984; Brockner and Rubin, 1985; Brockner, Shaw, and Rubin, 1979; Brockner, Rubin, and Lang, 1981; Nathanson et al., 1982; Rubin, Brockner, Small-Weil, and Nathanson, 1980) have attacked the escalation problem in a different manner. Rather than developing one specific escalation problem, they have conducted an extensive series of studies (using a wide variety of procedures) to identify factors that predict the tendency to escalate commitment to a previously selected course of action. They have found that the belief that one is very close to the goal, and thus has too much invested to quit, is a leading contributor to remaining in an escalatory situation. In addition, they found that individuals are far more likely to quit if remaining in the escalatory situation requires an active, rather than a passive, response. That is, many individuals escalate not because they have made a clear choice, rather because they have done nothing to stop a previously made decision—implicitly escalating commitment to the previous course of action. Many individuals escalate their commitment to a job/career not because they make a clear choice, but rather because they never actively confront the decision to stay or leave, which leads to maintaining the status quo. Rubin and Brockner also found that the presence of a "competitive other" (e.g., the competing bidder in the dollar auction game) provided an added source of motivation to escalate commitment to a previous course of action. Furthermore, they found that the salience of the costs necessary to continue the investment was an important predictor of the decision to continue. Finally, they found that the behavior of models had a very strong influence on the focal decision maker's behavior. That is, individuals learn whether or not to escalate commitment by observing the behavior of other individuals. This last finding is particularly important in an organizational context, where we are constantly surrounded by potential models.

Based on these studies, Rubin (1980) summarized the results of their research in terms of a set of recommendations on how to avoid escalation; the major points are

1. *Set limits on your involvement and commitment in advance.* In addition, once you set a limit, stick with it. Decision makers who set limits are eliminating the subsequent escalation bias that results out of the need to justify a previous decision. At the time of limit setting, the individual has not yet been trapped.
2. *Avoid looking to other people to see what you should do.* Because escalation is a commonly observed behavior, it is easy to look around for examples of others escalating, which allow you to falsely justify your tendency to escalate.
3. *Actively determine why you are continuing.* Many of us escalate not because we believe that it is the best decision, but to manage the impression of others—for example, a boss, a friend.
4. *Remind yourself of the costs involved.* When people become committed to a course of action, they often fail to consider the added costs of continuing. Rather, they assume the costs must be minor in comparison with the overall costs of the project.
5. *Remain vigilant.* Escalation sneaks up on us. As was earlier suggested, escalation is often a passive response. We need to constantly reassess the costs and benefits of continuing.

WHY DOES ESCALATION OCCUR?

Each of the previous sections has provided some clues concerning why escalation occurs. This question is central, for the key to eliminating nonrational escalation is being able to identify its causes. The existing literature clearly suggests that there are multiple reasons why escalation occurs. This section will attempt to provide a taxonomy of these multiple reasons. The first three classes of explanations (perceptual biases, judgmental biases, external management) are general to all the examples of escalation presented. The fourth class of explanation (competitive irrationality) will further differentiate the unilateral escalation paradigm from the competitive escalation paradigm. After presenting each class of explanations of the escalation phenomenon, the implications for the elimination of escalation will be examined.

Perceptual Biases

Consider the individual at the beginning of the chapter who made the decision to hire the employee who did not perform at the level expected. The perception of information obtained after the initial decision may be biased by his/her previous decision. That is, the evaluator may notice information that supports the hiring decision, while ignoring information that provides information against the initial decision. Similarly, the bank loan officer, after making the initial loan decision, may have a greater tendency to notice positive information about the company than negative information about the company. This can be predicted from the suggestion in Chapter 2 that we pay more attention to confirming than disconfirming information. Similarly, Staw (1980) and Caldwell and O'Reilly (1982) suggest that trapped administrators may protect their initial decision by actively seeking out information that supports their initial decision—information that suggests that the employee is performing well. Caldwell and O'Reilly empirically show that subjects who freely chose a particular course of action subsequently filtered information selectively to maintain their commitment to the course of action.

The perceptual biases that are likely to result after we make a commitment to a particular course of action suggest a number of correction procedures. As mentioned in Chapter 2, we need to vigilantly search for disconfirming information—as well as the confirming information that we intuitively seek. The need to search for disconfirming information seems particularly pronounced in the escalation scenario. In addition, it would be recommended that a check on a decision maker's perceptions be built in, even before a second judgment is made. That is, if the decision maker could have an objective outsider evaluate the openness (for disconfirming information) of your information-filtering system, one barrier to nonescalatory behavior could be reduced or eliminated.

Judgmental Biases

Once the subject has filtered the information that he/she will use in a subsequent decision, a decision still remains to be made. The central argument of this section is that the loss from the initial investment (e.g., bidding over a dollar in the competitive escalation paradigm, the initial R&D funding in the unilateral escalation paradigm) will systematically distort judgment toward believing in the rationality of continuing the previously selected course of action. The logic of this prediction lies in the framing concept developed in Chapter 3 (Arkes and Blumer, 1985; Northcraft and Neale, in press).

The central result of the framing literature is that individuals tend to be risk-averse for positively framed problems and risk-seeking for negatively framed problems. Assume that you are the bank loan officer described at the beginning of the chapter. You made an initial investment of $50,000 to the start-up venture. After a short time, you are faced with the decision of accepting a loss of that $50,000 or risking an added $50,000 in the hope that this added investment will eliminate the loss entirely. The risk-averse response is to accept the sure loss of $50,000, whereas the risk-seeking action is to try to recover the initial funds by allocating an additional $50,000.

From Chapter 3, we know that most of us prefer a 50 percent chance of a loss of $100,000 over a sure loss of $50,000—even if they have the same expected value. Based on this systematic preference, we expect most individuals would give the additional loan if the expected success of that added loan was 50 percent. However, now assume that you did not make the initial investment. You are now likely to evaluate the potential benefit of the second loan from a neutral reference point. From a neutral reference point, the decision is to quit now with no gain or loss or take a 50–50 chance of winning or losing $50,000. Most individuals would quit, choosing not to accept the gamble. Thus, high- and low-responsibility subjects in Staw's paradigm simply may have been responding from different reference points, as the framing concept would predict. Similarly, the loan officer who made the initial decision is including sunk costs in the frame, which is normatively wrong.

The framing explanation of the escalation phenomenon suggests the same solution as the approach argued by the accountants. We need to get individuals to assess the new decision point from a more *neutral* reference point that eliminates the extreme risk-seeking behavior observed among high-responsibility subjects. This can be accomplished by convincing the decision maker that the initial investment has proven to be a loss and that the second decision represents a new problem to be objectively examined ignoring sunk costs. If this is not feasible, we need to introduce a new decision maker to make the subsequent decision.

External Management

Returning to the hiring decision from the beginning of the chapter, even if the manager's perception and judgment led to the conclusion that the employee should be fired, the manager might not fire the employee. Why? To fire the employee publicly announces that a mistake was made in the earlier decision. Keeping the employee might be the preferred alternative in order to "save face." Thus, managing the impressions of others serves as a third reason for escalating commitment to a previously selected course of action. This is consistent with Caldwell and O'Reilly's work showing that individuals not only selectively perceive information, but that they also selectively provide information to others. Specifically, individuals who make an initial commitment to a particular course of action are more likely to provide confirming, rather than disconfirming, information to others.

In addition to avoiding the admission of failure to others, we also try to appear consistent. The consistent course of action is to increase your commitment to action that you previously chose. An interesting paradox results: To make the best choice suggests making the best decision for your organization based on future costs and benefits, ignoring the historical commitment that you previously made. Yet, empirical evidence (Staw and Ross, 1980) shows that you are likely to be rewarded more for escalating your commitment to the previously selected course of action. Thus, what is best for your organization is not what the organization will reward. Similarly, John F. Kennedy's book *Profiles in Courage* suggests that one of the most courageous decisions a politician ever has to make concerns favoring an action that he/she believes to be in the best interests of the constituency, yet that he/she knows will be disfavored by that very same constituency. The conflict would be particularly severe if this action consists of turning one's back on a previously supported direction— which leads to the accurate prediction that elected leaders will rarely make such decisions.

In the political example of the previous paragraph, we have a paradox without easy answers. At an organizational level, however, there is a lot that we can do about managers who manage impressions rather than make the best decisions. First, we can convey throughout the organization that impression management at the expense of high-quality decisions within the firm will not be tolerated. Second, we can strive to make the manager's values closer to those of the organization. The organization wants the best decision. The manager wants to make the decision that will be best for managing his/her future career. If the bank loan officer is not punished for the initial failure, then he/she is less prone to escalate commitment to the loan. Then how can we evaluate the performance of the loan officer? Again, I return to Chapter 2. To the extent that rewards are based on results, the loan officer will make decisions based on results—he/she will hide a bad result by escalating commitment. To the extent that rewards are based on the quality of the decision, the loan officer will be motivated to make the best possible decision at the second decision point.

The view expressed in the preceding paragraph that decisions should be evaluated based on process rather than on outcome is consistent with Peters and Waterman's (1982) discussion of Heinz's experimentation with "perfect failures." The perfect failure concept recognizes that many projects that have all the right elements are not successful. In fact, the system suggests that management recognize the learning that is acquired through perfect failures and celebrate when these failures occur. The central point is that Peters and Waterman are conveying to the managerial world that we must recognize good decisions based on process and not just on outcomes.

Competitive Irrationality

The previous three explanations of escalation are generalizable to both the Staw and dollar auction paradigms, as well as to a number of other traps. Competitive irrationality, however, offers an explanation of the dollar auction escalation that does not apply to the Staw paradigm. Thus, this explanation of escalation serves as the primary distinction between the two paradigms. Specifically, competitive irrationality refers to a situation in which two parties (there is only one actor in the Staw paradigm) engage in an activity that is clearly irrational in terms of the expected outcomes to both sides, yet in which it is hard to identify specific irrational actions by either party. Many people would argue that getting involved in the dollar auction is irrational, and although this is a very reasonable perspective, the argument is not without a plan. If it makes sense for you not to play, then it does not make sense for anyone else to play. If no one else plays, you can bid a small amount and get a bargain. Sounds logical. Once you make the initial bid, another individual bids, and the bind that we have already described appears. It was earlier argued that continuing to bid will then depend on your estimation of the likelihood of the other party quitting. Obviously, the same reasoning applies to the other party. If it is possible for someone to get a very cheap dollar (e.g., for 5 cents), it must be rational for one individual to be able to bid. Yet, we know what happens when multiple individuals adopt this attitude. Thus, perhaps competitive irrationality presents an unresolved paradox, rather than an explanation of escalation. The only recommendation that can be derived from the competitive irrationality explanation of escalation is that many situations may look like opportunities but prove to be traps unless the actions of others are fully considered.

Integration

This section has suggested four causes of our tendency to escalate commitment to a previously selected course of action. By referring to the four causes as additive, I am suggesting that they are not mutually exclusive. There is no conflict about which of the four explains escalation. Rather, each one can

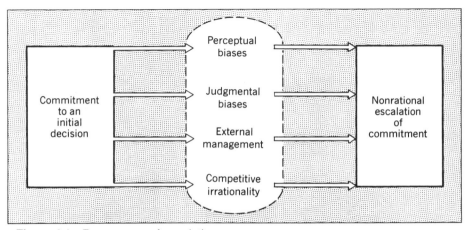

Figure 4.1 Four causes of escalation.

independently cause escalation, and more commonly, they act additively to increase a decision maker's nonrational tendency to continue a previous mistake. The four causes of escalation are graphically presented in Figure 4.1. To reduce escalation, we need to attack each of the four causes of its occurrence. Initial strategies for reducing each cause of escalation have been suggested. Finally, in trying to reduce escalation, it is critical to remember that we are trying to reduce the nonrational commitment to a course of action. Rational commitment remains a valuable attribute in organizational members. We will return to the topic of escalation when we consider multiparty contexts later in the book.

FIVE
CREATIVITY AND JUDGMENT

Innovative. Clever. Unique. Insightful. Illogical. Different. These words are connected to the alluring topic of "creativity." These words can be used to describe the outcomes of creative individuals. They can also be used to describe the traits commonly associated with creative individuals. For the purpose of this chapter, *creativity will be viewed as a cognitive process concerned with the development of an idea, commodity, concept, or discovery that is novel to its creator or some targeted audience.* In addition, creativity will be viewed as a process distinct from, yet compatible with, the logical processes of decision making identified in Chapter 1. The central thesis of this chapter is that the lack of creativity that exists in most individuals is a result of the judgmental deficiencies discussed earlier in the book. Thus, the key to creativity lies in breaking through many of the previously described heuristics.

To begin the chapter, attempt to solve the following classic creativity problem (used without original reference by many previous authors):

Quiz Item 1: Without lifting your pencil (or pen) from the paper, draw four (and only four) straight lines that connect all nine dots shown here:

Most people come up with unsuccessful attempts that look something like one of the following:

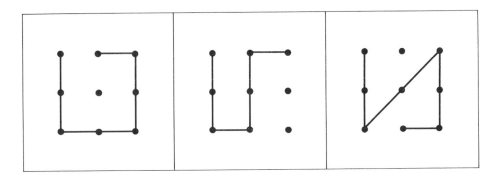

Why are most people unsuccessful? Most individuals attempt to apply all their *logical* tactics to the *perceived* problem: Connecting all nine dots without going outside the boundaries imposed by the nine dots. They make assumptions that frame the problem and constrain them from finding a solution. The most critical barrier to creative decisions is our assumptions. When our logical processes fail, creative solutions often lie outside our self-imposed assumptions. *Individuals make false assumptions about problems to fit the problems into their previously established decision processes.*

Back to the problem: Once the assumption about the barrier around the nine dots is broken, the following solution is fairly easy to achieve:

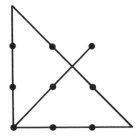

The solution is not achievable by trying additional alternatives within our commonly perceived assumptions. However, the problem is easily achieved after the assumption is removed.

Adams (1979) claims that at least 27 solutions exist. For example, it can be done with three lines:

Viewing creativity as an assumption-breaking process forms a central perspective of this chapter. This perspective, however, is not unique to this book. The assumption-breaking process is central to many other writings on creativity (e.g., Adams, 1979; De Bono, 1971; Winklegren, 1974). Inspired by this tradition, this chapter attempts to explain *why* individuals fail to break assumptions and lack creativity. We will make no attempt to review fully the literature on creativity, which many (including this author) view as a disappointing literature. Rather, we will propose a new perspective for explaining the assumptions that limit creativity.

Our explanation relies on the arguments concerning limitations to rationality found in the first four chapters of this book. Going back to the rational decision process described in Chapter 1, a perfect decision process would have a clear definition of the problem, all alternatives would be known, all relevant factors would be identified and properly weighted, and so forth. Because the rational model always makes the optimal decision, all decisions would be fully creative as well.

In contrast to this idealistic view, we have documented that our decisions are better explained by bounded rationality and characterized by a set of heuristics and biases. Consistent with this view, this chapter attempts to show that the assumptions that inhibit our creativity are created by our bounded rationality and use of heuristics. We start with an examination of the potential for assumptions at each of the steps in the logical decision process depicted in Chapter 1. We then go on to explore how the specific deviations from rationality described in earlier chapters create assumptions at the various stages of the decision process. After this explanation is offered, we will examine a number of heuristic-breaking heuristics for eliminating the assumptions that result from these limitations to rationality.

ASSUMPTIONS AT VARIOUS STAGES
OF THE DECISION PROCESS

Assumptions manifest themselves at various points in the decision process. This section explores the impact of these assumptions on the multiple steps of the rational decision process outlined in Chapter 1. Specifically, we examine the limiting effect of assumptions in defining the problem, identifying alternatives, and identifying and weighting factors.

Definition of the Problem

Individuals are quick to define the problem. Defining the task allows us to use our standard logical processes. However, as the nine-dot problem demonstrated, false assumptions at this stage can prevent us from finding the solution. Similarly, a manager who writes a job description (defining the problem) in a constrained manner may succeed in reducing the number of resumes that she needs to review, but she may also succeed in defining away the individual who was best for the job but lacked some unimportant "requirement."

Alternative Generation

Where do we look for alternatives? Do we just search for the standard alternatives? Are we making assumptions about the requirements necessary to view an alternative as viable? Frequently, the creative solution lies in identifying an alternative that most people would have excluded from consideration because of their assumptions. A vivid example of this limitation affected the author (and many others) in the famous hedge maze at Hampton Court in England. The hedge maze consists of very tall hedges that are constructed in a human-sized maze (a real highlight of a trip to England for a game player). As you enter the maze, signs implicitly lead you to walk to the left to "begin the maze." In actuality, turning to the left leads you to a complex set of dead ends. As you enter the maze, you are actually only seconds from the solution: You simply walk to the right (which is set up to be counterintuitive), turn a corner, and you are out. I walked to the left, tried to solve the maze quickly (to beat my spouse), then tried to eliminate the various dead ends logically. Unfortunately, I did not even consider the idea that the initial turn may have been wrong. I assumed that the maze originated to the left. After 75 minutes, I was frustrated and was convinced that I had negated all possible alternatives. I gave up and decided to go out the way I came in, leading me to find the solution to the problem (and my laughing spouse who claims to have been waiting for most of the time that I spent in the maze).

Criterion Identification and Weighting

What factors are relevant in selecting among alternatives? What assumptions do we make in factor identification? Again, creatively choosing between alternatives may result from breaking our assumptions about which criteria are important and the weights attached to each criterion. Consider the recent MBA selecting between multiple job offers: She eventually chooses a job that has the highest starting salary and a great deal of prestige (a well-known consulting firm). Over time, she realizes that the job was never consistent with her true values. What she wanted was a job with little travel that only demanded a 40 to 50-hour work week. Why did she take the wrong job? When she had the offers, she used the criteria that were the most salient (money, prestige). The more appropriate and creative choice required that she examine more carefully the assumptions that she was making concerning her preferences.

This section demonstrates that most decisions have more than one point at which creativity, and assumption breaking, may be necessary. However, this section simply shows that assumptions are likely to limit rationality at various decision points. The next section explores the psychological bases of these assumptions.

THE PSYCHOLOGICAL BASES
OF CREATIVITY
LIMITING ASSUMPTIONS

This section argues that the judgmental distortions identified in the first four chapters of this book create assumptions that limit creativity. We will attempt to show that these limitations to rationality lead the decision maker to simplify the optimal decision process and that these simplifications have serious implications for the creativity of the subsequent decisions. Specific attention will be given to the framing of problems, anchoring and adjustment, the representativeness heuristic, the availability heuristic, the tendency to escalate commitment, and cultural and environmental blocks.

The Framing of Problems

In Chapter 3, it was shown that individual choice was systematically affected by the way problems were framed: Individuals tend to be risk-averse to positively framed problems and risk-seeking to negatively framed problems. In addition, we tend to make the implicit false assumption that the frame in which the problem is presented is the only perspective on the problem. Using the term "frame" more broadly, most problems are framed with a variety of connotations, expectations, and such. Each time we choose a single frame, we limit the way that we look at the decision. This suggests that one basis of the assumptions that block creativity emanates from the framing of decisions.

The potential negative impact of framing on creativity can be illustrated by the often repeated story of the manager who asks "How can I get my employees to work harder?" If the manager is trying to increase performance, his/her frame on the problem is likely to eliminate the possibility of increasing performance by finding the answer to the question "How can I get my employees to work smarter?" Obviously, the nature of the framing concept suggests that it is most likely to create assumptions that inhibit creativity in the problem definition stage.

Anchoring and Adjustment

You have a problem to solve. You realize how you solved a similar problem. You use that strategy and try to make the appropriate adjustment. Unfortunately, this problem had a fundamental difference from the former problem that was disguised by your focus on their similarity, resulting in an unsuccessful solution. What happened? You were anchored to an initial strategy for solving the problem. Thus, the anchoring and adjustment heuristic can lead to shortcuts that inhibit a full search. Time is not spent on alternative strategies. Obviously, anchors can come from a variety of places. The key is to notice how your problem solving is anchored in a particular situation.

Representativeness

By leading individuals to assess the likelihood of an occurrence by the similarity of that occurrence to the stereotype of a set of occurrences, representativeness affects judgment. If we are evaluating alternatives to a problem, we are likely to select alternatives based on how similar they are to successful decisions in similar problems. Although this will often be a successful strategy, the creative alternative is likely to be one that the representativeness heuristic would lead us to ignore. Thus, although the representativeness heuristic serves most of us fairly well on a day-to-day basis, it may be that being creative consists of going beyond our existing heuristics—such as representativeness.

The impact of the representativeness heuristic on blocking creativity can be illustrated in the context of selecting graduate students. If the faculty bases its selection on how representative applicants are of past successes in the program, they are likely to replicate their past level of success. However, the use of this heuristic will also destroy the opportunity to find a new creative profile of students that might be equally or more successful.

Availability

By leading individuals to assess the likelihood of an event by the degree to which instances of occurrences are readily available in memory, availability affects judgment. Individuals are overly affected by very vivid events. For example, an individual is likely to select an alternative that previously led to a very vivid success or an alternative that was recently used. However, further consideration may have led us to a better alternative. The use of the availability heuristic enabled us to respond to the problem quickly, perhaps at the sacrifice of a more creative and less available result. Similar to the representativeness heuristic, the availability heuristic serves us fairly well on a day-to-day basis, but it may be that being creative consists of being less affected by such heuristics.

Escalation

Creative thinking requires that the individual is open to divergent ideas. If the first hole seems to be in the wrong place, what other holes would be appropriate to consider digging? This is the creative strategy. In contrast, the escalation literature predicts that once an individual digs a hole and obtains negative results, he/she is likely to continue nonrationally to dig in order to justify the initial decision to dig that hole. Thus, the strategy described by the escalation literature is in direct conflict with the need for divergent thinking that is central to the creativity process. The nonrational tendency to escalate commitment to a previously selected course of action leads us to make implicit assumptions about the rationality of our initial strategy, reducing our potential creativity at future stages of the decision process.

Cultural and Environmental Blocks

Most of the previous blocks have been specified at only a cognitive level. Many of the cognitive assumptions that we make about how to solve the problems arise from the culture and environment that surround us. This is vividly illustrated by Adams (1979, p. 54) with the following example:

Quiz Item 2: Assume that a steel pipe is embedded in the concrete floor of a bare room as shown in Figure 5.1. The inside diameter is 0.06 inches larger than the diameter of a table tennis ball (1.50 inches) that is resting gently at the bottom of the pipe. You are one of six people in the room, along with the following objects:

100 feet of clothesline
A carpenter's hammer
A chisel
A box of cereal
A file
A wire coat hanger

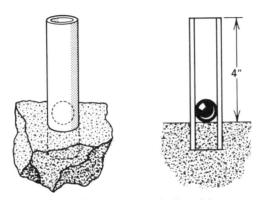

Figure 5.1 The ping-pong ball problem.

A monkey wrench

A light bulb

List as many ways as you can think of (in five minutes) to get the ball out of the pipe without damaging the ball, tube, or floor.

Adams argues that a creative person can come up with a number of solutions. Solutions include (1) filing the wire hanger in two, flattening the resulting ends, and making a large pair of tweezers to retrieve the ball; and (2) smashing the handle of the hammer with the monkey wrench and using the splinters to retrieve the ball. However, Adams suggests that it takes an unusually creative individual to identify the following solution: Have everyone in your group urinate in the pipe. Why is this solution so difficult to develop? Because our society has a taboo against solutions like these. As Adams notes, "urinating is somewhat of a closet activity." The important message is that we often make assumptions about problem solving based on the organization, culture, and society that surrounds our behavior.

A general pattern that emerges from examining these assumption creating blocks to creativity is that each of them leads us to seek a single (or limited set) right answer, leading us to abbreviate the decision process prematurely. Each may make the decision process more efficient. However, each also has the potential to stifle creativity.

This section has offered an approach for specifying why we make assumptions that block creativity. We have argued that the heuristics and frames that govern our decision processes also govern our creative abilities. This suggests that creativity is not a unique topic from decision making. We have argued that many of the reasons that explain our bounds to rationality also explain our lack of creativity. Thus, *we conceptualize the lack of creativity under the rubric of bounded rationality, with a particular focus on problems that require novel solutions*.

HEURISTIC-BREAKING HEURISTICS: STRATEGIES FOR BREAKING BLOCKS TO CREATIVITY

The focus of the chapter thus far has been to describe why most individuals are insufficiently creative. This focus is consistent with the focus of the first four chapters in being descriptive. The discussion so far in this chapter suggests (1) that the lack of creativity limits the quality of our decisions *and* (2) that individuals can be trained to improve their judgment by learning how to be more creative. The improvement of creativity is a central objective of this chapter. This implies that creativity is trainable—which I believe. This contradicts popular wisdom, which suggests that creativity is something that one is born with—some have it and some do not. Although there are individual differences in creativity, it is also true that all of us miss solutions because of the assumptions that we make. Thus, the lack of creativity is viewed similarly to heuristics; (1) it affects all of us, and (2) we can improve our judgment by reducing our lack of creativity.

This section is going to change the descriptive focus of this chapter and propose strategies for developing creativity that overcome the limitations identified in the previous section. Thus, this section will be prescriptive, consistent with the orientation in Chapter 6. However, the creativity literature has identified a number of useful prescriptions that are directed toward creative problem solving and deserve specific attention.

Wallas (1926) proposed that creative thinking was a four-stage process: (1) preparation, (2) incubation, (3) illumination, and (4) verification. This four-stage model, along with other similar models, has been used by many other authors to describe what creative individuals typically do and to prescribe what they should do to be creative. A general conclusion is that, although following these four stages cannot guarantee creativity, these four stages point out a number of useful ingredients for developing creativity. After examining these four stages, this section will extend the discussion by examining a number of specific strategies for breaking assumptions that block creativity.

1. Preparation (or Problem Definition)   Getzel (1975, p. 15) provides the following example concerning the importance of preparation before going on to the "action" part of problem solving:

> An automobile is traveling on a deserted country road and blows a tire. The occupants of the automobile go to the trunk and discover that there is no jack. They define the dilemma by posing the problem: Where can we get a jack? They recall that several miles back they had passed a service station and decide to walk to the station for a jack. While they are gone, another automobile coming from the other direction also blows a tire. The occupants of this automobile go to the trunk and, by happy coincidence needed for our example, they too discover that there is no jack. They define the dilemma by posing the problem: How can we raise the automobile? They look about and see that adjacent to the road is an old barn with a pulley for lifting bales of hay to the loft. They push the car to the barn, raise it on the pulley, change the tire, and drive off, while the occupants of the first car are still trudging toward the service station.

This example shows how the preparation (problem identification) of one group led to a significantly superior decision than that of another group. Preparation consists of obtaining a broader perspective of the problem through a wider search of information, clarifying the problem that needs to be solved, analyzing the resources that you have to address the problem, identifying missing resources, gathering additional resources, and assessing the assumptions that are being made about the problem. To the extent that the decision maker tries to move beyond the preparation prematurely (known as ready−fire−aim), the following problem-solving deficiencies are likely to result:

- You solve a problem, but it turns out to be the wrong problem. That is, you did not clearly understand the question and came up with a solution that does not solve the real problem. Rather, it solves the mythical problem that you thought existed.

- You make assumptions that keep you from finding the solution to the problem. We saw this in the nine-dot problem.
- You begin to work on the problem with insufficient physical resources, knowledge, or such. A common result is that by the time you realize that added resources are needed, you have invested a significant amount of time, money, and other factors in directions that are not productive. Many researchers find themselves in the middle of research projects that they wonder why they ever started. Insufficient problem definition may be the answer.
- You solve the short-term problem but not the long-term problem. That is, you identify the problem according to the existing symptoms. Your answers eliminate the symptoms but not the fundamental cause underlying the symptoms. Frequently, a broader perspective would have allowed for specifying the fundamental, long-term problem, rather than the superficial, short-term problem.

Finally, a critical part of preparation can consist of finding interesting problems to solve. This may sound confused: Why solve a problem that does not exist? Getzel (1975) asks and answers:

> Is not the world already teeming with dilemmas at home and in business, in economics and technology, in science and in art? The world is, or course, teeming with dilemmas. But the dilemmas do not present themselves as problems capable of resolution or even of sensible contemplation. They must be posed and formulated in fruitful and often radical ways if they are to be moved toward solution.

Similarly, Einstein argued that

> The formulation of a problem is often more essential than its solution, which may be merely a matter of mathematical or experimental skill. To raise new questions, new possibilities, to regard old questions from a new angle, requires creative imagination. . . ."

2. Incubation   Once the problem is defined, the next step in a logical, but uncreative, decision process is to converge toward a solution. Such logical decision processes are typically sequential, moving in a planned direction, conservative, and built on established patterns. This typically consists of identifying the immediately apparent alternatives, using obvious factors to evaluate the alternatives, and logically determining the best solution. Unfortunately, we often develop an early impression of the best solution, and most of our decision process consists of collecting confirmatory information for that decision (see Chapter 2).

In contrast, incubation is defined as a stage in the creativity process in which the individual explores unusual alternatives, eliminates assumptions that may hide alternatives, elaborates on the definition of the problem, and, in general, thinks in divergent ways to consider the problem. In contrast to the logical pattern of decision making, incubation will lead the individual to focus on low-probability (high payoff) alternatives and to think creatively and flexibly. De Bono (1971) describes incubation in terms of the concept *lateral thinking*: Lateral thinking is contrasted with logical (vertical) thinking by comparing the problem-solving process to the digging of a hole. Logic digs bigger and deeper holes. That is, logic escalates commitment to digging a particular hole. However, if the hole is in the wrong place, no amount of high-quality digging is going to put it in the right place. Lateral thinking is digging in different places to determine the right place to dig.

Many areas of research are criticized for telling the consumer of the research the obvious. Although the research may be extensive and of high quality, it may also be guilty of vertical thinking—digging the wrong hole very well. Like the manager, the researcher must consider the benefits of additional incubation. On the other extreme, however, incubation taken to an extreme becomes a rationalization for procrastination.

3. Illumination   This is the "aha" in problem solving. In its purest form, new ideas appear in a flash of insight. However, a more common, and still valid, form of illumination occurs when all the pieces fall into place. Although Wallas describes illumination as a stage in the creativity process, it is really the climax of the incubation stage.

4. Verification   This is the stage in which many highly "creative" people fail to be creative. After preparation, incubation, and illumination, the problem solver is ready to celebrate. However, all too often, he/she has been the victim of the confirmatory trap and the overconfidence bias. He/she has only tried to confirm that the innovation works. Furthermore, he/she approaches the task with a degree of overconfidence that is great for morale, yet potentially destructive to the innovation. Verification is the stage in which traditional logic and reason (the logical steps in decision making) are applicable for rigorously testing the validity of the innovation. An important aspect of this stage is to search for disconfirming evidence (see Chapter 2)—the true test of an innovation.

To this point, this section has focused on prescribing a set of stages that may help to organize the creative process. The creativity literature has also identified a number of specific strategies for developing creative solutions. Overall, the strategies will focus on how to break the blocks to creativity specified in the previous section. The specified strategies can be viewed as a partial checklist for developing creative solutions to a particular problem. The presentation will include a number of quiz items, which you are encouraged to solve before continuing the reading.

Assumption Breaking

Attempt to solve the following quiz item:

> *Quiz Item 3:* (Adapted from Winklegren, 1974) You are given four separate pieces of chain that are each three links in length (see the given state in Figure 5.2). It costs $100 to open a link and $150 to close a link. All links

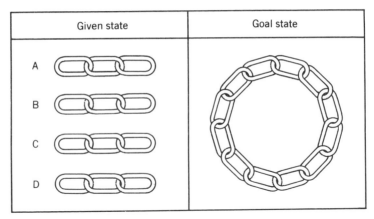

Given state	Goal state
A	
B	
C	
D	

Figure 5.2 Given and goal states for the necklace problem.

are closed at the beginning of the problem. Your goal is to join all 12 links of chain into a single circle (see the goal state in Figure 5.2). Your total budget for forming the single circle is $750. Solve it!

This quiz item is quite similar to the nine-dot problem that introduced the chapter. In the nine-dot problem, most people fail to solve the problem because of the false assumption that you cannot go outside the boundaries of the nine dots. In this (necklace) problem, most people fail to solve the problem because they assume falsely that after you open one link you can only insert one closed link into the opened link. For example, they try opening a link at the end of chain A, inserting an end link of chain B, and closing the joining link. They then open one end of the six-link chain and insert one of the other three-link chains, and so on. Unfortunately, this strategy will lead to the need to spend $1000 to solve the problem—beyond your budget. There are a number of action sequences that are essentially identical to this strategy, and all of them cost $1000.

In contrast, a few people have the insight to break the assumption that when you open one link, you are limited to inserting only one link into the opening. This leads to a variety of very similar successful solutions. For example, open all three links in chain A (cost = $300). Use one of them to combine chains B and C (cost = $150), use the second one to combine the free end of chain C to either end of D (cost = $150), and use the final open link to combine the remaining free end of chains B and D (cost = $150). The total cost equals $750.

As you can see, the solution is simple. However, very bright people can look at this problem for hours and not develop the solution. Why? Because we make assumptions about the problem that eliminate the solution. Frequently, we miss the optimal solution/choice to a problem not because we actively chose a different alternative over the optimal choice, but because we never considered the optimal choice as feasible. The reason for this oversight is typically caused by the assumptions that we make. Thus, the first proposed heuristic-breaking heuristic is to make it part of your standard decision processes to examine what you are assuming about a problem and its potential solutions.

The first strategy is a direct response to the argument that our limited rationality leads to assumptions that block creativity. We simply suggest that an awareness of this assumption-formation process can lead a decision maker to reduce this limitation by cognitively searching for the assumptions behind a decision.

Identify Subgoals When the Whole Task Appears Incomprehensible

Attempt to solve the following problem:

> **Quiz Item 4:** There are three identical spikes and six discs. Each disc has a different diameter. In addition, each disc has a hole in the middle large enough for any of the spikes to go through. At the beginning of the problem, the six discs are placed on spike A, one on top of another, with the largest disc on the bottom, then the next largest, and so on, with the smallest disc on top (see Figure 5.3). You are permitted to move one and only one disc at a time from one spike to another, with the restriction that a larger disc must never be moved on top of a smaller disc. The goal is to transfer all six discs from spike A to spike C (without a larger disc ever resting on a smaller disc). *Note:* You can use three pencils and six pieces of different size paper as a readily available substitute for the equipment shown in Figure 5.3. (This is a centuries-old problem presented by many authors including Winklegren, 1974).

Most people find this task to be overwhelming, or they immediately start moving the discs on a trial-and-error basis—a strategy that is not very suc-

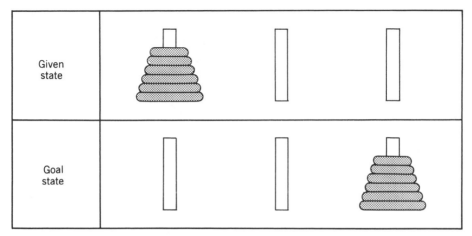

Figure 5.3 Given and goal states for the Tower of Hanoi problem.

cessful (if you find it easier than I describe, think about the problem with eight discs rather than six). A more useful strategy consists of thinking about the problem in terms of a sequence of actions to be solved (similar to a long computer program).

Your ultimate goal is to get all six discs stacked up on spike C. Because disc 6 has to be on the bottom, you have to get all the other discs off of disc 6 so that it is free to move. Also, you have to make sure that spike C is empty, so that disc 6 can be moved there. Fulfilling these requirements necessitates getting the five smallest discs on spike B (the five-disc problem)—a useful subgoal. In solving this subgoal, it should become apparent that it is necessary that you first get discs 1 through 4 on spike C (the four-disc problem) so that you can move disc 5 to spike B. To solve this four-disc problem, you need to get discs 1 through 3 on spike B (the three-disc problem) so that disc 4 can be moved to spike C. I am sure that you can easily solve this three-disc problem. Once you solve the three-disc problem, an interesting pattern emerges. You move disc 4 to spike C and want to move discs 1 through 3 on disc 4. Interestingly, you already know from your experience how to move disc 1 through 3 from one spike to another. Now that you have discs 1 through 4 on spike C, you move disc 5 to spike B. And now you already know from your recent experience how to move discs 1 through 4 from one disc to another. Once this is done, you are free to move disc 6 to spike C and repeat your knowledge of how to move discs 1 through 5 from one spike to another. You will then have the problem solved. Notice that you have now solved a problem that seemed quite difficult without performing any operation that was truly difficult. By analyzing how the problem could be broken into subgoals, a difficult problem turned into a series of fairly simple procedures.

Of course, you are not typically called on to solve Tower of Hanoi puzzles as part of your life as student, manager, or whatever. You are faced, however, with a variety of problems that *do* require subgoals. Computer programs have already been mentioned. The rationale for a subgoal approach generalizes to any problem that has multiple stages. The interesting task is to identify multi-stage problems that may not be presented as such.

Finally, a word of warning is in order. The subgoal approach will not work on all problems. Some problems require a single unique insight. Other problems have no subgoals. In either case, the subgoal approach will not lead to a solution. It is critical to identify whether or not the particular problem is in the domain of a subgoal approach. The important point is that we must approach decision making with the flexibility to use multiple different approaches.

Process Analysis

Quiz Item 5: (Adapted from Bartlett, 1978) A hobo can make one whole cigar from every five cigar butts he finds. How many cigars can he make if he finds 25 cigar butts?

Quiz Item 6: (Adapted from *Omni* magazine, 1981) Ten male senators are on their way to the Inaugural Ball. A crowd of disgruntled taxpayers attacks them with a volley of snowballs, knocking each senator's top hat to the ground. A helpful page retrieves the hats and hands one to each senator—but without checking to see who owns which one. What is the *exact* probability that *exactly* nine senators will receive their own hats? Do not use the assistance of a statistics book to solve this problem.

Both these problems are fairly simple using a heuristic-breaking heuristic called *process analysis.* By thinking about the processes (actions) involved by the actors in the problem, a problem solver can gain unique insights into the problems. Consider the hobo problem. The obvious answer is five. Unfortunately, this answer is wrong. Imagine the hobo on the park bench working with the 25 butts. What will he do with them? Create five cigars. Then why is five the wrong answer? The right answer lies in continuing to think about the bum in this situation. What will he do with the cigars? Smoke them. What will happen after he smokes the five cigars? He will get five butts and create a sixth cigar!

Similarly, consider the senator problem. Imagine the scene. Ten senators all lose their hats. How likely is it that exactly nine get the right hat? Try to imagine the return of the hats. If nine out of ten senators get the right hat back, what about the tenth hat and the tenth senator? If nine have the right hat, then there is only one senator and one hat left, meaning that the tenth senator must also have the right hat. Thus, the probability of exactly nine senators getting the right hat back is zero.

Now that you have had some practice with process analysis, try the following—it is a tough one:

Quiz Item 7: (Adapted from Bartlett, 1978) A conversation took place between two friends, a philosopher and a mathematician, who had not seen or heard from one another in years. The mathematician, who had an exceedingly good memory, asked the philosopher how many children he had. The philosopher replied that he had three. The mathematician then asked how old the children were. His friend, who knew how much most mathematicians enjoy puzzles, said he would give him a number of clues to the children's ages. The philosopher's first clue: "The product of the children's ages is 36." The mathematician immediately replied that this was insufficient information. The philosopher's second clue: "All the children's ages are integers; none are fractional ages (e.g., 1 ½ years old)." Still, the mathematician could not deduce the correct answer. The philosopher's third clue: "The sum of the three children's ages is identical to the address of the house where we played chess together often years ago." The mathematician still requires more information. The philosopher then gave his fourth clue: "The oldest child looks like me." At this point, the mathematician was able to determine the ages of the three children. Here is your problem: What were the ages of the three children?

This could be the hardest problem in this book. In trying to solve it, think about the information available to the mathematician after each clue. Why was he unable to solve the problem after the first three clues, but able to solve it after the fourth?

Let us analyze the likely thought processes of the mathematician. After the first clue, he knows that if you multiply the three numbers together, they will equal 36. There are an infinite number of possible combinations—thus the mathematician could not solve the problem at this point. After the second clue, the mathematician knows that all the ages are integers. This reduces the possibilities from an infinite number of possible solutions to the following eight:

A. $1 \times 1 \times 36$
B. $1 \times 2 \times 18$
C. $1 \times 3 \times 12$
D. $1 \times 4 \times 9$
E. $1 \times 6 \times 6$
F. $2 \times 2 \times 9$
G. $2 \times 3 \times 6$
H. $3 \times 3 \times 4$

However, after the second clue the mathematician has no way of deciding among these possibilities (although alternative A seems a bit unlikely). The third clue told the mathematician that the sum of the ages was equal to the address where they used to play chess. So the mathematician probably considered the sums of the eight possible combinations:

A. $1 + 1 + 36 = 38$
B. $1 + 2 + 18 = 18$
C. $1 + 3 + 12 = 16$
D. $1 + 4 + 9 = 14$
E. $1 + 6 + 6 = 13$
F. $2 + 2 + 9 = 13$
G. $2 + 3 + 6 = 11$
H. $3 + 3 + 4 = 10$

However, even after doing this, the mathematician with an extremely good memory (which suggests that he remembers the address where they used to play chess) still cannot determine the answer. Why not? There must be more than one answer that fulfills the requirements of multiplying to 36 and adding to the address where they used to play chess. Thus, the answer must be E or F. However, after the first three clues, the mathematician has no way of choosing between the two alternatives. After the fourth clue, that the *oldest* looks like the philosopher, the mathematician learns that there is an oldest! In choice E, there is no oldest child, because the two oldest are twins. Thus, the answer must be alternative F—2, 2, and 9.

This problem is clearly very difficult. Yet, even if you did not solve it, you should realize the potential insights that can be obtained by considering the actions and decision processes of the actors in the problem. Often, we are faced with situations where we cannot understand how a particular circumstance arose. Process analysis suggests that we can often gain a number of insights by thinking about the processes that were involved. Most of us, in contrast, tend to use a rational model based on surface evidence to understand our world.

All the heuristic-breaking heuristics presented up to this point have represented strategies that are likely to be counterintuitive to most readers. One might argue that they are the "creative" creativity techniques. In addition, there are a number of additional strategies that deal with breaking our heuristics that are commonly acknowledged in the creativity literature. These strategies tend to appear obvious, yet they are underused by decision makers.

Brainstorming

The best-known method of idea generation is probably brainstorming. The objective is to generate the greatest number of alternative ideas from uninhibited cognition. Initially, nothing is rejected or criticized. Any attempt to analyze, evaluate, or reject ideas is prohibited during a brainstorming session. "Freewheeling" is encouraged, nothing should be held back. Brainstorming breaks our tendency to eliminate quickly any solution that appears outside the boundaries of our assumptions. Although brainstorming is typically presented as a group problem-solving strategy, the logic of brainstorming is clearly extendable to individual problem solving. Get all your wildest ideas out without prejudgment.

One of the problems with brainstorming is the development of many shallow, poor-quality ideas. This could be a real problem if the ideas are taken too seriously. Thus, a useful companion strategy is *reverse brainstorming*—which consists of specifying everything that might be wrong with an idea. Thus, just as brainstorming increases the likelihood of finding the hidden great idea, reverse brainstorming allows us to find that hidden problem that makes the proposed solution useless. However, a word of caution: Reverse brainstorming must be used *after* brainstorming so as not to inhibit the positive benefit of brainstorming.

The Scientific Method

In many ways, the scientific method seems to be the antithesis of creativity. It is logical. It is orderly. It tends to be vertical. Yet, for many individuals, it will help them identify solutions that they would have never considered. Although many forms of the scientific method have been proposed, the steps generally include: (1) define the problem, (2) develop alternatives based on the existing information, (3) hypothesize the most likely solution, (4) gather data on the hypothesis, (5) incorporate the data into a proposed solution, (6) create an independent test of the solution, and (7) make a final determination. The scientific method leads people to follow a logical process—which may not occur based on intuitive strategies. More importantly, the scientific process builds in the potential to disconfirm what you thought would be true. As argued in Chapter 2, we tend only to seek anecdotal evidence that supports our position. The scientific method leads us to question the accuracy of our ideas.

Although a number of alternative strategies have been proposed in the creativity literature, most of them overlap with the ideas proposed here. In some cases, creativity techniques have been ignored because of their lack of a theoretical basis and empirical support. What has been proposed consists of a set of strategies that directly attack the bases of our blocks to creativity. Each of these techniques is supported by logic. However, future research needs to examine their effectiveness. In addition, this chapter has argued that these prescriptions respond to the limits to creativity defined earlier. This remains a topic meriting further investigation. Finally, these techniques are a mere sampling of heuristic-breaking heuristics. Other techniques have been and should continue to be identified. To illustrate this point, simply consider the following additions to the strategies presented previously: explore analogies, sleep on it, produce at least two solutions, be playful, explain it to someone else, call in a consultant. The point is that there are many strategies, and you should attempt to match the strategies to the cause of the lack of creativity—the assumptions that we make. Which strategy is most likely to eliminate the assumptions in a particular situation?

At this point, you should be aware of the reasons why we make assumptions and are often insufficiently creative, as well as some strategies for overcoming these barriers. However, we have developed our intuitive processes over many years. How can we change to become more creative in the ways specified? First, there is the issue of vigilance. Stay alert to situations where (1) assumptions are likely, (2) subgoals exist, (3) you can think about the process of the situation, (4) additional ideas may exist, (5) convergent thinking seems to have occurred quickly, or (6) the decision maker is failing to "test" the designated solution. Second, actively use some of or all the strategies suggested. If you incorporate these strategies into your decision processes, they will become second nature. Finally, learn to be aware of and evaluate your decision processes. By evaluating your decision processes, you can obtain feedback on your use of creative strategies.

SOME CONCLUDING COMMENTS

The relevance of our assumption-breaking approach to creativity can be further understood by considering its implications in a specific domain. Because of my biases and professional background, these concluding comments will briefly consider this approach to creativity in the research process. Davis

(1971) suggests that "interesting" research is created by breaking the "assumption ground" of the reader. That is, research will be interesting (creative) to the extent that the researcher demonstrates some piece of knowledge that contradicts the assumptions that others impose on the world. Many people question the value of research that confirms what they have already assumed to be true. But clear evidence that contradicts what you thought was true—that's interesting! The difference between the nine-dot problem and Davis's arguments lies in the target of the assumption breaking. In the nine-dot problem, the focus of the creativity lies in breaking your assumptions, whereas in Davis's definition of creativity, the focus lies in breaking the assumptions of the readers to whom the work is targeted.

In a related stream of thought, Kuhn (1970) argues that science is incremental (normal) until a revolution comes that contradicts the assumptions of a field of inquiry. Revolution formation is viewed as an unusually creative process in science, and as a very rare occurrence. Furthermore, Kuhn presents revolutions as an activity for a few lucky and gifted scientists, as opposed to being a trainable scientific process. Similarly, Adams (1979) makes the distinction between primary and secondary creativity in science, where primary creativity maps onto the scientific revolutions proposed by Kuhn. Although Kuhn's classic work has been a worthy development in training researchers to understand the scientific process, it may have also hindered the development of creativity. This book argues (1) that "revolutions" can be developed at varying levels of aggregation and (2) that researchers can be trained to create "revolutions" by questioning the assumptions that surround their research.

This chapter has suggested that we need to break more of our assumptions, it is also true that (like other heuristics) our assumptions have benefits in our decision processes. Specifically, they allow us to provide closure to a particular part of a problem and get on with solving the problem. Taken to an extreme, attempting to be infinitely creative can be counterproductive—keeping us from ever making a decision. One way of viewing this issue can be described on the following continuum:

"Normal" Decision Processes ---------------Creativity ----------------Absurdity

The central argument developed in this chapter is that most of us are insufficiently creative—we are too far to the left on the continuum. If we think about the research domain, most would agree that there is too much research that lacks creativity. This leads to admirable calls for "interesting" research. Frequently, the most enthusiastic admirers of these cries are those who are doing research that much of the field perceives as bordering on the absurd. We argue that researchers should be aware of this continuum and that the definition of creativity in various fields of inquiry should be openly debated.

This chapter encouraged a movement toward creativity but not an overreaction that leads to absurdity. Some individuals are very creative (or even absurd) in some domains, yet make too many assumptions that limit their decision processes in other domains (e.g., the logical decision maker at work that breaks all assumptions on the weekend). I hope that this chapter has provided you with some descriptions and prescriptions that are useful for thinking about creativity and where you lie on the continuum depicted here.

Finally, this chapter did not advocate a particular strategy for finding creative solutions. Rather, it is argued that decision makers need to understand the limits to rationality that limit creativity. This will allow for the discovery of underlying deficiencies that hinder creativity. In terms of tactical responses to a particular problem, this chapter encouraged flexibility in order to identify strategies that are appropriate to the situation and that are apt to respond to the blocks to creativity that are likely to be operating in the specific context.

SIX
IMPROVING DECISION MAKING

> The capacity of the human mind for formulating and solving complex problems is very small compared with the size of the problems whose solution is required for objectively rational behavior in the real world. . . .
>
> Herbert A. Simon

This quote articulates a central theme of the first five chapters of this book. These chapters have argued not that human beings are "bad" decision makers but that we fall short of objectively rational behavior. In addition, these chapters have identified specific ways in which the human mind fails to achieve fully rational behavior. These deficiencies clarify the need for ways to improve the decisions that we make.

The earlier chapters were primarily descriptive. This chapter departs from this direction temporarily to consider alternative prescriptive responses to the limitations to rationality that have been described. Although most individuals make judgments that are good enough to get by in everyday life and in the corporate world, the contention of this book is that there is plenty of room to improve on our deficient judgment. In addition, I argue that the topic of improving the quality of decisions is an important component of understanding managerial decision making.

In many areas of inquiry in the social sciences, descriptive and prescriptive work are not well connected. However, the area of decision making is a notable exception. In the area of decision making, descriptive and prescriptive research are more closely intertwined. A primary reason for this exception is that so much of the descriptive work is done against a prescriptive background. That is, descriptive researchers often describe decision making in comparison with a normative prescription. For example, the tendency to escalate was defined as a systematic bias in comparison with the decisions of a normative model. This means that prescriptive work can be seen as a set of trainable techniques to correct these previously identified deficiencies.

This chapter presents four alternative strategies for making better decisions than those that we would expect from using human intuition. These four strategies are (1) debiasing human judgment, (2) the use of linear models, (3) adjusting intuitive prediction, and (4) decision analysis. Each of these topics is based on fairly technical research. However, the presentation of the details of the research is not the purpose of this book. My purpose is to clarify to the uninformed reader what each strategy means at a fairly intuitive level. Based on this intuitive understanding, you can pursue a more detailed understanding through references in each of the sections.

The four strategies presented are not meant to represent a complete taxonomy of strategies for improving decisions. Rather, they are offered as four strategies that have received some attention from behavioral decision theorists. In addition, there may be more overlap between some pairs of strategies than between others. This chapter initially presents the strategies without illuminating clear connections between the strategies. After presenting the four alternative approaches, a comparative evaluation will be provided concerning the benefits and costs of each, as well as an evaluation of when each of the strategies would be most appropriate.

DEBIASING HUMAN JUDGMENT

Debiasing is a procedure for reducing biases arising from the cognitive strategies of the decision maker. Debiasing can be general (i.e., directed at a wide variety of biases) or specific (i.e., one bias) and can be temporary or permanent. This section will focus on debiasing efforts that are global and permanent. That is, we will be concerned with debiasing efforts that affect the entire range of judgmental deficiencies discussed in the first five chapters, and we will discuss debiasing of human judgment that is expected to create a permanent change in the individual's intuitive judgment.

Fischhoff (1982) has provided the most extensive discussion of procedures for debiasing human judgment. He proposes four strategies for eliminating unwanted biases in human judgment that are increasingly pessimistic about the ease of perfecting decision making: (1) warning about the possibility of bias; (2) describing the direction of the bias; (3) providing a dose of feedback; (4) offering an extended program of training with feedback, coaching, and whatever it takes to improve judgment. Fischhoff (1977) has shown that even when biases are explicitly described to subjects and they are asked to avoid the biases, biases remain. However, research on the overconfidence bias (Lichtenstein and Fischhoff, 1980) has found that intensive, personalized feedback was moderately effective in improving judgment. Overall, debiasing is a difficult process that needs to be guided by a psychological framework for understanding how to *change* human intuition.

Fischhoff's research is quite instructive for the development of a model to improve intuition. His work suggests that debiasing is quite difficult. In addition, his work suggests that feedback on an individual's own decisions is an important ingredient to successful judgment improvement. Both conclusions are consistent with the Lewinian three-stage change framework initially mentioned in Chapter 1. Table 6.1 outlines a comprehensive framework for improving human intuition that builds on the Lewinian framework, Fischhoff's debiasing research, and my own judgment training programs with MBA students and executives. In addition, the framework was the guiding model in the development and presentation of the first five chapters of this book.

Table 6.1   The Three-Stage Framework of Improving Judgment

	Stages		
	Unfreezing	Change	Refreezing
Implementation strategies	Quiz items that lead to failure Feedback	Clarification of the existence of specific judgmental deficiencies Explanation of the roots of these deficiencies Reassurances that these deficiencies should not be taken as a threat to the individual's self-esteem	Application Repeat training Feedback

Reading the table from left to right, the necessary stages for changing and improving judgment are outlined. The top half of the diagram repeats the Lèwinian stages. The bottom half specifies one view of how these stages could be implemented in the context of improving judgment. Each stage is examined more carefully below.

Unfreezing

Lewin told us that many behaviors at the individual, group, and organizational levels are ingrained, part of the organism's standard repertoire and thus quite difficult to change. He suggested that organisms find protection in the status quo. Translated into decision terms, organisms are often risk-averse and prefer the known (certain) outcomes of familiar behavior to the unknown outcomes of an innovative behavior. The importance of Lewin's unfreezing concept is central in changing the decision processes of individuals. This is true for at least three reasons. First, the individual has used his/her current intuitive strategy for many years. To want to change would be to admit that there was something wrong with past strategies. This is likely to be psychologically disturbing to many individuals. Thus, individuals may be motivated to avoid the emotionally disturbing information provided by the knowledge of judgmental deficiencies.

Second, individuals who are generally successful (it is assumed that this includes most MBA students, managers selected for special executive education programs, and I hope, readers of this book) have in the most part received positive reinforcement for many of their past decisions. According to reinforcement theory, individuals tend to continue behaviors that are positively rewarded. Many successful executives rose to the top using their intuitive strategies. This increases the individual's resistance to any information that his/her judgment is deficient in some observable manner.

Third, balance theory (Heider, 1958) suggests that individuals typically keep their cognitions in some consistent order. For the successful manager, the cognition "there is something fundamentally wrong with my decision processes" is inconsistent with his/her cognition about past success. The cognition "I am currently an excellent decision maker" is much more in balance and, according to balance theory, is therefore the cognition that is more likely to dominate.

Overall, a pattern emerges of an intelligent manager who has multiple reasons for believing in the quality of his/her decision processes and resisting any changes in intuitive strategies. In contrast, the first five chapters provided substantial evidence that there is significant room for improvement in the intuitive strategies of many bright, successful individuals. Thus, we conclude that improving intuition is an important activity for successful managers but that cognitive resistance to change is a predictable pattern.

To combat this resistance, early chapters in this book used a quiz and feedback format that was designed to unfreeze the reader. Most readers make a substantial number of mistakes on these items, which challenges the notion that the reader's decision processes were good enough and the book would have little to offer. Most readers respond by wanting to know where they went wrong and how they could have known to do better. When this occurs, the unfreezing process is taking place. The reader is no longer frozen to his/her past decision processes but wants to know what could be changed to create the desired improvement. In other cases (e.g., the dollar auction), a vivid example was described that had the potential for unfreezing the reader through identification with the individuals who fell victim to the judgmental deficiency. Thus, this chapter argues that creating change in judgment requires that the individual is exposed to some concrete evidence that leads the individual to question his/her current judgment strategies. A pure text format or lecture is unlikely to achieve this objective.

Change

The next stage consists of the change itself. The individual is now unfrozen from past behaviors and willing to consider an alternative. However, the change is far from guaranteed. The resisting forces are likely to still remain, and the individual is likely continually to reassess the desirability of the change. In terms of changing decision processes, there are four critical pieces that must be included in the change stage.

The *first* piece consists of clarifying the existence of specific judgmental deficiencies. This requires the abstraction from the concrete example that was used for unfreezing to identifying the more general bias that exists. The *second* piece provides an explanation of the roots of this deficiency. For a decision maker to fully understand the existence of the bias, he/she needs to understand why the bias exists. This often consists of clarifying the heuristic or phenomenon that underlies the bias. The *third* piece specifies what the "proper," or normative, decision process would be. This allows the decision maker to compare the intuitive deficient process with an improved process. Finally, the *fourth* piece provides the decision maker with reassurance that the deficiency should not be taken as a threat to the individual's self-esteem. The first three pieces can be threatening enough to increase the individual's resistance that was partially overcome in the unfreezing stage. Specifically, it is critical that the decision maker understand that biases exist in virtually all individuals, that they do not imply that he/she is not a good decision maker, only that room for improvement exists.

Refreezing

Once the change takes place, it is still easy for the individual to revert back to past practices. The old heuristics still exist and can be easily used. The new procedures are foreign and must become part of the decision maker's intuition. This takes place with practice over time. The individual needs to knowingly apply the new knowledge to multiple applications. Slowly, the new strategies will become second nature and will take their place as intuitive strategies. However, frequent application and repeat training are necessary to make the change last and become institutionalized as part of the individual's intuitive strategies.

This three-stage framework of change is most commonly seen in the organizational change literature. In that arena, the message of the framework is directed at change agents—individuals trying to implement some change in an organization. We see it as a guide to understanding a necessary set of conditions for creating cognitive change. It outlines some necessary conditions for changing the descriptions in the first five chapters of the book. And it provides a framework so that readers of the book can understand where they are in the change process.

LINEAR MODELS BASED ON EXPERT JUDGMENT

The judgment improvement strategy in the previous section responded directly to the biases discussed in the first five chapters of the book. Because the presentation of this book is based on a debiasing approach to judgmental improvement, the debiasing approach is the strategy most central to judgmental improvement in the context of this book. However, there are a number of reasons for examining alternative approaches. First, an individual will never be debiased entirely. Second, even if an individual could make the "rational" choice, the amount of time that it would take may not be worth the effort. In addition, the manager is often faced with the problem of creating a decision environment under which *others,* who may not be debiased, will be making decisions. Under these conditions, are there strategies that *respond to the limitations of human judgment* by creating alternative mechanisms to debiasing intuition?

The first alternative mechanism to debiasing consists of using an expert's judgments to build a linear model of his/her judgment that is effective in making future decisions. This strategy attacks the traditional view of expert decision making as being a mysterious phenomenon, incapable of the precise description that a model implies (Bowman, 1963; Slovic, 1982). The traditional view of expert decision making can be seen in a letter that I received from a well-known arbitrator when I asked the arbitrator to make a number of decisions as part of a study that examined the decision model of arbitrators (Bazerman, 1985):

> You are on an illusory quest! Other arbitrators may respond to your questionnaire; but in the end you will have nothing but trumpery and a collation of responses which will leave you still asking how arbitrators decide cases. Telling you how I would decide in the scenarios provided would really tell you nothing of any value in respect of what moves arbitrators to decide as they do. As well ask a youth why he is infatuated with that particular girl when her sterling virtues are not that apparent. As well ask my grandmother how and why she picked a particular 'mushmellon' from a stall of 'mushmellons.' Judgment, taste, experience, and a lot of other things too numerous to mention are factors in the decisions.

This section examines a strategy that does allow for capturing the arbitrator's decision model (or his grandmother's choice of a mushmellon). Evidence will be presented that in repeatable decision situations experts can be replaced by models based on their judgments and that these models can do better than the experts!

The statistical technique that is typically used is regression analysis (although other linear models are viable). Our purpose is not to examine the technical properties of such procedures, but to describe the essence of using regression analysis to capture an expert's decision processes. (Slovic and Lichtenstein [1971] review the use of regression analysis to capture decision processes). This approach necessitates that an expert makes decisions on a large number of cases, each of which is defined by the same set of factors. A regression equation can then be developed for that expert which describes his/her idiosyncratic model for making decisions. This procedure, referred to as *policy capturing,* has previously been used to investigate performance appraisal (Anderson, 1977; Naylor and Wherry, 1965; Zedeck and Kafry, 1977), promotion policy (Stumpf and London, 1981), and job choice (Zedeck, 1977), among many other managerial and nonmanagerial applications.

One compelling example of the use of linear models is provided by Dawes's (1971) work on graduate admissions decisions. He modeled the average judgment of a four-person committee. The predictors in the model were (1) a score from the Graduate Record Examination, (2) overall undergraduate grade point average, and (3) quality of undergraduate school. Dawes used the model to predict the average rating of the committee on 384 applicants. He found that the model could be used to reject 55 percent of the applicants without ever rejecting an applicant that the committee would have accepted. In addition, the weights used to predict the committee's behavior were better than the committee itself in predicting future faculty ratings of the accepted and matriculated applicants. Dawes estimated in 1971 that the use of a linear model as a screening device by the nation's graduate schools (not to mention the larger domains of undergraduate admissions, corporate recruiting, and so on) could result in an annual savings of about $18 million worth of professional time.

Researchers have found policy capturing to produce superior predictions across an impressive array of domains. In addition, research has found that more complex models produce only marginal improvements beyond a simple linear framework. Why do linear models work so well? Dawes (1979) argues that the underlying reason is that people are much better at selecting and coding information (i.e., what variables to put in the model) than they are in integrating the information (i.e., using the data to make a prediction). Einhorn (1972) illustrated this point in a study of doctors who coded biopsies of patients with Hodgkin's disease and then made an overall rating of severity. This rating had no predictive power of the survival time of the patients—all of whom died. The variables that the doctors selected to code, however, did predict survival time when optimal weights were determined with a multiple-regression model. The point is that the doctors knew what information to consider, but they did not know how to integrate this information into a valid prediction.

In addition to the difficulty that individuals have in integrating information, individuals are also unreliable. Given the same data, we will not always make the same decision. Our decisions are affected by such factors as mood, invalid subjective interpretations, and random fluctuations. In contrast, the model will always make the same decisions with the same inputs. Thus, the model captures the underlying policy that the expert uses but does not add the random errors that the expert adds in making decisions. Furthermore, the expert is likely to be affected by a number of biases. In contrast, the model only includes the actual data that are empirically known to have predictive power and is unaffected by the salience or representativeness of that data. This point was exemplified in the graduate school application of Mark Sonet (name has been changed). Sonet was a graduate student in the department of one of my early faculty positions. He was extremely bright, had a history of excellent board scores, had good grades, had been in a number of graduate programs before, and never seemed to make much progress toward completing his doctorate. I was looking over some recent admissions decisions and noticed an applicant that had excellent grades, excellent board scores, who had previous graduate school background, seemed to have found his real interests, and was rejected. It seemed apparent to me that the applicant was well above the standards of the department and would have been easily accepted by a Dawes-type admissions procedure. When I asked why the applicant was rejected, I was told that he looked too much like Mark Sonet!

A number of similar examples can be identified easily in financial decisions, corporate personnel decisions, bank loan decisions, routine purchasing decisions, and so on. The common aspect of these domains is that each requires the decision maker to make multiple routine decisions based on the same set of variables. These characteristics lend themselves well to the policy-capturing methodology, and ample evidence suggests that the linear model of the experts will outperform even the experts. In addition, the policy-capturing procedure allows the organization to see what factors are important in the decisions of experts. Thus, the feedback and training potential of linear models, independent of their superior predictive powers, make their use a valuable managerial tool. The application of policy capturing (and the variety of expert systems that are being developed in artificial intelligence) is clearly an underused decision procedure in the managerial environment.

Although the evidence suggests the ample power of the policy-capturing methodology, its use is not that well diffused. Why? Resistance. Early in the development of the methodology, technical arguments on the predictive ability of linear models emerged (Dawes, 1979). These have generally been addressed, and the literature provides strong support for the models. But this does not stop individuals from failing to believe in the predictive ability of the models. Stronger resistance comes in the form of ethical concerns and general resistance to change. The ethical concerns are well illustrated by a woman cited in Dawes (1979):

> When I was at the Los Angeles Renaissance Fair last summer, I overheard a young woman complain that it was "horribly unfair" that she had been rejected by the Psychology department at the University of California, Santa Barbara, on the basis of mere numbers, without even an interview. "How could they possibly tell what I'm like?" The answer is they can't. Nor could they with an interview (Kelly, 1954).

Dawes goes on to argue that for a decision maker to believe that he/she can predict better based on a half-hour interview than the information contained in a transcript based on three and one half years of work and the carefully devised aptitude assessment of graduate board exams demonstrates unethical conceit on the part of the decision maker.

The other main reason for resistance to the use of linear models is that linear models are threatening. "What will my role be if I don't make the decisions?" What does a bank loan officer do if she does not make decisions on loans? These questions are common and show the concern that people are not central to the use of linear models. But people are important. People determine the variables to put into the model. People make the initial decisions that are the ingredients of the model. People determine when the model needs to be updated. People monitor the performance of the model. Nevertheless, Lewin clarified that resistance to change can be expected, and the use of linear models is no exception to this expectation.

The models described have dealt with weights as determined by modeling the decisions of experts. Sometimes those data do not exist. Alternative procedures exist. These include having experts provide the weights, using equal weighting procedures, and determining optimal weights from a data base of outcomes. Each of these has desirable properties over human intuition in repetitive decisions where the same variables are used for prediction. However, a full discussion of these procedures is beyond the scope of this book. The reader is referred to Slovic and Lichtenstein (1971), Dawes and Corrigan (1974), and Dawes (1979).

Finally, a number of other procedures follow the policy-capturing approach of trying to model what it is that experts do. These alternative procedures deal with a wider domain of problems than those addressed by policy capturing. Examples include recent developments in artificial intelligence and expert systems. These paradigms seek to provide knowledge representations and inference mechanisms to the computer in ways that allow for capturing and improving on what experts know about problem solving in general and specific domains (Hayes-Roth, Waterman, and Lenat, 1983). Again, the examination of these other modeling procedures is beyond the scope of the book, but identifying their existence is relevant in the context of understanding the role of using models to replace intuition.

ADJUSTING INTUITIVE PREDICTION

The nature of managerial work requires reviewing the tentative decisions of others, transforming recommendations to decisions, and adjusting previously made decisions. This is a fundamentally different decision task than the decisions implied by the rational decision model specified in Chapter 1. Clearly, the decision maker wants to include the content of the previously made decisions and recommendations. Often, the initial decision was made with more information than you care to reevaluate. However, you are aware that the initial decision was influenced by a set of biases. How can you systematically adjust the initial decision to account for biases in order to make a better final decision? Before answering this question in a generic sense, consider the following managerial situation:

> You are the director of marketing for a retail chain that has 40 stores in 14 cities. Sales in these stores average between $2 million and $4 million, with mean sales of $3 million. Twenty-five of these stores have opened in the last three years. Plans for the future include opening 30 new sites in the next four years. Because of this growth, you have a site location analyst assigned to predict the sales in each potential site. Unfortunately, predicting sales in new markets is very difficult and even the best analyst faces a great deal of uncertainty. You are partially evaluated on the accuracy of the forecasts coming out of your department. The site location analyst has just handed you her latest forecast. It forecasts sales of $3.8 million for a new potential site. The facts verify that the demography of this area should place this location as one of the top producers in the chain. What is your reaction to the forecast?

At a naive level, there is reason to have confidence in the forecast. She knows more of the details than you about the facts that underlie the prediction.

In addition, your overview also predicts that the store will do well in comparison with existing stores. This evaluation is based on matching the prediction with the outcomes of representative sites. However, this rule of prediction is unsound, because it fails to take the decision maker's lack of predictability into account. One basic idea of statistical prediction that is often counterintuitive, is the concept of regression to the mean. That is, extremity of prediction should be moderated (toward the mean) by the degree of uncertainty in the prediction (Kahneman and Tversky, 1982). This can be illustrated in the preceding example. Assume that the site-location analyst was excellent. In fact, there was a perfect (1.0) correlation between her predictions and actual sales. In that case, it would be appropriate to use the $3.8 million prediction. However, also consider the case where there is a correlation of zero between her predictions (which are based on the demographic data) and actual sales—thus making the $3.8 million forecast meaningless. In this case, the only remaining information that is available is that the average store has sales of $2 million, and this becomes your best estimate. In cases of intermediate predictability, which is the common state, the forecast should fall between the mean store and the site location analyst's estimate—becoming progressively closer to the analyst as the predictability increases (Kahneman and Tversky, 1982). However, as we know from Chapter 2, intuitive prediction is nonregressive, and extreme forecasts are frequently made based on invalid data.

This analysis suggests that the director will want to reduce the forecast to somewhere between $2 million and $3.8 million depending on an assessment of the correlation between forecasts and actual sales. Essentially, the director should use his/her understanding of the nonregressiveness of human judgment (see Chapter 2) to determine a systematic adjustment to the initial decision. Notice that if we understand systematically the ways in which judgment deviates from rationality, similar adjustments can be determined for a vast array of biases. The next part of the section will outline a corrective procedure for our lack of regressiveness and apply it to the site location problem. The section will then examine the relevance of such procedures to other biases.

The preceding analysis provides a rough guide to the adjustment of the analyst's forecast. Kahneman and Tversky (1982) have formalized this process into a five-stage procedure that is useful for clarifying the logic behind the adjustment of intuitive judgment. You not only should examine the technical nature of the five-step process, but should also be thinking about the intuition that would be necessary to make the appropriate adjustments without going through the formal procedure. In other words, you should be thinking about how the systematic training suggested in the five-step process can help the manager think about decisions in such a way that he/she naturally recognizes the existence and direction of a wide range of biases across a wide range of settings.

1. *Selecting a comparison group.* This step consists of selecting the set of past observations to which the current forecast can be compared. In the site

location problem, the population of all company stores is an obvious group. However, alternatives exist. For example, it might be decided that only the stores opened in the last three years are appropriate for comparison. This might be decided if the recent stores are quite different from the established stores and are closer in description to the future stores. The existence of multiple comparison groups is common. The more inclusive group allows for the larger base for comparison, but its heterogeneity may reduce its comparability to the targeted forecast. Therefore, the decision maker must balance the simultaneous needs for a large *and* appropriate comparison group.

2. *Assessing the distribution of the comparison group.* If the group consists of all stores, we know the range and mean from the data presented previously. If we limited the group to recent stores, these data would need to be re-calculated. In addition, we might want to get additional data about the shape of the distribution around the mean.

3. *Intuitive estimation.* This step is to identify the nonregressive forecast of the expert—the site location analyst. This estimate ($3.8 million in the site location problem) provides the intuitive estimate that needs to be adjusted. The next two steps attempt to improve this forecast.

4. *Assessing the predictability of the analyst's forecast.* This is the most difficult step in the corrective procedure. It consists of estimating the relationship between the analyst's forecasts and actual sales. It may be possible to assess this by correlating past estimates to actual sales. In the absence of this data, you must determine some subjective procedure for this assessment. Kahneman and Tversky (1982) discuss this in more detail. For our purposes, however, the key point is that the nonregressive estimate assumes a perfect correlation of 1.0. In virtually all cases, we can produce a better subjective estimate than the implicit assumption of a 1.0 correlation that nonregressive estimates imply.

5. *Adjusting the intuitive estimate.* This step provides an estimate that reduces the nonregressiveness error described earlier. For example, this procedure should produce an estimate of $3.8 million when the correlation in step 4 was 1.0, an estimate of $2 million when the correlation was 0, and estimates proportionally in between when the correlation was in between. This can be formalized as (Kahneman and Tversky, 1982)

adjusted estimate = group mean + correlation (initial estimate − group mean)

In our example, it is easy to see that this leads to a prediction of $2.9 million when the correlation is .5, $3.35 million when the correlation is .75, and so on. The person making the adjustment should fully understand the logic of the procedure, then evaluate its relevance to the decision at hand. In arguing for this adjustment, it should be remembered that we are again likely to face a problem of resistance to change.

The preceding steps provide a clearly delineated process for debiasing an individual's nonregressive intuition. The formal procedure will typically improve the forecast. More importantly, a person who understands the process can use this understanding to intuitively assess the degree to which an initial estimate should be regressed to the mean. It is in this informal sense that we have a model for how to adjust a wider range of biased decisions. We simply understand the systematic properties of the bias of the analyst's decisions, then make the logical adjustment. We can similarly use this judgment improvement technique to evaluate and adjust our own intuitive judgments. This judgment improvement process requires that we examine the likely decision processes of ourselves and of others—a difficult process. However, with this in hand, we can consider and adjust from the systematic properties of all the biases discussed in the first five chapters of the book.

DECISION ANALYSIS

The previous sections provided alternative approaches to improve human intuition as a strategy to increase the quality of decisions. The first section concerned creating a permanent improvement in intuitive skills. The second section dealt with using a policy-capturing approach developed from expert judgment to improve decision making. And the third section dealt with adjusting intuition based on the biases that we know to describe intuitive processes. Each of the three sections prescribed corrective procedures that respond directly to the description of how we actually make decisions. Although each strategy was prescriptive, each was based on a description of judgment. The use of decision analysis, by contrast, is distinctly normative. It prescribes what we should do without a descriptive base. Obviously, this work is not consistent with the general descriptive thrust of this book. However, we provide an overview of this strategy because it is relevant to improving judgment and is an alternative direction to the strategies described previously.

Decision analysis is a set of normatively derived techniques that outline how we should make decisions. Decision analysis can be thought of as a set of explicit techniques that lead us through a rational decision process. They are typically recommended for decisions when the stakes are high and both time and available resources are substantial (Slovic, 1982). Decision analysis encompasses cost-benefit analysis and the use of decision trees, as well as more complicated procedures from the operations research literature. The objective of decision analysis is to provide a rational perspective for making decisions under uncertainty that will prescribe the best decision given the decision maker's goals, expectations, and values (Raiffa, 1968; Keeney and Raiffa, 1977).

Decision analysis can be an extremely complex procedure requiring very skilled expertise. In other situations, it requires minimal training that can be found in introductory textbooks on the topic. This section will not try to present a detailed technical treatment of decision analysis, not even in a simple form.

Rather, I will try to give you an overview of the ingredients and objectives of decision analysis. Decision analysis provides technical guidance for implementing the rational steps of decision making outlined in Chapter 1 under conditions of uncertainty. Thus, an overview of decision analysis overlaps with the steps specified in Chapter 1. For example, Hogarth (1981) lists the following as steps in decision analysis:

1. Structuring the problem.
2. Assessing consequences.
3. Assessing uncertainties.
4. Evaluating alternatives.
5. Sensitivity analysis.
6. Information gathering.
7. Choice.

Structuring the problem consists of identifying the decision makers, the alternatives, the criteria on which alternatives differ, the key uncertainties, and formalizing the structure of the problem. *Assessing consequences* consists of assigning a value for each alternative on each criterion and weighting the criteria according to their relative importance. *Assessing uncertainties* consists of formalizing the level of uncertainty in each area of uncertainty in the problem structure. *Evaluating the alternatives* consists of selecting the decision rule to apply (e.g., expected value, expected utility, etc.) and using this rule to make an initial decision. *Sensitivity analysis* assesses the amount of error in the inputs that would be needed for a different decision to result. This identifies the confidence the decision maker should have in the initial decision. This five-step process is likely to identify areas in which additional information is necessary. Identifying these deficiencies is the role of the *information-gathering* stage. Finally, after additional information is obtained, a final (and rational) *choice* about which alternative to select can be made.

It should be obvious that each of the steps listed may in actuality be a very complicated process, both in terms of analysis and in terms of mathematics. In addition, the inputs are still likely to come from individuals—who still possess the biases discussed extensively in the book. For these reasons, the implementation of formal decision analysis requires expertise for obtaining relatively unbiased inputs and for using the sophisticated analyses available for decision analysis.

In addition to its primary role as a rational procedure for making complex decisions, decision analysis identifies all the inputs and assumptions that went into the decision (Slovic, 1982). Thus, it can serve as a vehicle for communication among those involved in the decision. The decision analytic framework can be used to identify the location, magnitude, and importance of areas of disagreement. The decision analytic framework can identify why various individuals differ in their intuitive judgment—thus allowing for a clearer discussion of the dispute or areas in which additional information is needed. Finally, decision analysis allows for relatively easy updating of decisions as the inputs change—because the structure of the problem is so clearly formulated.

It should be obvious that the use of decision analysis does not eliminate the individual from the decision. The individual is needed at each stage of the process, and the inputs to the framework come from individuals. Decision analysis provides an orderly mechanism to aggregate the knowledge and judgment of various sources to help make the best possible decision for the organization. Thus, it is more appropriate to view decision analytic procedures as methods for structuring judgment, rather than replacing judgment.

A final benefit that accrues from the use of decision analytic procedures is the improvement in the logic of the intuitive processes of the decision makers involved. By following the decision analyses in formal decisions, we learn over-time to think in a more logical way. Although this is not the primary reason to adopt decision analysis, it is a desirable externality.

COMPARISON OF STRATEGIES FOR IMPROVING DECISIONS

Following an overview of four distinct strategies for improving decision making, there is a natural tendency to want to see a preferred strategy emerge. However, the picture that emerges as the four strategies are compared is one in which the four strategies achieve very different objectives and need different information as inputs. All started with the problem that judgment deviates from rationality and attempted to develop some way of improving on intuition. However, the four strategies achieve this general objective in different ways. These differences are summarized in Table 6-2. This section will discuss the differences of the four strategies in terms of their objectives, necessary ingredients, and primary advantages.

Objectives

The strategy of debiasing human judgment creates an improved intuitive decision maker through a change process that reduces the decision maker's susceptability to unwanted biases. No other strategy has this objective. Debiasing human judgment could be viewed as the personal development strategy for improving judgment. This is the only strategy of the four that is focused on the decision maker, as opposed to a decision or group of decisions. Thus, although this strategy is likely to have the most generalizable impact on the decision maker, it is probably the least useful for improving a specific decision or group of decisions. The main thrust of this book falls in this category.

The use of policy-capturing is the strategy that creates a routine mechanism for making multiple repetitive decisions. In addition, this strategy is the only one that attempts to maintain some aspect of the past decisions of experts. Furthermore, this strategy can easily be updated if the decision maker has the objective of constantly improving the decision-making procedure.

Table 6.2 A Comparison of the Four Decision-Making Improvement Strategies

	Debiasing	Linear Models	Adjusting Intuition	Decision Analysis
Primary objectives	Improving the permanent quality of an individual's intuition	Capturing the model of experts Making high-quality repetitive decisions	Adjusting an individual's intuition to account for biases known to affect judgment	Making a rational decision in unique situations
Necessary ingredients	Successful change process Knowledge of biases	Common set of independent variables	Knowledge of operative biases and the directionality and magnitude of the biases	Sophistication in decision analytic techniques Ample time Ample resources
Advantages	Generalizable across domains Personal development	Improves on expert's decisions Reliable Empirically validated	Improves the intuition of self Improves the intuition of others	Normative Adaptable to nonroutine decisions

The strategy of adjusting intuitive judgment is a particularly interesting strategy for the managerial environment. Managers are constantly faced with evaluating and adjusting the biased decisions of others. Typically, the manager does not want to repeat all the work that went into the initial decision. Rather, the manager is looking for guidance concerning how to evaluate and adjust the summary evaluation that a subordinate or peer provided. This is the perfect role for this third strategy.

Decision analysis attempts to make the optimal decision in the specific decision context. Accepting the decision analytical view of rationality as maximizing the utility of the decision maker, this strategy is optimal for unique decisions that are important and where resources are ample. Although the full use of a formal decision analytic procedure may be limited to a narrow range of situations, knowledge of decision analytic procedures may help a decision maker organize his/her decision process across a much broader array of settings. In fact, decision analysts often argue that the primary benefit of this procedure is that the "process" is illuminated.

These four different strategies have four different purposes. Thus, the four different strategies are not directly competing—they serve different needs.

One might conclude that the debiasing strategy is independent from the others because it focuses on the decision maker. Thus, it might be recommended that all decision makers should focus on a debiasing effort. In contrast, when the manager thinks about improving a decision or set of decisions, he/she has three alternative strategies that seem best suited for three very different contexts. The optimal strategy will be the one that best fits the strategy's objectives and the objectives of the decision maker. Finally, it is noteworthy that each of the decision-oriented strategies requires inputs from the decision maker, and a debiased decision maker is more likely to provide the appropriate inputs into these alternative strategies.

Necessary Ingredients

The information requirements for the four strategies also differ dramatically. The debiasing strategy simply requires an open mind, the knowledge for change, and a successful change program. Although the debiasing strategy may be the most difficult to implement because of resistance to change, there is little in the way of resource requirements to block implementation. In contrast, each of the other strategies needs some specific data, knowledge, and/or expertise. The policy-capturing strategy requires an historical database of past decisions where each decision is described by a common set of quantifiable independent variables (or some suitable alternative). In addition, some sophistication in the use of regression analysis and/or related techniques is necessary. Adjusting intuitive judgment requires knowledge of the operative bias and the ability to identify situations in which the bias is likely to take effect. In addition, the decision maker must have formal or informal knowledge of how to make the appropriate adjustment. Finally, decision analysis requires substantial time, resources, and expertise. Thus, in addition to evaluating the fit of the four strategies to the decision maker's problem, some consideration of the necessary ingredients is required.

Advantages

Each of the four strategies has a number of distinct advantages. The debiasing strategy has the advantage of producing improvement across all the decision maker's judgments. It offers the benefit of improving something within the decision maker, rather than the decision. Finally, we make many decisions in which we will never consider implementing any of the other strategies. In these cases, we have no choice but to trust our judgment. The debiasing strategy offers the opportunity of increasing the quality of the intuition that we trust. The policy-capturing approach offers the opportunity to understand the underlying model of experts. In addition, it provides feedback to the decision maker. The strategy is also the only method with a proven track record for improving the quality of decisions. Finally, this method offers a low-cost mechanism for making multiple repetitive decisions. Adjusting intuitive prediction offers the benefit of fitting into the common managerial context of evaluating and adjusting an initial decision, rather than making the original decision. Finally, the decision-analysis strategy offers us the best decision in unique situations. Decision analysis is the optimal strategy for important, unique decisions where few resource constraints exist. Again, we see in the comparison of the advantages of the four strategies unique benefits that call for a fit between the strategy and the goal of the decision maker.

This chapter has attempted to outline alternative strategies for dealing with the limitations that were presented in the earlier chapters of the book. Four unique strategies have been proposed. This book argues that the debiasing strategy is one that all managers should want to implement. In addition, a good decision maker should be aware of the other three strategies and implement these alternatives when they fit with the decision context.

By providing an overview of these three other strategies, this chapter places this book in the broader context of decision-making improvement strategies. It illustrates three additional strategies in the decision-making literature that augment the debiasing strategy found in this book. Finally, this chapter provides references to allow the interested reader to expand his/her examination of ways of improving decision making.

SEVEN
JUDGMENT IN TWO-PARTY NEGOTIATIONS

In negotiation, as in life, we tend to end up with less than our wildest dreams, but with a great deal more than is provided by the next best alternative.

Jeffrey Z. Rubin (1983)

The first six chapters dealt with individual decision making. That is, the chapters examined how individual judgment systematically deviates from rationality and how individuals can/should change based on the biases described. Little attention has been given to the other actors involved when a manager makes a judgment. The rationale for this approach has been the argument that we need to understand a number of basic principles of judgment before we examine how managerial judgment is affected by other individuals that managers encounter in organizational life. It is fairly obvious that many managerial decisions are multiparty decisions made in conjunction with other organizational actors.

Chapters 7 and 8 will now build on the information in the first six chapters to examine judgment in multiparty contexts in organizations. These chapters will selectively use information presented in the first six chapters, as well as information in the literatures on negotiation, third-party intervention, coalition behavior, group decision making, and competitive bidding. Thus, these chapters will not use every piece of information in the first six chapters, nor will they provide a comprehensive review of these multiparty contexts. Rather, they will selectively use information to identify what a judgmental perspective has to offer to each multiparty context.

Chapter 7 examines judgment in negotiated contexts between two parties. When two parties within or between organizations jointly make decisions and do not have identical preferences, they are negotiating. They may not be sitting around a bargaining table; they may not be making explicit offers and counteroffers; they may be making statements suggesting that they are on the same side. However, if they do not have identical preferences concerning some joint decision, they are negotiating. This suggests that negotiation is a pervasive activity that is central to organizational life. The purpose of this chapter is to examine how the ideas developed earlier in the book are manifested in competitive situations. In addition, this chapter examines additional sources of deviations from rationality that inhibit rational behavior in competitive situations.

This chapter will present relevant background material on negotiation and then propose a framework to integrate information on negotiator cognition into

the negotiation literature. There are many other topics in the negotiation literature that deal with decision making that are not discussed in this chapter (see
Lewicki and Litterer, 1985). Rather, this chapter extends the judgmental framework developed throughout this book to the negotiation context. The findings
on negotiator cognition in this chapter are based on experimental studies by
myself and my colleagues. Chapter 8 will deal with the remaining areas of
multiparty decision making in organizations (third-party intervention, coalition
behavior, group decision making, and competitive bidding). Chapter 8 will be
far more exploratory because little research has been done on the role of
cognition in these interactive decision situations.

This chapter is written to affect competitive decision making in two ways:
First, the chapter seeks to improve the quality of outcomes to a particular
negotiator who is familiar with the material in this chapter. In addition, the
chapter seeks to improve the quality of dispute resolution in terms of reducing
the likelihood of negotiations reaching an impasse when it is in the interest of all
parties for a settlement to be reached. This latter purpose is a very friendly
objective. Whereas the former objective seeks to help a specific negotiator, the
latter purpose attempts to improve the outcomes to both parties in the negotiation and the effectiveness of a society in dealing with conflict.

SOME BASIC FRAMEWORKS FOR
UNDERSTANDING NEGOTIATIONS

The Bargaining Zone

The Single-Issue Case   To illustrate this basic building block of negotiation,
consider the following example:

> An MBA from a very prestigious school, with a number of unique talents, is being
> recruited for a highly specialized position. The organization and the employee have
> agreed on all issues other than salary. The organization has offered $40,000, and the
> employee has requested $50,000. Both sides believe that they have made fair offers.
> However, both sides would very much like to see an agreement worked out. The
> student, although not verbalizing this information, would be willing to take any offer
> over $43,000 rather than losing the offer. The organization, while not verbalizing this
> information, would be willing to pay up to $47,000 rather than losing the candidate.

Ben Franklin offered some advice to our two parties: "Trades (e.g., an
employment agreement) would not take place unless it were advantageous to
the parties concerned. Of course, it is better to strike as good a bargain as
one's bargaining position permits. The worst outcome is when, by overreach-
ing greed, no bargain is struck, and a trade that could have been advantageous to both parties does not come off at all" (Raiffa, 1982).

Most recent discussions of the positions of parties in negotiations have used
Walton and McKersie's (1965) concept of the *bargaining zone*. A simplified

view of the bargaining zone concept is diagrammed here to describe the recruitment problem.

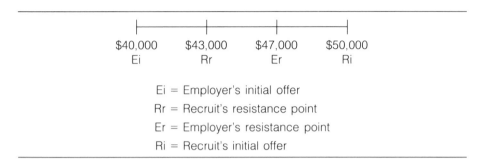

The bargaining-zone framework assumes that each party has some "resistance point" below (above) which the negotiator would prefer not reaching a settlement (impasse) over a settlement at that level. These points are represented by the two resistance points in the diagram. Notice that the two points overlap—that is, the employer's point is above the employee's point. There are a set of resolutions (i.e., all points between $43,000 and $47,000) that both parties would prefer over not reaching an agreement. When the resistance points of two parties overlap, a positive bargaining zone is said to exist. Furthermore, when a positive bargaining zone exists, a rational model of negotiation would dictate that the negotiators should reach a settlement—it is the rational thing to do. When the resistance points of the two parties do not overlap, a negative bargaining zone is said to exist. If a negative bargaining zone exists, no resolution should be possible because there are no settlements that are acceptable to both parties (in comparison with the parties' best alternatives other than a resolution).

Many people find the notion of a bargaining zone to be counterintuitive, because listening to a variety of negotiations leads to the conclusions that the resistance points of the parties never overlap, but that they simply meet at the point of agreement. This thinking is typically incorrect. In fact, at the point of agreement both parties are choosing that settlement in comparison to impasse. Obviously, their actual resistance (or indifference) points are overlapping, and the settlement point is actually one of many within the bargaining zone.

Returning to the recruiting example, we can see that the bargaining zone truly consists of the range between $43,000 and $47,000. If the employer could convince the recruit that an offer of $43,100 was final, we know the recruit would accept the offer. Similarly, if the recruit could convince the employer that $46,900 was the lowest salary that she would accept, we know the employer would agree to accept this wage. Thus, one of the key skills of negotiation is to determine the other party's resistance point, and aim for a resolution barely acceptable to the other party. However, Ben Franklin has warned us that if the two parties have too much greed, they may rigidly demand a bargain that is outside the other party's resistance point, and no bargain can be achieved. When this greed occurs, the parties may act in ways that prohibit the rational choice of finding a solution within the bargaining zone (e.g., the recruit holds to a demand of $46,000 and the employer holds to the offer of $44,000—both believing that the other side will "cave in").

The Multiple-Issue Case   The preceding analysis dealt with negotiation in a situation in which a single issue (salary) was disputed. Many negotiations, in contrast, consist of many disputed issues. For eample, consider the Camp David talks in 1978 (documented in Pruitt and Rubin, 1985).

> Egypt and Israel tried to negotiate the control of the Sinai Peninsula, a situation in which it appeared that the two sides had directly opposing goals. Egypt wanted the return of the Sinai in its entirety, whereas Israel, which occupied the territory since the 1967 war, refused to return this land. Efforts at compromise failed. Neither side found the proposal of splitting the Sinai acceptable.

An initial examination of this conflict suggests that a negative bargaining zone exists and that a negotiated resolution would not be possible. That is, if we mapped the *positions* of the parties onto the bargaining zone concept, the resistance points would not overlap and an impasse would be reached.

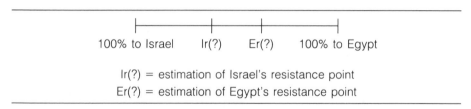

Ir(?) = estimation of Israel's resistance point
Er(?) = estimation of Egypt's resistance point

In contrast to this pessimistic and false prediction, the existence of multiple real issues and the development of *integrative bargaining* explains the resolution that eventually developed: As the Camp David negotiations continued, it became clear that while the *positions* of Egypt and Israel were incompatible, the *interests* of the two countries were compatible (Fisher and Ury, 1981). Israel's underlying interest was security from land or air attack. Egypt was primarily interested in sovereignty over land that was part of Egypt for thousands of years. What emerged was the existence of two real issues with differential importance to the two parties: sovereignty and military protection. The solution that emerged traded off these issues. The agreement called for Israel to return the Sinai in exchange for assurances of a demilitarized zone and new Israeli air bases.

To consider the agreement that the countries created, examine the more complex diagram presented in Figure 7.1. The utility of an agreement to Israel is represented on the horizontal axis, and the utility of an agreement to Egypt is represented on the vertical axis. Point *A* represents the solution of giving the land and total control to Egypt. Notice that this solution would be completely acceptable to Egypt and completely unacceptable to Israel. Point *B* represents

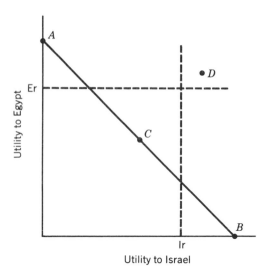

Figure 7.1 The Sinai negotiations.

the solution of Israel keeping the land and maintaining control over the land—completely acceptable to Israel and completely unacceptable to Egypt. Point C represents a straight compromise—for example, giving Egypt half the land and control over the returned land. As illustrated, this solution fails to meet the resistance points of both Israel and Egypt. It does not give Egypt sovereignty over the entire Sinai, and it does not give Israel sufficient security guarantees. The analysis of Point C clarifies why a negative bargaining zone appeared to exist in the diagram in the text. Point D (the eventual resolution), however, suggests a redefinition of the bargaining zone concept. In Figure 7.1, a positive bargaining zone exists to the extent that solutions exist that achieve the resistance points of both parties—the upper right-hand part of the figure beyond the dotted lines representing the resistance points of the two parties. What appears to have occurred in the Camp David accords is that the two parties realized the existence of a positive bargaining zone by considering the two *interests* of the parties and trading off those interests.

In the Sinai example, we observed that two fundamentally different interests underlied the positions of the two parties—sovereignty and security. It was possible to develop an integrative solution by the two countries trading off the issue that they cared less about for the issue that they cared more about. Point D allowed both sides to obtain their objective, while being compatible with the need of the other party. That is, Israel's utility was determined primarily by the degree to which it obtained security, whereas Egypt's utility was determined primarily by the degree to which it obtained sovereignty over the land. The next section examines alternative strategies for the development of integrative solutions.

The Development of Integrative Agreements

The preceding section suggested that the development of integrative behaviors can increase the likelihood of a negotiated compromise and improve outcomes to both parties. The treatment of integrative bargaining, however, was simply by example and provided only a limited picture of the nature of integrative agreements. This section builds on that treatment and develops a richer framework for understanding the development of integrative solutions.

Integrative agreements are solutions to conflicts that reconcile (i.e., integrate) the parties' interests and yield high joint benefit (Pruitt, 1983). Integrative agreements can be contrasted with compromises (distributive agreements), the latter being described by two parties conceding along an obvious dimension to some middle ground (e.g., what percentage of the Sinai will be held by Israel and Egypt). When integrative potential exists, integrative behavior will result in greater joint outcomes to the two parties than a simple compromise will produce. This is illustrated by the story of the two sisters who fought over an orange (Follett, 1940; Fisher and Ury, 1981). The two sisters agreed to split the orange in half—a compromise—allowing one sister to use her portion for juice and the other sister to use the peel of her half for a cake. The two parties in this conflict overlooked the *integrative* agreement of giving one sister all the juice and the other sister all the peel. Contrast this to the successful integrative behavior that was described in the Israel/Egypt conflict.

The preceding discussion of integrative bargaining is consistent with Walton and McKersie's (1965) initial presentation of two contrasting models of the negotiation process. Their distributive model views negotiation as a procedure for dividing a fixed pie of resources ("How much money is the recruit paid?" "How much of the Sinai does Israel keep?" "How much of the orange does each sister receive?"). Notice that in the one-issue case without underlying interests (i.e., the recruit), no integrative potential may exist. In contrast to the distributive model, Walton and McKersie's integrative model views negotiation as a means by which the parties can make trade-offs or jointly solve problems to the mutual benefit of both parties ("How can the Sinai situation be resolved to maximize the joint utility of Israel and Egypt?" "How can the orange be divided to maximize the joint benefit of the two sisters?").

Pruitt and his colleagues (see Pruitt, 1983) have conducted extensive experimental research on the development of strategies for pursuing integrative solutions. Pruitt (1983) summarizes these strategies by suggesting

> Integrative agreements sometimes make use of known alternatives, whose joint value becomes apparent during the controversy. But more often they involved the development of novel alternatives. Hence, it is proper to say that they usually emerge from creative problem solving. Integrative alternatives (those that form the basis for integrative agreements) can be devised by either party separately, by the two of them in joint sessions, or by a third party such as a mediator.

Before examining Pruitt's alternative strategies for creating integrative agreements, consider the following situation:

ABC, Inc., a consumer-oriented manufacturer, has identified an outstanding recruit from a high-caliber competitor. In fact, two departments are interested in hiring this recruit: marketing and sales. Both departments desire this individual's skills as a systems analyst and value her background in consumer goods. Like many organizations, ABC is rapidly computerizing their internal systems. However, the number of individuals trained in both the nature of the industry and computer systems is limited. The immediate problem concerns how to deal internally with the mutual desire of the two departments to hire this recruit. How should the two departments deal with their conflict? (*Reader's note:* Before continuing, identify as many possible solutions as you can.)

A couple of obvious solutions exist. The two departments could use a free-market approach and compete against each other as separate entities in trying to hire the recruit. However, ABC is likely to end up paying more than necessary to hire the recruit, and the process is likely to seem peculiar to the recruit. Another obvious alternative is to compromise. One example would be to split the recruit's time, 50 percent in marketing and 50 percent in sales. However, this leads to a number of administrative problems and at least one of the parties is likely to feel that 50 percent of the time is insufficient for their objectives. Both solutions *assume* that the two departments must split a fixed resource. Chapter 5 suggested that individuals often make assumptions that create barriers to creative solutions. This is frequently true in the negotiation context. Specifically, the search for integrative bargains can be viewed as the search for creative solutions that lie outside distributive assumptions. The following paragraphs examine approaches for searching for potential integrative solutions that are derived from Pruitt's five alternative strategies for the development of integrative solutions.

Obtaining Added Resources (Pruitt uses the term "expanding the pie")
The recruiting problem, like many conflicts, results largely because of a resource shortage. One approach to integrating the interests of two parties when the conflict exists because of a resource shortage is to expand the resources available. Can they use similar recruiting procedures to identify a second recruit? If so, each department can achieve its objective of hiring a recruit with the appropriate background.

This solution lies outside the immediate domain of the conflict. It involves changing the salient question from "How do we allocate this recruit?" to "How do we increase the number of recruits we have to split?" Obtaining added resources is a useful strategy when additional resources may exist, but premature assumptions about the location of the conflict are blocking the search for these added resources. In addition, this strategy is only viable when the interests are not mutually exclusive. That is, there is nothing about the marketing department's interest in hiring a consumer-oriented systems analyst that conflicts with the sales department's interests. In contrast, many conflicts are characterized by the parties having mutually exclusive interests. In these cases, expanding the pie is unlikely to be a successful integrative strategy.

Trading Issues (Pruitt uses the term "logrolling") Trading issues consists of having each party concede on low-priority issues in exchange for concessions on higher-priority issues. Each party gets the part of the agreement that it finds to be most important. After the Sinai problem was redefined into two issues (sovereignty and security), very effective issue trading took place. In the recruiting example, assume that the computerization issues facing both the sales and the marketing department were twofold: (1) the long-term need to hire qualified computer professionals and (2) the immediate need to handle its share of the work in a merger of the sales and marketing data bases for more effective analyses by both departments. Obviously, the recruit would be valuable to either department. However, it may be that the primary interests of the two parties are different. For example, it may be that marketing is primarily concerned with developing a high-quality group of computer professionals, whereas sales is primarily interested in handling the immediate database merger with maximum efficiency. In this specific example, issues could be traded to achieve the primary underlying interests of both parties. An agreement could be reached that called for the marketing department to hire the recruit and then the marketing group to take full responsibility for the database merger (reducing the workload of the sales group).

Trading issues can also be facilitated by refocusing the kinds of questions asked by the parties. Appropriate questions would include: Do the parties have different underlying interests? If so, what issues are most important to marketing? Which are most important to sales? Trading issues is a very effective strategy when the parties are blocked by a surface-level statement of the issue(s) being disputed. It is also a very effective strategy when the dispute is defined as a multi-issue dispute. To develop issue-trading solutions, it is necessary to have information about the interests of the parties so that exchangeable concessions can be identified.

Nonspecific Compensation In nonspecific compensation, one party gets what it wants and the other party is paid on some *unrelated* issue. Compensation is defined as nonspecific when the "unrelated" issue is external to the main issue (i.e., the recruit) being negotiated. For example, assume that the sales and marketing departments also had been arguing about an issue unrelated to the defined dispute; which department should pay for acquiring a database that is relevant for both sales and marketing. Nonspecific compensation might consist of an agreement whereby the two departments agreed that the sales department would hire the recruit and would also pay the entire bill for acquiring the mutually desired database.

Nonspecific compensation is conceptually very similar to trading issues. Under trading issues, two or more issues *within* the domain of the conflict are traded. Under nonspecific compensation, additional issues are brought into the conflict to create the potential to trade off issues. Thus, nonspecific compensation can be viewed as trading issues with a broader definition of the conflict.

Nonspecific compensation is also likely to be affected by the kinds of questions asked by the two parties. Useful questions to ask to facilitate the development of integrating agreements through the use of nonspecific compensation include: What could each party supply to the other party in exchange for favorable terms of the focal issue (i.e., the recruit)? How much does each side value the recruit? How much does each side value the additional issues that can be redefined as part of the conflict? Like trading issues, the development of agreements using the nonspecific compensation strategy requires information about the interests of the parties so that exchangeable concessions can be identified.

Cost Cutting The cost cutting strategy calls for one party to get what it wants and for the other party to have its costs associated with the concession reduced or eliminated. The result of high joint benefit occurs not because the party that receives the recruit has changed its demand, but because the second party suffers less. Assume that the recruit is a highly priced, extremely skilled individual. In addition, assume that the marketing department really values the high level of skill, but the sales department simply needs added personnel with computer skills. An integrative agreement could be arranged that called for marketing to hire the recruit and for the marketing department to transfer a lower-skilled employee (with a lower salary) to the sales department.

Cost cutting often takes the form of specific compensation, where the party who makes the major concession receives something in return that satisfies the precise goals that were frustrated by the concession. Cost cutting is also conceptually similar to trading issues in terms of the existence of some trade-off. However, it is a unique strategy in terms of concentrating on the reduction or elimination of the costs to one party of the other party achieving its objectives.

Like previous strategies, cost cutting is likely to be affected by the kinds of questions asked by the two parties. Useful questions to ask to facilitate the development of integrating agreements through the use of cost cutting include: What costs would be imposed on sales if marketing hired the recruit (or vice versa)? The development of cost cutting solutions necessitates an understanding of the costs to each party of the other party achieving its objectives. Like trading issues, the development of agreements using cost cutting requires information about the interests of the parties so that the costs to each side can be identified.

Bridging Bridging is the development of a new option that satisfies the most important interests underlying the demands of both parties. Under bridging, neither side achieves its initially stated objective, rather the parties search for new, creative solutions that are hidden by the original statement of the conflict. For example, assume that both sales and marketing want the following from hiring the recruit: (1) some of the skills of the employee, (2) the ability to continue to use these skills over an extended period of time, and (3) performance of the department's share of the work associated with the earlier suggested problem of merging the sales and marketing databases. One bridging solution would consist of hiring the recruit into a staff position with the management information systems department, with the understanding that the person would be assigned initially to the sales/marketing database merger and that this person would continue to be available for special projects to both sales and marketing in the future (and billed out at internal rates).

Bridging involves a reformulation of the conflict by assessing a wider variety of potential solutions that can fulfill the underlying interests of both parties in the focal conflict. Bridging necessitates a clear understanding of the underlying interests of the two parties. The search for bridging solutions consists of removing the parties from the immediate definition of the conflict, identifying the interests of the parties, and brainstorming for a wide variety of potential solutions that can bridge these interests.

Each of Pruitt's five strategies for identifying integrative agreements requires that someone breaks out of the existing definition of the conflict. Typically, either party or a third party can use these strategies to develop alternatives that integrate the interests of the parties. Each of these strategies, where successful, results in resolutions of higher joint benefit than simple compromises. Thus, the search for creative solutions that lie outside the assumptions of the conflict is a useful approach to increasing the joint resources obtained by the conflicting parties.

NEGOTIATOR COGNITION

It was earlier suggested that when resistance points overlap (i.e., a positive bargaining zone exists), a settlement should always occur. In contrast, common observation is that the two parties often fail to agree despite overlapping resistance points. Walton and McKersie asserted that "intangibles," or psychological factors and conflict dynamics, result in the perceptual disappearance of the positive bargaining zone during negotiations. *If it is rational for a settlement to occur whenever a positive bargaining zone exists, what specific processes account for negotiators failing to reach an agreement despite overlapping resistance points?*

The first five chapters provided a useful direction for responding to this question. These chapters provided ample evidence that individuals do not always make decisions in the ways prescriptive models recommend. Rather, individual rationality is bounded. Furthermore, the bounds to rationality were argued to be describable in terms of a set of systematic deviations from rationality.

This section explores the role of systematic distortions in describing negotiator cognition. It is argued that a judgmental perspective offers a novel and complementary approach for thinking about how to improve the effectiveness of dispute resolution in organizations. In developing this approach, this section uses information from the first five chapters and augments this information by considering deviations from rationality that are unique to competitive situations. Thus, the goal is not simply to apply the information in the earlier chapters, but to provide a more general argument that cognitive limitations provide a set of answers to the question of why negotiators fail to reach an agreement when a positive bargaining zone exists. We will not examine every cognitive limitation that affects negotiators. Rather, we will selectively sample from what we know about cognitive limitations to illustrate the potential of a judgmental perspective to negotiation. Specific attention will be given to the following issues in negotiator cognition: (1) the mythical fixed pie of negotiation, (2) the framing of negotiator judgment, (3) the nonrational escalation of conflict, (4) negotiator overconfidence, (5) the winner's curse, and (6) the lack of perspective taking by negotiators.

This section argues that negotiator judgment can be improved by first describing the ways in which negotiators deviate from rationality and prescribing (based on the ideas in Chapter 6) a strategy for eliminating these deficiencies from the negotiator's cognitive repertoire. The core of this section consists of six subsections that describe the deviations from rationality listed above in the context of negotiation. Each subsection clarifies how negotiator decisions differ from a prescriptive analysis of negotiator behavior and discusses how negotiators can be trained to respond to these deviations.

1. The Mythical Fixed Pie of Negotiations   Pruitt (1983) and Walton and McKersie (1965) have argued that integrative agreements are nonobvious solutions to conflict that reconcile the parties' interests and yield higher joint benefit. In addition, it was pointed out that negotiators often fail to reach the integrative solutions that are possible (e.g., the sisters who fought over the orange). Why did the sisters use a distributive bargaining strategy to a problem that, at least retrospectively, had integrative potential? I argue that *the fixed-pie assumption of the distributive model represents a fundamental bias in human judgment.* That is, negotiators have a systematic intuitive bias that distorts their behavior; they assume that their interests *directly* conflict with the other party's interests.

Regardless of the basis for this mythical fixed-pie perception of bargaining, most conflicts are not purely distributive problems. Why? Most conflicts have more than one issue at stake, with the parties placing different values on the differing issues. Once this condition exists, the conflict is objectively no longer a fixed pie. Consider a Friday evening on which you and your spouse are going to dinner and a movie. Unfortunately, you prefer different restaurants and different movies. It is easy to adopt a distributive attitude toward each event to be negotiated. In contrast, if you do not assume a fixed pie, you may find out that you care more about the restaurant selection and your spouse cares more about the movie choice. Similarly, purchasing goods is often treated as a distributive problem. Often, however, a retailer is suddenly willing to reduce the purchase price if payment is made in cash (no receipt, and so on). Although you care only about price, he or she also cares about the form of payment.

The fundamental assumption of a fixed pie probably results from a competitive society that creates the belief that most situations are win–lose. This win–lose orientation is manifested objectively in our society in athletic competition, admission to academic programs, corporate promotion systems, and so on. Individuals tend to generalize from these objective win–lose situations and let their experience create expectations for situations that are not objectively fixed pies. Faced with a mixed-motive situation requiring both cooperation and competition, it is the competitive aspect that becomes salient—resulting in a win–lose orientation and a distributive approach to bargaining. This, in turn, results in the development of a strategy for obtaining the largest share possible of the perceived fixed pie. Such a focus inhibits the creativity and problem-solving necessary for the development of integrative solutions.

The tendency of negotiators initially to approach bargaining with a mythical fixed-pie perception has been documented by Bazerman, Magliozzi, and Neale (1985). Their simulation allowed individuals acting as buyers and sellers to complete transactions on a three-issue integrative bargaining problem with as many opponents as possible in a fixed amount of time (30 minutes)—with total profit the goal. The profit available for various levels of the three issues, for each transaction completed, for sellers and buyers, can be seen in Tables 7.1a and b (ignore Tables 7.1c and d for now), respectively. Buyers achieve their highest profit levels and sellers their lowest profits at the A level of delivery, discount, and financing, whereas sellers achieve their highest profits and buyers their lowest profits at the I levels. A negotiated transaction consisted of the two parties agreeing to one of the nine levels for each of the three issues. As can be observed, a simple compromise solution of E–E–E results in a $4000 profit to each side. However, if the parties are able to reach the fully integrative solution of A–E–I, (by trading issues) then each would receive a profit of $5200. The mythical fixed-pie bias argues that negotiators approach a competitive context with a fixed-pie assumption and only relax this assumption when provided with evidence to the contrary.

Figure 7.2 plots the average of buyer and seller profit of all agreements (sample size, 942 transactions) reached in each five-minute segment of the exercise (aggregated across six runs of the market simulation). The diagonal line in this figure shows the joint profits to the two parties if they make simple compromises (e.g., E–E–E). The curved line shows the efficient frontier available to the negotiators. The *efficient frontier* is defined as the set of agreements for which there is no point that would simultaneously improve the outcomes to both parties. This figure shows that negotiators start the exercise by obtaining agreements that would be predicted by a mythical fixed-pie hypothesis (i.e., the transactions approach the distributive point of $4000, $4000). However, as the negotiators gain experience, the myth is disproved and far greater integrative behavior is observed (i.e., the transactions approach the fully integrative point of $5200, $5200).

The pervasiveness of the fixed-pie perception, as well as the importance of integrative bargaining, can be seen in the recent housing market. When in-

Table 7.1 Buyer and Seller Schedules for Positively and Negatively Framed Negotiations

Table 7.1*a* Seller Net Profit Schedule						Table 7.1*b* Buyer Net Profit Schedule					
Delivery Time		Discount Terms		Financing Terms		Delivery Time		Discount Terms		Financing Terms	
A	$ 000	A	$ 000	A	$ 000	A	$4000	A	$2400	A	$1600
B	200	B	300	B	500	B	3500	B	2100	B	1400
C	400	C	600	C	1000	C	3000	C	1800	C	1200
D	600	D	900	D	1500	D	2500	D	1500	D	1000
E	800	E	1200	E	2000	E	2000	E	1200	E	800
F	1000	F	1500	F	2500	F	1500	F	900	F	600
G	1200	G	1800	G	3000	G	1000	G	600	G	400
H	1400	H	2100	H	3500	H	500	H	300	H	200
I	1600	I	2400	I	4000	I	000	I	000	I	000

Table 7.1*c* Seller Expense Schedule (Gross Profit = $8000)						Table 7.1*d* Buyer Expense Schedule (Gross Profit = $8000)					
Delivery Time		Discount Terms		Financing Terms		Delivery Time		Discount Terms		Financing Terms	
A	$−1600	A	$−2400	A	$−4000	A	$ 000	A	$ 000	A	$ 000
B	−1400	B	−2100	B	−3500	B	−500	B	−300	B	−200
C	−1200	C	−1800	C	−3000	C	−1000	C	−600	C	−400
D	−1000	D	−1500	D	−2500	D	−1500	D	−900	D	−600
E	−800	E	−1200	E	−2000	E	−2000	E	−1200	E	−800
F	−600	F	−900	F	−1500	F	−2500	F	−1500	F	−1000
G	−400	G	−600	G	−1000	G	−3000	G	−1800	G	−1200
H	−200	H	−300	H	−500	H	−3500	H	−2100	H	−1400
I	000	I	000	I	000	I	−4000	I	−2400	I	−1600

Source: Bazerman, Magliozzi, and Neale (1985).

terest rates first shot past 12 percent in 1979, the housing market came to a dead stop. Sellers continued to expect the value of their property to increase. However, buyers could not afford the monthly payments on houses they aspired to own, because of the drastically higher interest rates. Viewing the problem as a distributive one, buyers could not afford the prices that sellers were demanding. This fixed-pie assumption (which was prevalent throughout the industry) led to the conclusion that transactions would not occur until seller resistance points decreased, buyer resistance points increased, and/or interest rates came down. However, once the industry began to view real estate transactions integratively, some relief was provided. Specifically, sellers cared a great deal about price—partly to justify their past investment. Buyers cared about finding some way to afford a house that they aspired to own—perhaps

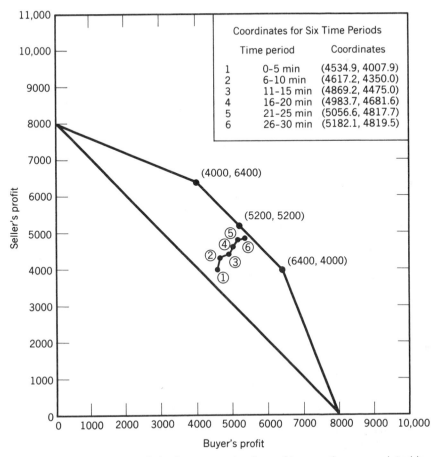

Figure 7.2   Average profit for buyers and sellers of transactions completed in each five-minute segment of the market (aggregated across markets).

their first house. The integrative solutions were the wide variety of creative financing developments (e.g., seller financing) of the early 1980s, which allowed sellers an artificially high price in exchange for favorable financing assistance to the buyer. Creative financing integrated the interests of buyers and sellers, rescuing an entire industry from our common fixed-pie assumptions.

The preceding arguments suggest that although some fixed pies exist objectively, most resolutions depend on finding favorable trade-offs between negotiators, trade-offs that necessitate eliminating our intuitive fixed-pie assumptions. Chapter 5 argued that individuals are often limited in finding creative solutions by the false assumptions that they make. The fixed-pie perception is a fundamentally false assumption that hinders finding creative (integrative) solutions. A fundamental task in training negotiators lies in identifying and eliminating this false assumption and institutionalizing the creative process of integrative bargaining.

2. The Framing of Negotiator Judgment Consider the following two scenarios:

> You are a wholesaler of refrigerators. Corporate policy does not allow any flexibility in pricing. However, flexibility does exist in terms of expenses that you can incur (shipping, financing terms, and so on), which have a direct effect on the profitability of the transaction. These expenses can all be costed out in dollar-value terms. You are negotiating a $10,000 sale. The buyer wants you to pay $2000 in expenses. You want to pay less expenses. When you negotiate the transaction, do you try to minimize your expenses (reduce these losses from $2000) or maximize net price—price less expenses (increase the net price from $8000)?

> You bought your house in 1981 for $60,000. You currently have the house on the market for $109,900, with a real target of $100,000 (your estimation of the true market value). An offer comes in for $90,000. Does this offer represent a $30,000 gain in comparison with the original purchase price, or a $10,000 loss in comparison with your current target?

The answer to the question posed in each scenario is "Both." Each is a "Is the cup half full or half empty?" situation. From a normative perspective, and based on our intuition, the difference in the two points of view is irrelevant. However, as described in Chapter 3, Kahneman and Tversky (1979, 1982; Tversky and Kahneman, 1981) have demonstrated that important differences exist in how individuals respond to questions framed in terms of losses versus gains. This difference is critical in describing negotiator behavior.

To exemplify the importance of "framing" to negotiation, consider the following labor–management situation suggested by Neale and Bazerman (1985): The union claims that they need a raise to $12 an hour and that anything less would represent a loss given current inflation. Management argues that they cannot pay more than $10 an hour and that anything more would impose an unacceptable loss. What if each side had the choice of settling for $11 an hour (a certain settlement) or going to binding arbitration (a risky settlement)? Because each side is viewing the conflict in terms of what they have to lose, following Tversky and Kahneman's (1981) findings, each side is predicted to be risk-seeking and unwilling to take the certain settlement. Changing the frame of the situation to a positive one, however, results in a very different predicted outcome: If the union views anything above $10 an hour as a gain, and management views anything under $12 an hour as a gain, then risk-aversion will dominate, and a negotiated settlement will be likely. Using an example conceptually similar to this scenario, Neale and Bazerman (1985) found that negotiators with positive frames are significantly more concessionary and successful than are their negative counterparts.

In the Bazerman, Magliozzi, and Neale (1985) study described earlier, it was found that the frame of buyers and sellers systematically affected their negotiation behavior. Negotiators were led to view transactions in terms of either (1) net profit (gains) or (2) expenses (losses) away from the gross profit of the transactions. The net profit (gain) payoff tables were previously described in

Tables 7.1*a* and *b*. To create a negatively framed or "losses" condition, these tables were converted into "expenses" that the subject would incur—that would be taken away from the $8000 gross profit that would be received for each completed transaction. The transformation can be seen for sellers and buyers in Tables 7.1*c* and *d*. Because net profit is defined to be equal to gross profit minus expenses, Tables 7.1*a* and *b* are objectively equal to Tables 7.1*c* and *d*. For example, the seller's profit for A–E–I is $5200, the sum of 0 + $1200 + $4000 (Table 7.1*a*). In Table 7.1*c*, this same transaction would result in expenses of $2800, the sum of $1600 + $1200 + 0. When $2800 is subtracted from the $8000 gross profit, the same net $5200 is received. Although both frames of the schedule yield the same objective profit result, positively (gain) framed negotiators experienced the risk-aversion necessary to have an incentive to compromise. This incentive to compromise led negotiators with a positive frame to (1) complete a larger number of transactions and (2) obtain greater overall profitability than did negotiators with a negative frame.

The implications of the framing effect can be of critical importance in affecting the likelihood of a resolution when a positive bargaining zone exists. Both sides (in many contexts) in negotiation typically talk in terms of why they need a certain wage, price, or such, thus setting the reference point (the benchmark against which gains and losses are measured) by their stated (often extreme) goals. If this occurs, the negotiators will adopt a negative frame to all reasonable proposals, exhibit risk-seeking attitudes, and be less likely to reach a settlement. A critical role of interested third parties may therefore be their skill at influencing the parties to alter their negative frame (and concomitant risk-seeking orientation) toward a positive frame that is more conducive to a negotiated settlement.

What determines whether a negotiator will have a positive or negative frame? The answer lies in the selection of a perceptual anchor. Consider the anchors available to a union negotiator in simply negotiating a wage: (1) last year's wage; (2) management's initial offer; (3) the union's estimate of management's resistance point; (4) the union's resistance point; or (5) your bargaining position, which has been announced publicly to your constituency. As the anchor moves from 1 to 5, what is a modest *gain* in comparison to last year's wage is a *loss* in comparison to the publicly specified goals. As the anchor changes from 1 to 5, the union negotiator moves from a positive frame to a negative frame. For example, for workers who are currently making $10 an hour and demanding an increase of $2 an hour, a proposed increase of $1 an hour can be viewed as a $1 an hour gain in comparison to last year's wage (anchor 1) or a loss of $1 an hour in comparison to the goals of the union's constituency (anchor 5). To avoid the adverse effects of framing, the negotiator should be aware of his/her frame and examine the context from alternative frames.

It is easy to see that the frames of negotiators can result in the difference between an important agreement and impasse. In addition, framing has important implications for the tactics that negotiators can use. The framing effect suggests that in order to induce concessionary behavior from an opponent, a negotiator should always create anchors that lead the opposition to a positive frame and negotiate in terms of what the other side has to gain. In addition, the negotiator should make it salient to the opposition that they are in a risky situation where a sure gain is possible.

Finally, the impact of framing has important implications for mediators. To the extent that the goal is compromise, a mediator should strive to have both parties view the negotiation in a positive frame. This is tricky, however, because the anchor that will lead to a positive frame for one negotiator is likely to lead to a negative frame for the other negotiator. This suggests that when the mediator meets with each party separately, he or she needs to create differing anchors to create risk aversion in both parties. Again, if the mediator is to affect the frame, he/she also wants to emphasize the risk of the situation and create uncertainty, leading both sides to prefer the sure settlement.

3. The Nonrational Escalation of Conflict   Consider the following situation:

> It is 1981. PATCO (The Professional Air Traffic Controllers Organization) decides to strike to obtain a set of concessions from the U.S. government. It is willing to "invest" the temporary loss of pay during the strike to obtain concessions. No government concessions result or appear to be forthcoming. PATCO is faced with the option of backing off and returning to work under the former arrangement or increasing their commitment to the strike to try to force the concessions they desire.

In this example, PATCO has committed resources to a course of action. PATCO is then faced with escalating that commitment or backing out of the conflict. This example illustrates the concept of escalation (see Chapter 4) in negotiation. The escalation literature would have predicted that PATCO was far more likly to persist in their course of action than a rational analysis would have dictated.

It is easy to see the process of the nonrational escalation of commitment unfold in a wide variety of actual conflict situations. The negotiation process commonly leads both sides initially to make extreme demands. The escalation literature predicts that if negotiators become committed to their initial public statements, they will nonrationally adopt a nonconcessionary stance. To the extent that a negotiator believes that he/she "has too much invested to quit," intransigence is the likely behavior. Furthermore, if both sides incur losses as a result of a lack of agreement (e.g., a strike), their commitment to their position is expected to increase, and their willingness to change to a different course of action (i.e., compromise) is expected to decrease. For example, it could be argued that in the Malvinas/Falklands conflict, once Argentina had suffered the initial loss of life, it had the information necessary rationally to pursue a negotiated settlement. Analysts from around the world commented on Argentina's poor military position. In addition, Britain was threatening to use nuclear weapons if necessary. The escalation literature, in contrast, accurately predicts that the loss of life (a significant commitment to a course of action) would lead Argentina to a further escalation of its commitment not to compromise on the return of the Malvinas to Britain.

One important result from the escalation literature is that public announcement of one's commitment increases one's tendency to escalate nonrationally (Staw, 1981). Once the general public (or constituency) is aware of the commitment, the decision maker is far less likely to retreat from his or her previously announced position. This suggests that escalation can be reduced if negotiators and third parties avoid the formation of firmly set public positions, because this provides the ignition for the nonrational escalation of conflict. Implementation of this recommendation is, however, contradictory to everything known about how negotiators (e.g., labor leaders, representatives of management) behave when they represent constituencies. A firmly set public position is typically perceived as necessary to build constituency support and allegiance and to be seen as loyal and tough. Thus, it may be that what is best for the constituency is not the same as what the constituency will reward.

An understanding of escalation can also be very helpful to a negotiator in understanding the behavior of the opponent. When will the other party really hold out? The escalation literature predicts that the other side will really hold out when they have "too much invested" in their position to give in. This suggests that there are systematic clues concerning when you can threaten the opponent and win versus when the threat will receive an active response— owing to a prior public commitment to a course of action. Strategically, this suggests that a negotiator should avoid inducing any statements or behaviors from the opponent that will create the perception of having too much invested to quit.

4. Negotiator Overconfidence   Consider the following scenario:

> You are an advisor to a major-league baseball player. In baseball, a system exists for the resolution of compensation conflicts that calls for a player and a team owner who do not agree to submit final offers to an arbitrator. Using final-offer arbitration, the arbitrator must accept one position or the other, not a compromise. Thus, the challenge for each side is to come just a little closer to the arbitrator's perception of the appropriate compensation package than the opposition does. In this case, your best intuitive estimate of the final offer that the team owner will submit is a package worth $200,000 a year. You believe than an appropriate wage is $400,000 a year but estimate the arbitrator's opinion to be $300,000 a year. What final offer do you propose?

This scenario sets up a common cognitive trap for negotiators. Individuals are systematically overconfident in estimating the position of a neutral third party and in estimating the likelihood that a third party will accept their position. In the baseball example, if the arbitrator's true assessment of the appropriate wage is $250,000, and you believe it to be $300,000, you are likely to submit an inappropriately high offer and overestimate the likelihood that the offer will be accepted. Consequently, the overconfidence bias is likely to lead the advisor to believe that less compromise is necessary than a more objective analysis would suggest.

As demonstrated in Chapter 2, individuals are overconfident in their assessment of the probability (confidence judgement) that their judgment will be accurate. Farber (1981) discusses this problem in terms of negotiators' divergent expectations. That is, each side is optimistic that the neutral third party will adjudicate in its favor. Assume that (1) the union is demanding $8.75 an hour, (2) management is offering $8.25 an hour, and (3) the "appropriate" wage is $8.50 an hour. Farber (1981) suggests that the union will typically expect the neutral third party to adjudicate at a wage somewhat over $8.50, whereas management will expect a wage somewhat under $8.50. Given these divergent expectations, neither side is willing to compromise at $8.50. Both sides will incur the costs of impasse and aggregately do no better through the use of a third party. In the baseball scenario, if one side had a more objective assessment of the opponent's offer and the position of the arbitrator, it could use this information strategically to its advantage in final-offer arbitration.

Research demonstrates that negotiators tend to be overconfident that their positions will prevail if they do not "give in." Neale and Bazerman (1983; Bazerman and Neale, 1982) show that negotiators consistently overestimate the probability, under final-offer arbitration, that their final offer will be accepted. That is, although only 50 percent of all final offers can be accepted, the average subject estimated that there was a much higher probability that his or her offer would be accepted. In terms of Walton and McKersie's bargaining zone, overconfidence may inhibit a variety of settlements, despite the existence of a positive bargaining zone. If we consider a final offer as a judgment as to how much compromise is necessary to win the arbitration, it is easy to argue that when a negotiator is overconfident that a particular position will be accepted, their resistance point becomes more extreme, and the incentive to compromise is reduced. If a more accurate assessment is made, the negotiator is likely to be more uncertain and uncomfortable about the probability of success. One strategy to reduce this uncertainty is to compromise further. Based on the biasing impact of this overconfidence, Neale and Bazerman (1985) found "appropriately" confident negotiators to exhibit more concessionary behavior and to be more successful than overly confident negotiators.

Interestingly, individuals and organizations become aware of their overconfidence over time. When final-offer arbitration was first introduced into baseball, the final offers of the two parties involved in any arbitration were drastically disparate, largely owing to their overconfidence. Baseball negotiators have since learned that they fare better by coming closer to the arbitrator's actual position. This is demonstrated by the fact that over the years final offers of competing parties converged dramatically.

Training negotiators to recognize the cognitive patterns of overconfidence should include the realization that overconfidence is most likely to occur when a party's knowledge is limited. Most of us follow the intuitive cognitive rule: "When in doubt, be overconfident." This suggests that negotiators should be aware of the benefits of obtaining objective assessments of worth from a *neutral* party, realizing that this neutral assessment is likely to be systematically closer to the other party's position than the negotiator would have predicted intuitively.

5. The Winner's Curse Imagine that you are in a foreign country. You meet a merchant who is selling a very attractive gem. You have purchased a few gems in your life but are far from being an expert. After some discussion, you make the merchant an offer that you believe (but are uncertain) is on the low side. He quickly accepts, and the transaction is completed. How do you feel? Most people would feel uneasy with the purchase after the quick acceptance. Yet, why would you voluntarily make an offer that you would not want accepted? To put this problem in context, read and answer the problem in Exercise 7.1 as proposed by Samuelson and Bazerman (1985).

The "Acquiring a Company" exercise is conceptually similar to the gem merchant problem. In the "Acquiring a Company" exercise, one firm (the acquirer) is considering making an offer to buy out another firm (the target). However, the acquirer is uncertain about the ultimate value of the target firm. It only knows that its value under current management is between $0 and $100, with all values equally likely. Because the firm is expected to be worth 50 percent more under the acquirer's management than under the current ownership, it appears to make sense for a transaction to take place. Although the acquirer does not know the actual value of the firm, the target knows its current worth exactly. What price should the acquirer offer for the target?

Exercise 7.1 **Acquiring a Company**

In the following exercise you will represent Company A (the acquirer), which is currently considering acquiring Company T (the target) by means of a tender offer. You plan to tender in cash for 100 percent of Company T's shares but are unsure how high a price to offer. The main complication is this: The value of Company T depends directly on the outcome of a major oil exploration project it is currently undertaking. Indeed, the very viability of Company T depends on the exploration outcome. If the project fails, the company under current management will be worth nothing—$0 a share. But if the project succeeds, the value of the company under current management could be as high as $100 a share. All share values between $0 and $100 are considered equally likely. By all estimates, the company will be worth considerably more in the hands of Company A than under current management. In fact, whatever the ultimate value under current management, *the company will be worth 50 percent more under the management of A than under Company T.* If the project fails, the company is worth $0 a share under either management. If the exploration project generates a $50 a share value under current management, the value under Company A is $75 a share. Similarly, a $100 a share value under Company T implies a $150 a share value under Company A, and so on.

The board of directors of Company A has asked you to determine the price they should offer for Company T's shares. This offer must be made *now, before* the outcome of the drilling project is known. From all indications, Company T would be happy to be acquired by Company A, *provided it is at a profitable price.* Moreover, Company T wishes to avoid, at all cost, the potential of a takeover bid by any other firm. You expect Company T to delay a decision on your bid until the results of the project are in, then accept or reject your offer before the news of the drilling results reaches the press.

Thus, *you (Company A) will not know the results of the exploration project when submitting your price offer, but Company T will know the results when deciding whether or not to accept your offer. In addition, Company T is expected to accept any offer by Company A that is greater than the (per share) value of the company under current management.*

As the representative of Company A, you are deliberating over price offers in the range of $0 a share (this is tantamount to making no offer at all) to $150 a share. What price offer per share would you tender for Company T's stock?

My tender price is: $_____ per share.

Source: Research in Experimental Economics, Vol. 3, 1985, JAI Press Inc., Greenwich, Conn.

The problem is analytically quite simple (as will be demonstrated shortly), yet intuitively quite perplexing. The responses of 123 MBA students from Boston University are shown in Figure 7.3. The figure shows the dominant response was between $50 and $75. How is this $50 to $75 decision reached? One common, naive explanation is that "on average, the firm will be worth $50 to the target and $75 to the acquirer; consequently, a transaction in this range will, on average, be profitable to both parties."

Now consider the logical process that a normative response would generate in evaluating the decision to make an offer of $60 per share (a value suggested naively to be "profitable to both parties"):

> If I offer $60 per share, the offer will be accepted 60 percent of the time—whenever the firm is worth between $0 and $60 to the target. Because all values are equally likely, the firm will, on average, be worth $30 per share to the target when the target accepts a $60 per share offer and will be worth $45 per share to me, resulting in a loss of $15 per share ($45 − 60).

Consequently, a $60 per share offer is ill considered. It is easy to see that the same kind of reasoning applies to *any* positive offer. On the average, the acquirer obtains a company worth 25 percent less than the price it pays. Thus, the best the acquirer can do is not to make an offer ($0 per share). Even though in all circumstances the firm is worth more to the acquirer than to the target, any offer leads to a negative expected return to the acquirer. *The source of this paradox lies in the target's accepting the acquirer's offer when the acquirer least wants the firm—when it is a "lemon."* In this example, the target rejects the $50 a share offer when the firm is worth between $60 per share and $100 per share. (The same problem existed in the gem merchant case.) Unfortunately, only 9 of 123 subjects correctly offered $0 per share. Recent replications with MIT masters students in management have shown similar results.

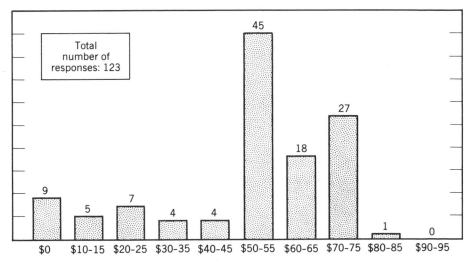

Figure 7.3 The distribution of price offers.

Finally, even subjects who believe that they will be paid according to their performance exhibit the same pattern of responses as depicted in Figure 7.3.

Most individuals have the analytical ability to follow the logic that the optimal offer is $0 per share (no offer). Yet without assistance, most individuals would make a positive offer (typically between $50 and $75 per share). Thus, individuals systematically exclude information from their decision processes that they have the ability to include. They fail to realize that their expected return is *conditional* on an acceptance by the other party and that an acceptance is most likely to occur when it is least desirable to the negotiator making the offer.

The key feature of the "winner's curse" in the bargaining context is that one side has much better information than the other side. Although we are all familiar with the slogan "buyer beware," our intuition seems to have difficulty putting this idea into practice when asymmetric information exists. Most people realize that when they buy a commodity they know little about, their uncertainty increases. The evidence presented here indicates that against an informed opponent, their expected return from the transaction may decrease dramatically. Practically, the evidence suggests that people undervalue the importance of accurate information in making transactions. They undervalue a mechanic's evaluation of a used car, a professional inspector's assessment of a house, or an independent jeweler's assessment of a coveted gem. Thus, the knowledgeable gem merchant will accept your offer selectively, taking the offer when the gem is probably worth less than your estimate. To protect yourself, you need to develop or borrow the expertise to balance the quality of information. Although the experimental evidence presented was highly artificial, the negative effects of the winner's curse should be considered by any negotiator dealing with a better-informed opponent.

6. The Lack of Perspective-Taking by Negotiators This chapter has explored a number of ways in which negotiators are affected by systematic deviations from rationality. Yet experience and empirical evidence suggest that there are some individuals who are more or less accurate in their competitive judgments (Bernstein and Davis, 1982; Davis, 1981). These individual differences may be related to the ability of a negotiator (individual) to take the perspective of his or her opponent. It is important to note that taking the perspective of an opponent is not done for purely philanthropic reasons; rather, in achieving any set of objectives, there is valuable information to be gleaned from taking the perspective of the other negotiating party. Davis (1981) developed a construct and measure of the ability to take others' perspective and see things from their point of view. He found that individuals with high perspective-taking ability (PTA) are more accurate than are those with low PTA in judging others. Furthermore, the accuracy with which those with high PTA judge others increased with experience, whereas those with low PTA did not exhibit similar improvement in accuracy (Bernstein and Davis, 1982). Interestingly, this systematic limitation to effective competitive judgment is not related to standard measures of intelligence.

Neale and Bazerman (1983) found that individuals with high PTA are better able to adopt the perspective of their bargaining opponents. They would also be more aware of the perspective of the opponent's constituency (e.g., labor or management) than would individuals with low PTA. This added information from perspective-taking should increase one's ability to predict accurately the opponent's goals, expectations, and resistance point. This is extremely important in developing a bargaining strategy (Rubin and Brown, 1975; Siegel and Fouraker, 1960; Walton and McKersie, 1965) and facilitating compromise. Neale and Bazerman (1983) found that PTA positively affects the concessionary tendencies of negotiators and the likelihood that a settlement will be reached. In addition, PTA was found to affect positively the outcome obtained by a negotiator. Furthermore, Bazerman and Neale (1982) have suggested that training mechanisms should be developed to increase the PTA of negotiators. This is consistent with the literature on negotiator role reversal—that having each bargainer verbalize the viewpoint of the other increases the likelihood of a negotiated resolution (see Pruitt, 1981). Thus, increasing the tendency of negotiators to take their opponents' perspective should be a central focus of mediators. Research (Kochan and Jick, 1978; Neale and Bazerman, 1983) suggests that increased information that is derived in this way often results in behavior that is more conducive to a negotiated settlement.

The proceding paragraphs provide strong evidence that perspective-taking is an important ingredient in a high-quality negotiator. In addition, Bazerman and Neale (1983) have provided evidence that most individuals lack a sufficient amount of PTA. That is, individuals appear systematically to ignore valuable information that is available from considering the concurrent decisions of the other party. Overall, *negotiators tend to act as if their opponent was a fairly inactive party to the negotiation* (Bazerman and Carroll, 1987).

This tendency can be seen in the escalation and winner's curse biases described earlier. Why do bidders get involved in Shubik's dollar auction exercise (see Chapter 4)? One explanation is that people see the potential for profit early in the auction and fail to take the perspective of what the auction will look like to other bidders. If the bidders consider the dollar auction from the point of view of two competing bidders, it is easy to see the benefit of staying out of the auction. The tendency to ignore the active behaviors of the opponent also explains the behaviors of negotiators in the winner's curse exercise. Why did individuals make positive bids? Because they viewed the opponent as a passive ingredient in the negotiation process, rather than as an active participant who would *selectively* accept offers. Finally, this tendency to view the opponent as passive can be seen in Perrow's (1984) recent work on "normal accidents." Perrow provides substantial evidence that the primary reason for ship accidents concerns the naive assumptions that each ship makes about the likely behaviors of the opposing ships. Our interpretation is that these accidents demonstrate a lack of perspective-taking by the ship captains. Overall, there is substantial evidence that competing decision makers fail to consider the impact of the active behaviors of the other party in negotiations. The central message of this section is obvious: Consider the decisions of the other party before you commit to a course of action as a negotiator. This piece of advice is counterintuitive to most individuals; most individuals falsely act as if the opponent is a passive party to the negotiation.

CONCLUSIONS

This chapter extends the book by examining judgment in the negotiation context. Specifically, the chapter has examined a number of biases described earlier in competitive situations and has identified a few additional biases specific to the negotiation context. This chapter presents an alternative approach to the study of negotiation. Most recent work on negotiation is prescriptive (e.g., Fisher and Ury, 1981; Raiffa, 1982). The work described in the latter half of this chapter follows a distinctly different approach. Rather than prescribing what a negotiator should do, this chapter has described the decision processes of negotiators. If the biases of negotiators can be identified, a complementary approach (to prescriptive approaches) to negotiation can be developed. Specifically, we can improve negotiation effectiveness by improving the judgmental abilities of negotiators.

EIGHT
JUDGMENT IN MULTIPARTY ORGANIZATIONAL CONTEXTS

Chapter 7 dealt with reexaming judgment in the context of negotiating with another party. The evidence presented suggested that the research on judgment from the first six chapters was very applicable to describing judgment in a two-party negotiation context. In addition, the evidence suggested that the unique context of negotiation required unique theory to explain some aspects of the judgments of negotiators. Chapter 7 was able to benefit from a growing literature on the judgment of negotiators. As we move to other multiparty organizational contexts (third parties in organizations, coalition behavior, groups, competitive bidding), there is far less empirical evidence from a cognitive/judgmental perspective. Consequently, this chapter's role is to provide logic and speculation about a set of unresearched topics based on the literatures from these multiparty contexts and the information on judgment developed in the first six chapters. This has a number of implications. First, frameworks will be developed based on my research biases. Few claims of empirical support will be provided. Second, the frameworks are at a very early stage of development. Third, this chapter should receive a more critical reading, with each reader developing more of his/her own ideas of the judgmental process involved in these multiparty contexts. Fourth, this chapter will identify a number of areas waiting for initial research.

Although this chapter is comparatively less developed than other chapters, it clarifies the role of this book. This book attempts to provide a bridge between the behavioral decision area and the field of organizational behavior. in Chapter 7, we saw the role of judgmental processes in understanding negotiations. However, the field of organizational behavior offers many other multiparty contexts that are relatively untouched by the power and insights of the behavioral decision theory literature. This chapter highlights many of these areas, and it offers some early views of what the decision theory literature will bring to each. If this book is to serve as a useful vehicle for the dissemination of the behavioral decision theory literature to organizational behavior, we must have some insights concerning the benefits of this link and how this link can be achieved. These are the central roles for this chapter.

The core of this chapter will be divided into four distinct sections, representing the four topics mentioned earlier. Each organizational context has received attention in the organizational behavior literature. However, little concern has been directed toward the judgment of the actors in these contexts. This chapter sees the judgments of organizational actors as the central mechanism that determines the behavior of multiparty entities in organizations. Thus, we believe that the behavioral decision theory approach provides a very useful vehicle, if not the most useful vehicle, for understanding and improving these organizational contexts.

Each section is organized to provide an overview of the literature in the area. We then develop the role of judgment in that section. Finally, we consider the benefits of such a perspective for achieving a better understanding of the multiparty context. Following the pattern of Chapter 7, the overview of relevant literature will be selective, with respect to both the particular domain of multiparty activity and the judgment literature. The primary goal in this chapter is to begin discussion of how the judgment perspective can inform these areas of decision making in organizations.

THIRD PARTIES IN ORGANIZATIONS

When most people think about third parties, they think about judicial bodies— the court system, arbitrators, mediators, and perhaps a variety of dispute counselors. A central theme of a growing body of literature (see Bazerman and Lewicki, 1983; Lewicki, Sheppard & Bazerman, 1986; Sheppard, 1983) is that acting as a third party is a major part of managerial behavior. This complements the view developed in Chapter 7 of negotiation as a central part of managerial life. The literature on the manager as third party notes that the manager is often in the position of dealing with conflicting positions of subordinates. How should he/she intervene? How will he/she intervene? What norms does he/she bring to the conflict?

The inclusion of third-party behavior as part of the managerial role is not new to organizational behavior. Weber's (1949) theory of bureaucracy viewed the hierarchy as a mechanism for solving any problem that could not be solved at a lower level. For example, if a dispute existed between two subgroups and no formal procedure existed for dealing with the situation, his theory noted that the decision will be directed up the hierarchy until a decision could be reached. A manager, acting as a third party, would make the decision. However, more recent literature has focused on alternative strategies for resolving disputes in organizations. For example, Kochan (1980) argues that mediation has the desirable property of helping the parties to work toward their *own* agreement. If the employees "own" the agreement, the agreement will be more readily accepted and more likely to last over time. Despite such newer insights, the investigation of the role of manager as a third party remains an underresearched area of organizational inquiry.

The importance of third parties in organizations has been recognized in an impressive array of contexts, ranging from daily managerial behavior to the role of an ombudsman to the judicial system as it affects organizations. However, the skills of third parties have been viewed as an art form—some have it and some do not. This was exemplified by the labor–management arbitrator cited in Chapter 6 who felt that his decisions could not be captured by a scientific model. Although we accept the role of third party behavior as being influenced by expertise, the art form view is found to be unacceptable. There are a number of insights that a scientific, judgmental perspective can raise in improving our understanding of how third parties do and should operate in organizations.

This discussion can be focused by considering two generic examples of the choices facing third parties in organizations.

> You are a manager with two divisions reporting to you. You have a limited budget that must be divided between the two divisions. You have asked the two division managers to reach an agreement on the proportion of the budget that each division needs and should receive. Not surprisingly, the needs of the two managers exceed the amount of funds that you have to disperse.

> Again, you have reporting responsibilities for two divisions. This time they are in dispute about the price at which Division A should sell goods to Division B. Division A argues that the market price is fair, whereas Division B argues for the variable cost to Division A. The organization prefers to have transactions occur within the firm whenever possible.

In responding to these situations, both the labor-relations literature (Kochan, 1980) and the procedural justice literature (Thibaut and Walker, 1975) describe the variety of procedures you could use to intervene. You could make the decisions for the parties unilaterally—you arbitrate. You could facilitate the process so as to help the parties themselves reach their own mutually agreeable resolution—you mediate. In addition, you can probably generate a number of alternative intervention styles that you might consider in your decision to intervene. Unfortunately, little is known about how managers choose among alternative intervention strategies, and virtually nothing is known about the context under which each strategy is likely to be most effective.

Initial groundwork on this topic can be seen in Sheppard's (1983, 1984; Lewicki and Sheppard, 1985) generic model of alternative intervention strategies. This research shows that the styles that managers most frequently decide to exercise are not the styles that have been most frequently identified in the labor relations literature. Instead of using arbitration or mediation styles, managers often behave like "inquisitorial judges" (collecting information on a dispute from the parties and then rendering a decision), or "conflict deflectors" (dubbed "kick in the pants," in that the manager tells the conflicting parties to resolve the dispute themselves or he/she will resolve it for them). In addition, it is interesting to note that Sheppard finds that managerial preference for mediation is not matched by actual behavior. Sheppard's work highlights the need to understand the choices of alternative third-party intervention styles better and brings the topic of alternative forms of third-party intervention into the domain of managerial behavior.

Past work on third-party intervention, with its focus on alternative forms of intervention, has ignored an equally important aspect of the third-party process—the judicial decision processes of the third party. Often, the third party must make a decision between conflicting parties. What norms and/or biases govern these decisions? What norms and/or biases would affect the decision maker in the scenarios depicted here? In an organization, a rational model would suggest that the conflict should be resolved in the manner that maximizes the outcomes to the total organization. This perspective will be illustrated next under the "global perspective" norm of distributive justice in organizations. However, we will also consider three other norms. (equity, equality, and anchoring) that challenge the predictive power of this global perspective. After reviewing these competing perspectives, we will examine some initial evidence coming from the labor–management domain.

Global Perspective

The most clearly articulated goal for how a manager should resolve disputes comes from the profit maximization goals inherent in a free-market economy. That is, the manager should resolve the dispute such that the settlement maximizes the profit of the larger entity—namely, the organization. This presumes that the interests of the disputants are only of indirect interest. That is, the interests of the parties only matter to the extent that they affect the global welfare of the organization (e.g., one valuable party may quit if the resolution is unacceptable).

Although this norm is consistent with the philosophical basis of capitalist economies, it is inconsistent with a number of other philosophical principles and goals that are known to affect managers and other third parties. It is also consistent with the rational actor model that was specified in Chapter 1 and attacked based on systematic deviations from rationality that were elaborated on throughout this book. In the context of the decisions of third parties, a number of alternative principles that imply deviations from this model of rationality can be inferred in philosophical and psychological writings on distributive justice. These alternative principles are specified in the other three norms delineated following.

Equity

A second principle that third parties might follow is the *equity norm.* This norm suggests that disputes should be resolved in the way that recognizes the legitimate rights of the disputants. What budget has each party earned? What salary is deserved by the multiple subordinates that you must choose among? The equity principle assumes that some notion of fairness can be determined for the particular context. The equity principle is consistent with the equity theory of motivation, which suggests that employees are motivated to receive a just return for their inputs in proportion to the return on inputs of relevant others (Adams, 1963, 1965). In the salary case, the implications of this point are obvious. In a budget scenario, equity might be operationalized in terms of demonstrated capacity to use the resources, past performance, or such. Implicit in the equity principle is the idea that individuals and groups should receive a proportion of the disputed resources according to some notion of their rights or inputs to the organization. Kahneman, Knetsch, and Thaler's (1985) recent work suggests that most individuals will forgo the optimal decision (in a value-maximizing sense) in order to make the equitable decision.

Equality

In contrast to the arguments in favor of a global perspective or equity, Rawl's (1971) egalitarian theory of justice argues that resources should be distributed equally to all individuals in a society (e.g., an organization) except in those cases where an unequal distribution actually works to everyone's advantage. This notion of *equality* suggests that most disputes should be resolved such that both disputants receive equal shares of the disputed resources (e.g., half way between the two pricing systems identified in the transfer pricing problem). Although the socialistic implications of this norm are not consistent with our generally capitalistic economy, Starke and Notz (1981), among others, argue that the tendency to compromise (which is operationally a decision to follow the equality norm) is common among amateur and experienced third parties.

Anchoring

Although the positions just identified can be defended based on philosophical and economic models of third-party decision making, Kahneman and Tversky's anchoring and adjustment argument (Chapter 2) suggests that human beings have a systematic tendency to make judgments by selecting an anchor and making only minor adjustments from that anchor. This position suggests that third parties are likely to select the most commonly available anchor (the existing distribution of disputed resources) and make an incremental adjustment to that decision. This suggests that budget disputes will be resolved such that this year's budget is not very different from last year's, that salary increases will be made so that the new salary structure will primarily maintain last year's salary structure, and so forth. A global perspective, equity, or equality will only be created to the extent that minor adjustment from the status quo can create these conditions.

The comparison between alternative norms of arbitration was the focus of a recent study by Bazerman (1985). This study examined the norms used by experienced arbitrators in the labor–management context. Because the third party in this study was not part of a more global organization, the global perspective norm was not evaluated. Although the arbitration literature has focused historically on whether arbitrators follow an equity norm or split-the-difference (equality), Bazerman found that the most common practice of arbitrators was to use the anchoring norm to maintain the status quo. That is, they made minor adjustments to last year's contract, thereby maintaining an approximation of the agreements that were accepted in the past. This suggests that managerial behavior might be described as inappropriately using past norms to guide their decisions concerning the distribution of limited resources. For example, are budgets decided starting with a clear slate or are they adjustments from last year's budget? Both a global perspective norm and an equity norm would suggest the need for a clean slate view of budget formation, because adjustments implicitly follow the anchoring norm. However, most budget setting practices are better described by the anchoring norm. Similarly, Chapter 2 gave the example of salary raises being determined as an adjustment to last year's salary structure as an example of the anchoring and adjustment heuristic. If we think of the performance appraisal system as the organization's method of distributing limited resources (raises) through an arbitration system (i.e., the employees are not asked to try to resolve the dispute themselves), this system again fits under the anchoring norm of arbitrator decision making. Although this limited empirical evidence suggests that the use of anchors is a common approach to distributive justice by third parties, we ask if it is acceptable given the logic behind the alternative norms of distributive justice. Many managers, when confronted with these arguments, feel a need to rethink how they deal with the distribution of scarce resources.

This section has provided the beginning of an emerging literature on the *decisions* made by third parties in organizations. Most managers have third-party styles and an implicit decision strategy for disputes, but they are often unaware of their style and decision strategy. By systematically studying third-party decisions, we can identify effective styles and strategies and develop feedback and training procedures for effective managerial behavior in the context of being a third party. This section noted the importance of the anchoring and adjustment heuristic in describing the behavior of third parties. Future research needs to identify other systematic heuristics that describe the behaviors of managers in the role of third parties.

COALITION BEHAVIOR IN ORGANIZATIONS

The discussion of negotiations dealt with two actors. The discussion of third parties simply added one additional actor. Decision processes in organizations, however, often include many more actors, and decisions are only made when they have sufficient support. This support may be in the form of a vote or the perception that there is sufficient support for the decision from "the people with power." Obtaining this support is referred to as *coalition behavior*. The argument that coalition behavior is important in organizations is well accepted. For example, consider the case of the federal government: There are a variety of coalitions that might form around a particular issue, each of which will result in a different outcome for the country and different outcomes to various interest groups. It is easy to see the importance of successful coalition behavior for being a successful politician.

Interestingly, it is easy to view the political behavior of organizational actors in the same manner. Although the manager wants what is "best for the organization" (like the politician who wants what is "best for the country"), the various managers have differing ideas on what is best for the organization. Not surprisingly, their different views on what is best for the organization are often correlated with what is best for the manager. This scenario suggests that managers are often forming alliances that can later be used in influencing organizational decisions and actions. This argument implies that coalition behavior is an important part of managerial behavior.

The roots of the study of coalition behavior as a research topic of organizational scholars can be traced to Cyert and March (1963), who suggested that an organization's goals can be described by the goals of the organization's dominant coalition. Pennings and Goodman (1977) used Cyert and March's framework to define organizational effectiveness as the fulfillment of the goals of the organization's dominant coalition. Other theoretical uses of the coalition concept are evident in the organizational writings of Thompson (1967), Pfeffer and Salancik (1978), and Mintzberg (1983).

Although organizational theorists have extensively discussed the importance of the behavior of coalitions in organizational functioning, empirical research has been limited to disciplinary work in game theory, social psychology, and political science (Murnighan, 1978). Each of these areas has adopted a different philosophical approach and methodology that has raised different research questions. In addition, each discipline has remained independent in its efforts to understand coalition behavior. Unfortunately, this separation has created a barrier to fully understanding coalition behavior as an organizational process.

Murnighan (1986) attributes the lack of cross-fertilization of coalition ideas into the organizational arena to the arguments that (1) the formal mathematical language of coalition theory may be less tractable than most areas that are viewed as a part of organizational behavior and (2) the empirical research on coalition behavior has been conducted almost solely in the laboratory. Although parts of these explanations may be accurate, they do not tell the whole story. There are certainly other areas in the behavioral sciences with similar limitations that have made their way into the organizational literature. The coalition literature has also been limited in the selection of topics investigated. This section will briefly overview the topics that have been studied in the various disciplinary areas of coalition behavior. Attention will then be directed to the potential of a judgmental perspective for increasing what we know about coalitions and for making the topic more relevant to the field of organizational behavior.

Game Theoretic Approaches

Game theoretic approaches to coalition behavior have focused on the development of sophisticated mathematical representations of the coalition-oriented behavior of maximally rational actors. In this literature, a "game" is defined by the payoffs available to each possible coalition, including one-person coalitions (what a party receives by not joining any larger coalition). The models developed by game theorists focus on the game's characteristics, assume that individuals will act rationally, and emphasize the generality of the solutions to a wide variety of contexts (Murnighan, 1978). Conflicting views exist within the literature, largely because of different assumptions about what constitutes "rational" behavior by an actor faced with a multiparty coalition task.

Social Psychological Approaches

Social psychological models have focused on the impact of the amount and kind of resources that each of the actors brings to a potential coalition-formation setting. These models are similar to game theoretic models in their focus on how coalition members will divide the rewards to the coalition. However, in addition, social psychological models make predictions about *which* coalitions will form. Most social psychological frameworks also assume that actors will attempt to maximize their outcomes. However, outcome-maximization predictions are not necessarily the same as the expectations for a rational actor from a game theoretic view. Rather, social psychological approaches are intended to be descriptive rather than normative, as in the game theoretic case, and take into account behavior that is not purely "rational" (Murnighan, 1978).

Political Approaches

The political perspective to coalition behavior focuses on the ability to implement the goals of the coalition following its formation. Thus, the political approach has a distinctly longer time focus than either the game theoretic or social psychological approaches. Evidence of this approach is manifested in the measurement and frequent use of the coalition's *duration* as a dependent variable in political analyses of coalitions (Murnighan, 1978). The political literature is rich in its description of coalition behavior, and much of it is in the form of case studies. However, it lags behind the other literatures in theory formation, perhaps because of the complexity of the descriptive scenarios that it wishes to capture.

Although other approaches to coalitions exist, most work falls into one of the three categories just described. A review of these literatures suggests that little overlap or infiltration has occurred between areas (Murnighan, 1978) and that the research in these areas has had virtually no impact on the study of coalitions in organizational behavior. Is the study of coalitions useful for understanding how decision-making entities behave in organizations? Although the lack of such research might suggest that the answer is "no," the intuitive answer appears to be "yes." Theorists and practitioners alike can easily identify the relevance of coalition behavior for understanding organizational issues. Whether the problem is to identify the sources of power of important actors in an organization, to identify the likely behavior of a key decision-making group such as an executive committee or a task force, or to understand how corporate networks form and operate, concepts of coalition behavior are central. Given the anecdotal evidence on the importance of coalitions to organizations and the rich literatures that exist to help answer these questions, what is necessary to advance coalition behavior as an organizational topic?

In the early part of his book on negotiation, Raiffa (1982) argues that the best prescriptive advice to a negotiator must take into account the best prediction of the actual behavior of the opponent. He argues it does far less good to tell the negotiator how to respond against a rational actor when the actual actor is unlikely to behave in a perfectly rational manner. Consider this in relation to the lack of infiltration of coalition research into organizational behavior: All three of the disciplinary directions to coalition behavior take fairly rationalistic views of the coalition process. They make predictions of outcomes based on what would occur if the actors followed what seemed to be rational behavior according to the researcher. This has led to a literature that is far less useful for organizational behaviorists who are in the business of providing descriptions and advice that are useful in managerial behavior. A far more useful direction would be to try to describe the actual coalition behavior of organizational members in a manner that helps an organizational actor understand what is going on and use this understanding to make better subsequent decisions. This section attempts to move in this direction by exploring the power of the behavioral decision theory literature to explain actual coalition behavior in organizations, in ways that are more descriptive and have more action implications than the rationalistic arguments in the existing literatures. The remainder of this section will develop specific predictions from the behavioral decision theory literature to explain (1) the decisions of actors to form a coalition and (2) coalition stability.

Coalition Formation

Game theoretic views and social psychological views of coalition formation make predictions of which coalitions will form based on rationalistic criteria. Although these models have demonstrated good predictive validity, we argue that the actual behavior of potential coalition members could be better described by focusing on the bounds to rationality that affect coalition formation. Specifically, the concepts of availability, overconfidence, the lack of perspective taking ability can be applied to the topic of coalition formation to make specific predictions about how actual coalitions will deviate from the rationalistic models described earlier.

The availability heuristic suggests that the perceived probability of an event (e.g., forming a specific coalition) is influenced by the degree to which that event is easily available in memory or imagination. Although this will often lead to efficient methods of forming a coalition, it has the danger of overlooking alternative coalition combinations by focusing exclusively on readily available forms of coalition formation. This is exemplified in the area of the formation of boards of directors—a coalition empowered to make many of the most important decisions that an organization faces. Research has shown that directors are chosen in ways that lead to the formation of an elite group (a megacoalition) that networks through overlapping board memberships (Bazerman and Schoorman, 1983; Schoorman, Bazerman, and Atkin, 1981). Many argue that these interlocks are created deliberately by the elite group to serve as a coordinating force within corporate America and serve against the best interests of the antitrust legislation that is aimed at creating a free market. An alternative interpretation is that existing boards are innocent of such wrongdoing and that they simply rely on available information when choosing additional board members. What individuals are most available? Individuals who are already serving as board members of other firms. (*Note*: The representativeness heuristic could be used to explain the same behavior to the extent the other board members are representative of the individuals in which the focal organization would be interested.)

Overconfidence effects also can have a pervasive impact on which coalitions form. Chapter 2 demonstrated that individuals have inappropriate confidence in their fallible judgment, and Chapter 7 provided evidence that this effect generalized to negotiators in their assessment of the likelihood of success in negotiation contexts. This section offers the prediction that individuals also are likely to be overconfident in their ability to form a particular coalition. For example, when William Agee (of the Bendix Corporation) was building a coalition among stockholders for the takeover of Martin Marietta Corporation, he was overconfident in his ability to form that coalition and complete the takeover. Some analysts also attribute Martin Marietta's ability to reverse the tables and consider a takeover attempt of Agee's Bendix Corporation to Agee's lack of perspective-taking ability in considering the response of Martin Marietta and overconfidence in his own plan (Lampert, 1983). In the end, Agee agreed to sell Bendix to Allied, a "white knight," in order to save Bendix from the hostile attack by Martin Marietta. It can be argued that Agee was forced into this situation because of a lack of perspective-taking at an early stage in the development of this coalition context.

Coalition Stability

Turning to the area of coalition stability, we again obtain rationalistic predictions from the existing literature. However, the behavioral decision theory literature makes predictions that systematically supercede these rationalistic arguments. Specifically, framing, anchoring, escalation, and the fixed-pie assumption all provide guidance in making predictions about actual behavior in the formation of coalitions.

Consider a situation in which an existing coalition is in power. As the present coalition literature predicts, there are often alternative coalitions that could be formed that increase the power of any particular coalition member (however, each of these alternative coalitions would exclude other current coalition members). Agreement by coalition members to maintain the existing coalition can be viewed as risk-averse behavior (accepting the known coalition relationship), whereas exploring alternative coalitions can be viewed as risk-seeking behavior (such exploration may dramatically increase or decrease the focal members' outcomes). Viewing coalition stability in this way, the framing effect (Chapter 3) would predict that coalition stability will be higher when coalition members have a positive, as opposed to negative, frame. As we earlier showed, the same objective situation can often be perceived in either frame.

The escalation literature predicts that individuals tend to make decisions in ways that escalate their commitment to a previously chosen course of action. This would predict that individuals would maintain an existing coalition beyond the point when it becomes rational to pursue alternative coalitions. This point is further emphasized by our tendency to anchor our new decisions (the coalition formation in the future) by a previously existing anchor (the existing coalition).

Finally, our discussion of the notion of a mythical fixed-pie (Chapter 7) also may be relevant to explaining the maintenance of existing coalitions. Consider the situation in which a dominant coalition exists, and it is in this coalition's best interest to expand and add new members. Such a view requires that the existing coalition members can see that the additions will increase the resources that the total coalition will have available. We would predict, however, that existing coalition members will have a tendency not to recognize the full potential of expanding the pie and including others into their elite circle. Returning to the topic of interlocking directorates, the argument that a small network of directors exists that maintains social-class elitism by excluding other viable director candidates presumes that a fixed amount of power exists in society. Thus, this view implicitly assumes that this coalition of board directors remains stable because of this fixed-pie perception. It can be argued that the corporation's pie could be expanded, and therefore that the directors are acting irrationally, if other individuals were added to these high-level decision-making bodies.

In summary, the existing coalitions literature has demonstrated its predictive validity. However, the prediction power is far from perfect. This section argues that the behavioral decision theory literature offers an undeveloped direction for furthering our understanding of coalition behavior. In addition, the focus on the role of judgment raises new questions that may help make the area of coalition behavior more useful to the organizational audience. The suggestions offered here, if empirically valid, provide specific guidance to organizational actors in thinking about their coalition behavior. The views offered not only help organizational actors in critiquing their own behavior, but also in understanding the behavior of other organizational actors. Obviously, empirical research is needed before we can place confidence in the predictions made in this section.

GROUP DECISION MAKING

Chapter 7 and the earlier parts of this chapter have dealt with decision making in explicitly competitive situations. In contrast, this section examines group decision making, a context under which the multiple actors may or may not be in competition. The study of group decision making has been recognized as an important part of organizational behavior (see Guzzo, 1982). This recognition exists both in the academic literature and in anecdotal accounts of organization members. Although most recognize the potential power in the use of groups for making decisions, most also recognize the difficulties in getting groups to perform at the optimal level.

This section will *not* offer a comprehensive discussion of group decision making, as this is readily available elsewhere (e.g., Brandstatter, Davis, and Stocker-Kreichgauer, 1982; Guzzo, 1982; Steiner, 1972). Rather, this section will highlight some important findings about group decision making and explore the potential benefits from the simultaneous examination of the group decision making and individual judgment literatures. Attention within the group decision-making literature will be focused on the "risky shift" and "groupthink" phenomena, the two most well-known findings in this literature. The relevance of individual judgment to these phenomena will be discussed. Finally, we will consider the impact of groups on the decision heuristics addressed in the earlier parts of this book.

Risky Shift

Over the past two decades, considerable evidence has been added to Stoner's (1961) initial demonstration that groups make riskier decisions than the mean of the decisions previously made by the individual members of that group. Rarely in the history of behavioral science has a single laboratory study stimulated as much empirical research as did Stoner's (1961) study of the risky shift. Stoner's results were a surprise, even to him, as he was simply trying to test the old "fact" that groups are more cautious and less creatively daring than are individuals.

Stoner's procedure consisted of having a small number of participants respond individually to a series of choice dilemmas. The subjects' task was to advise the actor in the dilemma as to how much risk he should take. The following is a sample item.*

---

*Source: From *Risk Taking* by Nathan Kogan and Michael A. Wallach. Copyright © 1964 by Holt, Rinehart and Winston. Reprinted by permission of CBS College Publishing.

Mr. A, an electrical engineer, who is married and has one child, has been working for a large electronics corporation since graduating from college five years ago. He is assured of a lifetime job with a modest, though adequate, salary, and liberal pension benefits upon retirement. On the other hand, it is very unlikely that his salary will increase much before he retires. While attending a convention, Mr. A is offered a job with a small, newly founded company which has a highly uncertain future. The new job would pay more to start and would offer the possibility of a share in the ownership if the company survived the competition of the larger firms.

Imagine that you are advising Mr. A. Listed below are several probabilities or odds of the new company's proving financially sound.

Please check the lowest probability that you would consider acceptable to make it worthwhile for Mr. A to take the new job.

_____ The chances are 1 in 10 that the company will prove financially sound.
_____ The chances are 3 in 10 that the company will prove financially sound.
_____ The chances are 5 in 10 that the company will prove financially sound.
_____ The chances are 7 in 10 that the company will prove financially sound.
_____ The chances are 9 in 10 that the company will prove financially sound.
_____ Place a check here if you think Mr. A should not take the job no matter what the probabilities.

After the subjects responded to 12 items individually, the participants assembled as a group and discussed each of the 12 items until group agreement was reached. The discovery that groups are on the whole more risk-prone than individuals was called the "risky shift" phenomenon. As findings began to accumulate, it became clear that the shift observed by Stoner (1961) using the 12-item Choice Dilemma Questionnaire (CDQ) as a means of operationalizing risk produced replicable results. Historically, the 12 responses were aggregated to determine a single score in which a lower score designated a riskier course of action.

Although the risky shift, using the CDQ, has been remarkably stable across a wide variety of experimental settings and types of experimental subjects, the shift for the various items of the CDQ differ substantially in both direction and magnitude. Some items consistently produce risky shifts, some items produce no significant shift, and two items regularly generate cautious shifts (i.e., the groups are less risky than individuals). In addition, new items similar in form to the CDQ have been constructed and tested that consistently generate cautious shifts (Cartwright, 1973).

Added questions concerning the risky shift paradigm were provided by contradictory research in "real-life" situations (e.g., investors, juries, consumers) and laboratory research that did not employ the CDQ. Sometimes a risky shift occurred, sometimes a cautious shift occurred, and sometimes no shift occurred. Based on such evidence, Cartwright (1973, p. 45) concluded that

. . . it is now evident that the persistent search for an explanation of "the risky shift" was misdirected and that any adequate theory will have to account for a much more complicated set of data than originally anticipated.

The fixation on laboratory studies using the CDQ has obscured the most critical question: When does a risky versus cautious shift occur? The black-box approach of using the total CDQ scores is incapable of delineating the processes underlying group-induced risk shifts. The remainder of our discussion focuses on two explanations of the risky shift phenomenon. The first is the most well-accepted explanation in the current social psychological literature, and the second is an explanation that can be derived from the behavioral decision theory literature.

Moscovici and Zavalloni (1969) and Doise (1969) have been responsible for developing a coherent and empirically validated explanation of the inconsistent effects of the risky shift phenomenon. They argue that the behavior of groups can be better characterized in terms of a "group polarization" effect. That is, group discussions tend to enhance the predominant view in the group. Thus, if the individuals were initially in favor of a moderately high degree of risk, then the group discussion will enhance the individual evaluations of the favorability of the risk, thus enhancing the group's evaluation of the risk. These researchers have found consistent support for this hypothesis. For example, they have reevaluated the CDQ and found that the group responses are more risk-seeking on items on which the individual were already fairly risk-seeking. However, on items where individuals were initially in favor of a moderately low degree of risk, group discussion enhanced the importance of minimal risk and a cautious shift appeared.

The group polarization argument provides a mechanism for understanding how individual opinions are affected in group discussion. The framing effect from Chapter 3 provides an explanation of the risky shift results in terms of how individuals versus groups actually make decisions. This explanation stems from Vinokur's (1971) suggestions that individuals *and* groups will choose that option that maximizes their expected utility. Although interesting, Vinokur's suggestion fails to clarify when the maximization of expected utility will lead to risky versus cautious shifts. Clarification of this question comes from the framing concept. As presented in Chapter 3, individuals will tend to be risk-averse in positively framed situations, while being risk-seeking in negatively framed situations. We might hypothesize, however, that groups encourage the verbalization of the problem in multiple alternative frames by varying group members—thus diluting the impact of any one specific frame (Bazerman, 1984). This suggests that groups will move away from the classical utility curve toward an expected value (or risk-neutral) decision strategy. Examining Figure 3.1, this perspective would suggest that (1) judgments made by individuals will tend to follow the classical utility curve and (2) group decisions will tend to adjust toward the risk-neutral line. *This analysis would predict a risky shift on positively framed items and a cautious shift on negatively framed items.* Neale, Bazerman, Northcraft, and Alperson (1986) provide preliminary empirical evidence in support of this position, and against the polarization argument. This analysis has the potential for clarifying group-induced shifts and the existence of the risky shift paradigm. Examination of the CDQ finds that this instrument is positively framed, which leads to the prediction of a risky shift. Would we currently be reexamining "the cautious shift" paradigm had Stoner (1961) initially conducted his experiment with a negatively framed instrument?

Groupthink

Perhaps the best-known effect in the group decision-making literature is the "groupthink" effect. Janis (1972) used this term to refer to the suppression of ideas that are critical of the direction in which a group is moving because of a concurrence-seeking tendency. Janis argues that moderately or highly cohesive groups use their cognitive resources to develop rationalizations in line with shared illusions about the invulnerability of the group's decision. He used the groupthink argument to describe a number of historical fiascos. For example, Janis analyzed the Bay of Pigs invasion.

Kennedy's Bay of Pigs invasion ranks as one of the poorest decisions ever made by the United States government. American intelligence officers with little background or experience in military matters attempted to place a small brigade of Cuban exiles secretly on a beachhead in Cuba with the ultimate objective of overthrowing the Castro government. The result was a fiasco. Janis analyzes this historical event in terms of the suppression of critical doubts in Kennedy's decision-making group.

Janis explains the Bay of Pigs fiasco and many other poor decisions by arguing that, in cohesive groups, the desire for concurrence leads to the following symptoms that inhibit the expression of critical ideas:

1. An illusion of invulnerability.
2. Collective rationalization.
3. Belief in the inherent morality of the group.
4. Stereotypes of out-groups.
5. Direct pressure on dissenters.
6. Self-censorship.
7. Illusion of unanimity.
8. Self-appointed "mindguards."

These symptoms are then argued to lead to a number of deficiencies in the decision-making process. These include (Janis and Mann, 1977):

1. Incomplete survey of alternatives.
2. Incomplete survey of objectives.
3. Failure to examine risks of preferred choice.
4. Failure to reappraise initially rejected alternatives.
5. Poor information search.
6. Selective bias in processing information at hand.
7. Failure to work out contingency plans.

It is easy to observe that Janis is arguing that groupthink interferes with the steps of rational decision making as outlined in Chapter 1.

Groupthink can be viewed as the use of a heuristic that limits effective decision making. Specifically, individual behavior in these groups assumes that the simple rule of not being the only deviant will result in improved decisions or that the improvement by the expression of critical doubts is not worth the conflict that would result. Just as the heuristics described in Chapter 2 limit effective individual decisions, groupthink limits the effectiveness of decisions at a group level.

The behavior of individuals described by the groupthink hypothesis is compatible with the discussion of the overconfidence effect described in Chapter 2. In Chapter 2, overconfidence was based on the individual's trust in his own fallible judgment. In this section, we see individuals suppressing their critical thoughts because of inappropriate confidence in the decision-making talent of the group.

The Impact of Groups on Decision-Making Heuristics

Before leaving the topic of group decision making, it is relevant to consider the impact of using groups rather than individuals on the judgmental deficiencies that were presented in the first part of this book. Much of the group decision-making literature has been devoted to the examination of the comparative benefits of individual and group decision making (Maier, 1967). An additional approach for examining this issue is to consider the impact of using groups on the decision heuristics identified in the early chapters of this book. Unfortunately, very few studies have been conducted that explore the existence of these deficiencies at the group level. However, a few exceptions exist, and these studies are reviewed here.

Argote, Seabright, and Dyer (1986) have investigated the use of the representativeness heuristic in both individual and group behavior. Their results find groups to exhibit the representative heuristic in the same directional pattern as individuals. In addition, they find the magnitude of the biasing effect to be greater in groups than individuals. Bazerman, Giuliano, and Appelman (1984) found groups to escalate commitment to a previously selected course of action nonrationally. In addition, the average degree of nonrational escalation in groups was equal to that of individuals. The difference, however, was that there was much more variance in the behavior of groups. Many more groups than individuals did not escalate their commitment. However, groups that did escalate their commitment tended to do so to a greater degree than did individuals. It seems that the added inputs from multiple members of the group afford the opportunity to realize the irrationality of the escalation pattern. However, if this realization does not occur, the group provides added support for the initial decision and rationalizations for a decision to escalate commitment.

There is an obvious need for more research that examines decision heuristics and biases in group behavior. These initial results suggest that the decisional problems identified in this book are likely to be descriptive of group decisions as well. However, the key is to identify specific differences such that group decision making can be improved and selectively used in situations in which group decisions are more likely to be optimal than are individual decisions. Unfortunately, much research is needed to get us to the point of providing such advice.

COMPETITIVE BIDDING

Each of the previous multiparty contexts has dealt with situations in which the focal actor is in direct contact with the other parties. That is, he/she was negotiating with an opponent, intervening between two other negotiators, negotiating the formation of a coalition, or making a group decision with other organizational actors. Many decisions in organizations, in contrast, require an organizational actor to make competitive decisions while indirectly interacting with many other parties. An example of this occurs in the context of *competitive bidding*. Competitive bidding raises judgmental issues for the decision maker. Consider the following scenarios.

> Your consulting firm is trying to acquire a young, highly regarded MBA student from a prestigious university. A large number of other organizations are also interested in this apparently talented individual. In fact, your firm seems to be competing against these other firms for her services. Finally, she accepts your offer. Will she prove to be as productive as you believe? Will it be worth the costs of hiring her?

> As the owner of a small movie theater, you must bid against a number of other theaters for the rights to exhibit first-run films. A new film is scheduled to be released in six months that is expected to be the hottest property since *E.T.* Like your fellow theater owners, you must bid for the rights to show the movie, sight unseen. You submit your bid, and it is high enough to win the right to show the movie in your theater. You "beat" a large number of nearby competitors. Is it time to celebrate?

> Your conglomerate is considering a new acquisition. Many other firms are also "bidding" for this firm. The target firm has suggested that they will gladly be acquired by the highest bidder. The actual value of the target firm is highly uncertain—the target firm does not even know what they are "worth." With at least a half dozen firms pursuing the target, your bid is the highest, your offer is accepted and you obtain the acquisition. Have you been successful?

> You are the owner of a baseball team. A hitter with an erratic performance (the "inconsistent slammer") has declared his free agency. In the free-agent draft, 11 teams (including yours) drafted the player and appear to be interested in negotiating for his services. After negotiating with each team, the player accepts your offer, explaining that "your team offered the best package." Is the player going to be worth the money you have offered to pay him?

Situations in which multiple parties pursue the same limited target are common. You can generate many other situations in which you were one of the many bidders and a few situations in which you were (part of) the scarce resource that was being pursued. In each of the scenarios given here, a naive analysis would suggest that you should be glad to have "won" the competitive situation, because you would not have offered more than you thought the commodity was worth. In fact, individuals in these situations often behave as if they won something. However, research evidence (see Bazerman and Samuelson, 1983) argues that you are likely to have become the most recent victim of the "winner's curse" in competitive bidding.

Bazerman and Samuelson posit that under certain circumstances the most likely reason you were the highest bidder is the fact that you significantly overestimated the actual value of the commodity. Figure 8.1 provides a graphic depiction of the winner's curse in competitive bidding (Bazerman and Samuelson, 1983). Shown on the figure is the distribution of bidder estimates of the true value of the commodity (curve E) and also the distribution of bids (curve B). As assumed in the depiction, the mean of the estimate distribution is equal to the true value of the commodity (thus, no aggregate underestimation or overestimation is expected), and the bid distribution is determined by a leftward shift of the estimate distribution—that is, bidders discount their estimates (roughly) a fixed amount in making bids. The figure suggests that a winning bid

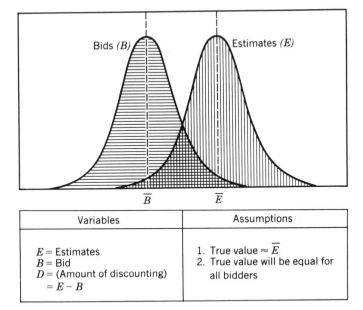

Variables	Assumptions
E = Estimates B = Bid D = (Amount of discounting) $= E - B$	1. True value $\approx \overline{E}$ 2. True value will be equal for all bidders

Figure 8.1 Graphic illustration of the winner's curse.
Source: M. H. Bazerman and W. F. Samuelson, "I Won the Auction but Don't Want the Prize." Journal of Conflict Resolution, Vol. 27, pp. 618–634. Copyright © 1983 by Sage Publications, Inc. Reprinted by permission of Sage Publications Inc.

(from the right tail of the distribution) is likely to exceed the actual value of the commodity to the degree to which the number of bidders is sufficient to fill out the distribution and if the uncertainty about the commodity is large enough to create the depicted dispersion in the distribution of estimates. That is, Bazerman and Samuelson predicted that the winning bidder in auctions of *highly uncertain* commodities (necessary to create dispersion in estimates and bids) with a *large number of bidders* (to fill out the distributions of estimates and bids) would commonly pay more than the commodity was worth. Their experimental data confirmed this prediction.

Why does the winning bidder fall prey to the winner's curse? The answer lies in the failure of bidders to draw a key inference: *If a particular bidder assumes that his/her bid will win the auction, this information should tell the bidder that he/she is likely to have overestimated the value of the commodity in comparison with other bidders.* Based on this reasoning, bidders should (but do not) adjust downward their estimates of the true value of the commodity and lower their bids accordingly.

The winner's curse effect in the competitive bidding context is conceptually related to the winner's curse effect in negotiation that was discussed in Chapter 7. In the negotiation setting, the winner's curse occurred because of the failure of negotiators to consider the decisions of the other negotiator. In the current setting, the winner's curse occurs because of a failure of bidders to consider the implications of being higher than a large number of other bidders. The key integrative conclusion is that individuals are not very good at integrating the implications of the decisions of competitive others into their own decisions. Again, following up a theme from Chapter 7, individuals are not very good at incorporating the perspectives of competitive others into their own decision processes.

The importance of the winner's curse in competitive bidding can be seen in the context of corporate takeovers. Corporate takeovers in the 1980s have provided ample evidence that acquiring companies often compete against one another and pay too much for what they get. As many as one third of all acquisitions prove to be failures, and an additional one third fail to live up to expectations (*Wall Street Journal,* 1981). The analysis of Bazerman and Samuelson suggests that potential acquirers should temper their optimism by recognizing that the winning bidder is likely to acquire a company that is worth far less than the expected value estimated by the acquirer who made the highest offer. More specifically, Bazerman and Samuelson point out that competitive decision makers should be particularly concerned about the winner's curse when there are a large number of bidders and high uncertainty around the true value of the commodity.

This section has shown that judgmental deficiencies are an important concern in the competitive bidding context. In addition, it has been suggested that competitive bidding is a common situation in organizations. Yet, the analysis of competitive bidding has been left in the hands of normative researchers (see Case, 1979) who provide excellent analyses but fail to focus on the judgment of the relevant actors. The analysis of judgment has a great deal to add. For example, how do different bidding procedures descriptively affect the various competitive actors? In what circumstances does bidder judgment deviate from rationality? How can bidders be trained to be more effective? And finally, how do the decisions of groups and organizations differ from those described for the individual in terms of the rationality of their competitive bidding strategies? These remain important unanswered questions.

CONCLUSIONS

This chapter argued that a descriptive understanding of individual judgment has a great deal to offer to the variety of organizational contexts in which multiparty decisions are made. Unfortunately, this chapter has been limited primarily to conceptual development and speculation, because very little empirical research has been done in these areas. To the extent that the ideas in this chapter are on target, an understanding of judgment has the potential to revolutionize research on multiparty decision making, just as it has revolutionized our descriptive understanding of the individual decision-making process.

NINE
JUDGMENT IN MANAGERIAL DECISION MAKING: BARRIERS AND OPPORTUNITIES

I started this book as an organizational behavior researcher with the belief that the behavioral decision theory literature had a lot to offer to my field. I found that the behavioral decision theory literature was of great interest to managerial students in undergraduate, masters, doctoral, and executive programs. In addition, a growing number of my colleagues in organizational behavior were developing an interest in this area—but the diffusion process was slow. I also met many excellent organizational behavior researchers who knew virtually nothing about this area. Thus, I chose to write a book that would take a number of basic ideas in the behavioral decision theory literature (Chapters 1 through 3) and show that they had the power to inform a number of other areas that are recognized more as a part of the organizational behavior literature (escalation, creativity, negotiation, coalition behavior, and so on). This book represents my current views on the connection.

This endeavor has led to a number of positive conclusions and a number of frustrations. On the positive side, ample evidence exists that the behavioral decision theory literature provides a new perspective for understanding some well-traveled areas of organizational behavior, and, where empirical evidence exists, there are encouraging signs that the behavioral decision theory provides new insights and new directions. For example, on the topic of negotiation, a new direction for understanding why negotiators fail to reach mutually beneficial agreements was outlined, as well as a new approach for training negotiators to improve their effectiveness. However, on many other topics this book identified the lack of research connecting the behavioral decision theory literature to organizational behavior topics. This was a source of frustration, because making connections without supporting data makes any empirical researcher (i.e., me) a bit nervous.

I am more convinced than ever that the behavioral decision theory literature should and will continue to infiltrate the organizational arena. However, I am more aware than ever of the limited degree to which the behavioral decision theory literature has been used in organizations. This was evidenced in my search for supporting research when none existed. Overall, the infiltration of behavioral decision theory into organizational behavior is at its very early stages.

Despite these limitations to the overall mission of the book, I believe that we have accomplished a number of objectives. This book takes many of the most critical findings in the behavioral decision theory literature and presents them in a form that is more accessible and usable in the managerial domain. This book uses the behavioral decision theory literature to provide an integrated conceptual overview of the topics of escalation and creativity. In the past, these literatures have been viewed as part of decision making, but they have never been well integrated with the behavioral decision theory literature. We have attempted to provide the conceptual link necessary to bridge this gap. This book uses the behavioral decision theory literature to identify a new direction for negotiation research and research on a variety of other multiparty contexts in organizations (third-party intervention, coalition behavior, groups, and competitive bidding). This last contribution identifies where I think the infiltration of behavioral decision theory can be most helpful. How can we combine our existing knowledge of these multiparty contexts that describe behavior in organizations with the rich knowledge of how individuals make *judgments* to provide better conceptual frameworks of how decisions are made in organizations? This book attempts to begin the investigation of this unified topic.

A great deal of potential research that falls under the rubric of the title of this book has not been fully explored. This is due to the lack of research from which to draw. This is consistent with the argument that the connection between the two fields of inquiry is at a very early stage of development. The final pages of this book provide some closing messages to the practitioner and to the organizational behavior researcher that will highlight some things that I was unable to accomplish fully in this book.

MESSAGES TO THE PRACTITIONER

I argued in Chapter 1 that most managers are fairly good decision makers. After providing great detail on what they do wrong in making decisions, I still believe that managers are fairly good decision makers. However, as Simon (1957; March and Simon, 1958) told us long ago, there are bounds to their rationality. These bounds affect all of us, even the best of decision makers. I argue that reducing the degree of biases can improve decision making for good and bad decision makers alike.

An optimistic, but naive, view of this book would expect that its readers would immediately improve their decision making. I say naive because it is premature to expect the change process attempted in these pages to be refrozen in a Lewinian sense (see Chapter 6). If unfreezing did not take place, the book failed. If you were not provided with sufficient information for the change, the book failed. But the responsibility for the refreezing of the changes in your decision processes lies with you. Refreezing requires a period when you constantly are reviewing your decision processes for the errors identified in this book. Refreezing requires that you think about these biases and review the concepts in this book. And refreezing requires that you are vigilant in your search for biases in the more complex world of decisions that you face. It is far easier to identify a bias while reading a book about decision making than it is to identify a bias when you are in the middle of an organizational crisis. Over time, you learn to make adjustments that, at first, require constant attention.

At this point in the book, it would be nice to roll out the ideal training program for improving decision making. However, the astute reader would know by now that I do not believe that such a thing exists. Rather, creating lasting internal improvement in decision making is a complex task that will occur gradually over time. It will include some knowledge of prescriptive models of decision making. It will also include an awareness (initially created by this book) of the deficiencies that affect judgment, enhanced by a motivated reader who will return to the ideas in this book to verify that change and refreezing are occurring over time. I believe that this long and complicated process is the most viable strategy for creating long-term improvement in decision-making ability.

The information in this book also has the potential to help inform you about the decisions of others. Chapter 6 discussed the formal topic of correcting the biased decisions of others. More informally, this book helps you think about the decision processes of others. We are often faced with situations in which we think that another individual is thinking about a problem in an inaccurate manner. However, we lack a way to articulate what is wrong with their logic. We think that they are wrong, but do not know why. The information in this book provides some systematic clues for understanding and explaining the biases of others. This can be practiced by examining tonight's newspaper or watching a sporting event on television. Reporters, sportscasters, and other public information providers constantly make statements that verify the intuitive decision processes outlined in this book.

Finally, I hope that this book raises your awareness of the importance of the decision *process*. Too many managers "want results." Unfortunately, as this book demonstrates, we make many decisions under uncertainty. Thus, many good decisions turn out badly and many bad decisions turn out well. To the extent that the manager rewards results, and not decision process, he/she is likely to be rewarding behaviors that will not be functional in the future. The position of this book is that an understanding of the decision process is the first step in providing the manager with the tools to evaluate decision processes.

MESSAGES TO THE ORGANIZATIONAL BEHAVIOR RESEARCHER

The major message to the researcher is that opportunities are ample. The behavioral decision theory literature has just begun to have an important influence on organizational behavior. I use this closing section to comment on some directions that I expect to emerge in the near future.

I am influenced in making these suggestions by the work of Davis (1971) who discussed the determinants of interesting research. He told us that interesting research contradicts the assumption ground of the reader (see Chapter 5). He told us that interesting research finds new connections that the reader did not know existed. He told us that interesting research leads the reader to think about problems that he/she never thought about before. Davis's ideas lead to the argument that future breakthroughs will not come from simply applying the behavioral decision theory literature to a wide variety of organizational problems. Thus, I am not advocating hundreds of studies that examine the availability heuristic (or framing, escalation, representativeness, and so on) in performance appraisal (or selection, career choice, motivational choice, or such). Rather, the important contributions will come from extensions that are not obvious. They will come from new conceptual connections. And they will come from understanding how the managerial context affects the intuitive issues discussed in this book.

Another way of presenting the ideas in the preceding paragraph is to suggest that future major contributions will come from identifying new or unanswered conceptual questions in organizational behavior that can be informed, but not fully answered, by behavioral decision theory. That is, what is it about coalitions or groups or competitive bidding that can lead to new questions that are informed by the behavioral decision theory literature, yet need additional conceptual thought to be fully answered? How can the literatures be combined so that we can understand the topic better because of the inclusion of behavioral decision theory? Such research is much harder to define than simply applying the behavioral decision theory literature, but I think that the rewards can be substantially higher. This intersection of ideas is my primary suggestion for new research directions and is illustrated in Figure 9.1.

The preceding paragraphs offer a global perspective of my suggestions for the future connection between behavioral decision theory and organizational behavior. The remainder of the section expands on earlier suggestions for specific topics that I think offer fertile ground for future research.

Coalition Behavior

Coalitions have been an enigma to organizational research for the last two decades. Their importance is well documented in the organizational theory literature. The disciplines (game theory, social psychology, and political sci-

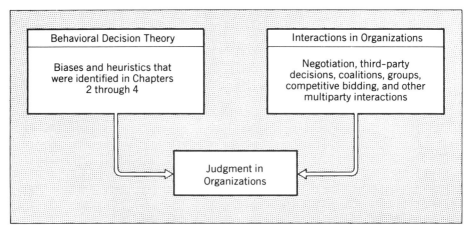

Figure 9.1 The integration of behavioral decision theory and organizational behavior.

ence) have offered interesting models. Yet the topic has never become particularly useful to the field. I believe that we can better understand coalitions by understanding the decisions of coalition actors. And in thinking about these decisions, we can gain a great deal by thinking about how their decisions will deviate from the rationalistic assumptions of the game theoretic, social psychological, and political science models. To respond to this topic, it will be necessary to do more than experiment with the host of biasing influences posited in Chapter 8. Rather, it will be necessary to conceptually identify which biases are likely to be manifested in a coalition setting, specify why these biases are operative, and then address these issues within interesting laboratory and field research.

Group Decision Making

Group decision making has had a long and important history. However, it has never been well linked to individual decision theory. An important issue in this literature has been the comparison between group and individual decisions (Steiner, 1972). However, we have remained at the level of specifying a set of factors that favor the individual, specifying a set of factors that favor the group, and identifying resulting differences in outcomes. The behavioral decision theory literature offers a new base for comparisons. It allows us to begin thinking about differences in *process* deficiencies that are often manifested in making decisions. This is represented in the research by Argote, Seabright, and Dyer (1985) and Bazerman, Giuliano, and Appelman (1984) reviewed in Chapter 8. However, future work needs to elaborate on these process differences and develop more thorough conceptual explanations that distinguish between individuals and groups in their use of biased decision procedures.

Third-Party Intervention

Many authors (e.g., Kochan and Bazerman, 1986) have argued that the management of conflict is becoming more important than ever as a result of a number of societal changes. This theme inspired much of the work on negotiation discussed in Chapter 7. Sheppard (1984) and others have done a very good job of documenting the importance of third-party roles in the manager's job. However, we argued earlier that we know very little about the decision processes of third parties. Again, we are not calling for experimental evidence that simply shows that third parties are influenced by the variety of biases identified in this book. Rather, we need to understand the context of third-party intervention and determine how that context interacts with what we know about judgment to improve our understanding of third parties. Kahneman, Knetsch, & Thaler (1985) have recently begun to examine the role of fairness in leading to decisions that are inconsistent with the predictions of a rational model. This work has obvious relevance as we begin thinking about the decisions of managerial third parties.

Competitive Bidding

Unlike coalitions, groups, and third parties, the topic of competitive bidding is not commonly viewed under the rubric or organizational behavior. Yet, organizational actors are often on one side or the other of a competitive bidding process. When multiple firms try to hire the same individual, they are competitively bidding. When multiple consulting firms are offering their services to the same potential client, they are competitively bidding. You can easily generate other examples. In addition, individuals are often uncertain about how to respond in these awkward situations. Normative models of competitive bidding exist, but good descriptive work in this area is lacking. Chapter 8 provided one example (the winner's curse) of the importance of systematic deviations from rationality in the context of competitive bidding. Other work is needed. I believe that a judgmental perspective can provide the vehicle to bring issues of competitive bidding into the mainstream of organizational behavior.

The Search for Additional
Heuristics and Biases

The heuristics and biases that are identified in this book are a sample of the total population of biases that affect our decisions. The heuristics and biases specified in the behavioral decision theory literature are individual cognitive biases that are not specific to any particular context or setting. In contrast, the winner's curse (discussed in Chapters 7 and 8) is specifically generated by the existence of competitive others. I expect that a number of other interesting heuristics and biases are caused by the existence of competitors, hierarchies, and other forms of interaction that are prevalent in organizations. However, the separation between behavior decision theory and organizational behavior has provided a barrier to their discovery.

The Expanded Use of the Social Cognition Literature

The behavioral decision theory literature is often viewed as a subsegment of the field of social cognition. The field of social cognition concerns the exploration of the intuitive cognitive strategies that individuals use to make sense of their interactive world (Nisbett and Ross, 1980). For example, the field of social cognition examines the ways in which individuals attribute cause to particular occurrences, and how these attributions affect subsequent behavior. We see many examples of the use of attribution theory in organizational behavior (e.g., in performance appraisal). However, most of this work takes the form of application. More work needs to be done on how the organizational world interacts to create new ideas that use the disciplinary base of social cognition (some suggestion on the link between social cognition and negotiation are presented in Bazerman and Carroll, 1987).

FINAL COMMENTS

I have argued throughout this book that the behavioral decision theory literature provides an important and underused disciplinary base for organizational behavior. One view of this suggestion is that we need more application from behavioral decision theory to organizational behavior. That is *not* my position. Rather, I argue that the most important advances are going to come from identifying the new conceptual ideas that emanate from the joint consideration of behavioral decision theory and organizational behavior. This suggests that neither organizational behavior nor behavioral decision theory can do it alone. Instead, future advances necessitate coordinated interaction.

My closing messages to the researcher were written to an organizational behavior audience (the targeted audience for the book). However, the suggestions for research clearly called for the intellectual integration *between* behavioral decision theory and organizational behavior. Thus, this set of recommendations is also meant to apply to behavioral decision theorists. To the behavior decison theory audience, I argue that searching for new ideas within the defined boundaries of behavioral decision theory is likely to offer diminishing marginal returns. The identification of new effects by bringing in ideas from outside the field offers new horizons to expand the knowledge and impact of behavioral decision theorists.

These suggestions for future research also have implications for areas other than organizational behavior. We see the ideas of behavioral decision theory moving into other applications (accounting, marketing, medicine). Again, major conceptual contributions will come not from straight applications, but from identifying the unique theoretical questions that are raised by these fields and addressed, but not fully answered, by behavioral decision theory. Again, the intellectual integration between behavioral decison theory and these fields of inquiry offer great potential.

This book outlines directions that may help us better understand a central aspect of organizational life—the decisions of managers. The success of this book is tied to the success of the future interaction between behavioral decision theory and organizational behavior. I hope that this book has helped this interaction at its very early stage of development.

REFERENCES

Adams, J. L. (1979). *Conceptual blockbusting*. San Francisco: San Francisco Book Co.

Adams, J. S. (1963). Toward an understanding of inequity. *Journal of Abnormal and Social Psychology* **67,** 422–436.

Adams, J. S. (1965). Inequity in social exchange. In L. Berkowitz (Ed.), *Advances in experimental social psychology,* Vol. 2. New York: Academic Press.

Alpert, M., and Raiffa, H. (1969). *A progress report on the training of probability assessors.* Unpublished manuscript.

Anderson, B. L. (1977). Differences in teachers' judgmental policies for varying numbers of verbal and numerical uses. *Organizational Behavior and Human Performance* **19,** 68–88.

Argote, L., Seabright, M. A., and Dyer, L. (1986). Individual versus group: Use of base-rate and individuating information. *Organizational Behavior and Human Decision Processes,* in press.

Arkes, H. R., and Blumer, C. (1985). The psychology of sunk costs. *Organizational Behavior and Human Performance* **35,** 124–140.

Aronson, E. (1968). *The social animal.* San Francisco: Freeman.

Bar-Hillel, M. (1973). On the subjective probability of compound events. *Organizational Behavior and Human Performance* **9,** 396–406.

Bartlett, S. (1978). Protocol analysis in creative problem-solving. *Journal of Creative Behavior,* **12,** 181–191.

Bazerman, M. H. (1982). Impact of personal control on performance: Is added control always beneficial? *Journal of Applied Psychology* **67,** 472–479.

Bazerman, M. H. (1983). Negotiator judgment: A critical look at the rationality assumption. *American Behavioral Scientist* **27,** 211–228.

Bazerman, M. H. (1984). The relevance of Kahneman and Tversky's concept of framing to organization behavior. *Journal of Management* **10,** 333–343.

Bazerman, M. H. (1985). Norms of distributive justice in interest arbitration. *Industrial and Labor Relations Review* **38,** 558–570.

Bazerman, M. H., Beekun, R. I., and Schoorman, F. D. (1982). Performance evaluation in a dynamic context: The impact of a prior commitment to the ratee. *Journal of Applied Psychology* **67,** 873–876.

Bazerman, M. H., and Carroll, J. S. (1987). Negotiator cognition. In L. L. Cummings and B. M. Staw (Eds.), *Research in organizational behavior,* Vol. 9. Greenwich, Conn.: JAI Press.

Bazerman, M. H., Giuliano, T., and Appelman, A. (1984). Escalation in individual and group decision making. *Organizational Behavior and Human Performance* **33,** 141–152.

Bazerman, M. H., and Lewicki, R. J. (1983). *Negotiating in organizations.* Beverly Hills, Calif.: Sage.

Bazerman, M. H., Magliozzi, T., and Neale, M. A. (1985). The acquisition of an integrative response in a competitive market. *Organizational Behavior and Human Performance* **34,** 294–313.

Bazerman, M. H., and Neale, M. A. (1982). Improving negotiation effectiveness under final offer arbitration: The role of selection and training. *Journal of Applied Psychology* **67,** 543–548.

Bazerman, M. H., and Neale, M. A. (1983). Heuristics in negotiation: Limitations to dispute resolution effectiveness. In M. H. Bazerman and R. J. Lewicki (Eds.), *Negotiating in organizations.* Beverly Hills, Calif.: Sage.

Bazerman, M. H., and Samuelson, W. F. (1983). I won the auction but don't want the prize. *Journal of Conflict Resolution* **27,** 618–634.

Bazerman, M. H., and Schoorman, F. D. (1983). A limited rationality model of interlocking directorates: An individual, organizational, and societal decision. *Academy of Management Review* **8,** 206–217.

Bazerman, M. H., Schoorman, F. D., and Goodman, P. S. (1980). *A cognitive evaluation of escalation processes in managerial decison making.* Paper presented to 40th Annual Meeting of the Academy of Management, Detroit.

Bernstein, W. M. and Davis, M. H. (1982). Perspective taking, self-consciousness, and accuracy in person perception. *Basic and Applied Social Psychology* **3,** 1–19.

Bowman, E. H. (1963). Consistency and optimality in managerial decision making. *Management Science* **9,** 310–321.

Brandstatter, H., Davis, J. H., and Stocker-Kreichgauer, G. (1982). *Group decision making.* London: Academic Press.

Brockner, J., Nathanson, S., Friend, A., Harbeck, J., Samuelson, C., Houser, R., Bazerman, M. H., and Rubin, J. Z. (1984). The role of modeling processes in the "Knee Deep in the Big Muddy" phenomenon. *Organizational Behavior and Human Performance* **33,** 77–99.

Brockner, J., and Rubin, J. Z. (1985). *Entrapment in escalating conflicts.* New York: Springer-Verlag.

Brockner, J., Rubin, J. Z., Fine, J., Hamilton, T., Thomas, B., and Turetsky, B. (1982). Factors affecting entrapment in escalating conflicts: The importance of timing. *Journal of Research in Personality* **16,** 247–266.

Brockner, J., Rubin, J. Z., and Lang, E. (1981). Face-saving and entrapment. *Journal of Experimental Social Psychology* **17,** 68–79.

Brockner, J., Shaw, M. C., and Rubin, J. Z. (1979). Factors affecting withdrawal from an escalating conflict: Quitting before it's too late. *Journal of Experimental Social Psychology* **15,** 492–503.

Caldwell, D. F., and O'Reilly, C. A. (1982). Responses to failures: The effects of choices and responsibility on impression management. *Academy of Management Journal* **25,** 121–136.

Cambridge, R. M., and Shreckengost, R. C. (1980). Are you sure? The subjective probability assessment test. Unpublished manuscript. Langley, Va.: Office of Training, Central Intelligence Agency.

Campbell, D. T. (1969). Reforms as experiments. *American Psychologist* **24,** 409–429.

Cartwright, D. (1973). Determinants of scientific progress. *American Psychologist* **28,** 222–231.

Case, J. H. (1979). *Economics and the competitive process.* New York: New York University Press.

Chapman, L. J., and Chapman, J. P. (1967). Genesis of popular but erroneous diagnostic observations. *Journal of Abnormal Psychology 72,* 193–204.

Cyert, Richard M., and March, J. G. (1963). *A behavioral theory of the firm.* Englewood Cliffs, N.J.: Prentice-Hall.

Davis, M. S. (1971). That's interesting! *Philosophy of Social Science,* 309–344.

Davis, M. (1981). A multidimensional approach to individual differences in empathy. *JSAS Catalogue of Selected Documents in Psychology* **10,** 85.

Dawes, R. M. (1971). A case study of graduate admissions: Applications of three principles of human decision making. *American Psychologist* **26,** 180–188.

Dawes, R. M. (1979). The robust beauty of improper linear models in decision making. *American Psychologist* **34,** 571–582.

Dawes, R. M., and Corrigan, B. (1974). Linear models in decision making. *Psychological Bulletin* **81,** 95–106.

DeBono, E. (1971). *Lateral thinking.* New York: Harper.

Doise, W. (1969). Intergroup relations and polarization in individual and collective judgments. *Journal of Personality and Social Psychology* **12,** 136–143.

Einhorn, H. J. (1972). Expert measurement and mechanical combination. *Organizational Behavior and Human Performance* **7,** 86–106.

Einhorn, H. J., and Hogarth, R. M. (1978). Confidence in judgment: Persistence in the illusion of validity. *Psychological Review* **85,** 395–416.

Einhorn, H. J., and Hogarth, R. M. (1981). Behavioral decision theory: Processes of judgment and choice. *Annual Review of Psychology* **32,** 53–88.

Farber, H. S. (1981). Splitting-the-difference in interest arbitration. *Industrial and Labor Relations Review* **35,** 70–77.

Feldman, J. M. (1981). Beyond attribution theory: Cognitive processes in performance appraisal. *Journal of Applied Psychology* **66,** 127–148.

Festinger, L. (1957). *A theory of cognitive dissonance.* Evanston, Ill.: Row, Peterson.

Fischhoff, B. (1975a). Hindsight ≠ foresight: The effect of outcome knowledge on judgment under uncertainty. *Journal of Experimental Psychology: Human Perception and Performance* **1,** 288–299.

Fischhoff, B. (1975b). Hindsight: Thinking backward. *Psychology Today* **8,** 71–76.

Fischhoff, B. (1977). Cognitive liabilities and product liability. *Journal of Products Liability* **1,** 207–220.

Fischhoff, B. (1980). For those condemned to study the past: Reflections on historical judgment. In R. A. Shweder and D. W. Fiske (Eds.), *New directions for methodology of behavior science: Fallible judgment in behavioral research.* San Francisco: Jossey-Bass.

Fischhoff, B. (1982). Latitudes and platitudes: How much credit do people deserve? In G. Ungson and D. Braunstein (Eds.), *New directions in decision making,* New York: Kent.

Fischhoff, B., and Beyth, R. (1975). "I knew it would happen":—Remembered probabilities of once-future things. *Organizational Behavior and Human Performance* **13,** 1–16.

Fischhoff, B., Lichtenstein, S., Slovic, P., Derby, S., and Keeney, R. (1981). *Acceptable risk.* New York: Cambridge University Press.

Fischhoff, B., Slovic, P., and Lichtenstein, S. (1977). Knowing with certainty: The appropriateness of extreme confidence. *Journal of Experimental Psychology: Human Perception and Performance* **3,** 552–564.

Fischhoff, B., Slovic, P., and Lichtenstein, S. (1981). Lay foibles and expert fables in judgments about risk. In T. O'Riordan and R. K. Turner (Eds.), *Progress in resource management and environmental planning,* Vol. 3. Chichester: Wiley.

Fisher, R., and Ury, W. (1981). *Getting to yes.* Boston: Houghton Mifflin.

Follett, M. P. (1940). Constructive conflict. In H. C. Metcalf and L. Urwick (Eds.), *Dynamic administration: The collected papers of Mary Parker Follett.* New York: Harper.

Friedman, M. (1957). *A theory of consumption function.* Princeton, N.J.: Princeton University Press.

Friedman, M., and Savage, L. J. (1948). The utility analysis of choices involving risk. *Journal of Political Economy* **56,** 279–304.

Getzel, J. W. (1975). Problem-finding and the inventiveness of solutions. *Journal of Creative Behavior* **9,** 12–18.

Guzzo, R. A. (1982). *Improving group decision making in organizations.* New York: Academic Press.

Harrison, E. F. (1981). *The managerial decision making process,* 2nd ed. Boston:Houghton Mifflin.

Hayes-Roth, F., Waterman, D. A., and Lenat, D. B. (1983). *Building expert systems.* Reading, Mass.: Addison-Wesley.

Hazard, T. H., and Peterson, C. R. (1973). *Odds versus probabilities for categorical events* (Technical report. 73-2). McLean, Va.: Decisions and Designs, Inc.

Heider, F. (1958). *The psychology of interpersonal relations.* New York: Wiley.

Hershey, J. C., and Schoemaker, P. J. H. (1980). Prospect theory's reflection hypothesis: A critical examination. *Organizational Behavior and Human Performance* **3,** 395–418.

Hogarth, R. H. (1981). *Judgment and choice: The psychology of decision.* New York: Wiley.

Holloway, C. (1979). *Decision making under uncertainty: Models and choices.* Englewood Cliffs, N.J.: Prentice-Hall.

Huber, P. (1980). *Managerial decison making.* Glenview, Ill.: Scott, Foresman.

Hughes, E. J. (1978). The presidency versus Jimmy Carter. *Fortune,* December 4, p. 58.

Janis, I. L. (1972). *Victims of groupthink.* Boston: Houghton Mifflin.

Janis, I. L., and Mann, L. (1977). *Decision making.* New York: Free Press.

Joyce, E. J., and Biddle, G. C. (1981). Anchoring and adjustment in probabilistic inference in auditing. *Journal of Accounting Research* **19,** 120–145.

Kahneman, D., Knetsch, J. L., and Thaler, R. (1985). *Perceptions of unfairness.* Conference on the Behavioral Foundations of Economic Theory, University of Chicago.

Kahneman, D., and Tversky, A. (1972). Subjective probability: A judgment of representativeness. *Cognitive Psychology* **3,** 430–454.

Kahneman, D., and Tversky, A. (1973). On the psychology of prediction. *Psychological Review* **80,** 237–251.

Kahneman, D., and Tversky, A. (1979). Prospect theory: An analysis of decision under risk. *Econometrica* **47,** 263–291.

Kahneman, D., and Tversky, A. (1982). Psychology of preferences. *Scientific American,* 161–173.

Keeney, R. L., and Raiffa, H. (1977). *Decisions with decision processes in applied settings.* New York: Academic Press.

Kelly, G. (1954). *The psychology of personal constructs.* New York: Norton.

Kochan, T. (1980). Collective bargaining and organizational behavior research. In B.

Staw and L. Cummings (Eds.). *Research in organizational behavior,* Vol. 2. Greenwich, Conn.: JAI Press.

Kochan, T. A., and Bazerman, M. H. (1986). Macro determinants of the future of the study of negotiation in organizations. In R. J. Lewicki, B. H. Sheppard, and M. H. Bazerman (Eds.), *Research in negotiation in organizations,* Vol. 1. Greenwich, Conn.: JAI Press.

Kochan, T. A., and Jick, T. (1978). A theory of public sector mediation process. *Journal of Conflict Resolution* **22,** 209–240.

Koriat, A., Lichtenstein, S., and Fischhoff, B. (1980). Reasons for confidence. *Journal of Experimental Psychology: Human Learning and Memory* **6,** 107–118.

Kuhn, T. S. (1970). *The structure of scientific revolutions,* 2nd ed. Chicago: University of Chicago Press.

Kunreuther, H., Ginsberg, R., Miller, L., Sagi, P., Slovic, P., Borkan, B., and Katz, N. (1978). *Disaster insurance protection: Public policy lessons.* New York: Wiley.

Lampert, H. (1983). *Till death do us part: Bendix vs. Martin Marietta.* San Diego, Calif.: Harcourt Brace Jovanovich.

Lewicki, R. J. (1980). *Bad loan psychology: Entrapment in financial lending.* Academy of Management Annual Meeting.

Lewicki, R. J., and Litterer, J. A. (1985). *Negotiations.* Homewood, Ill.: Irwin.

Lewicki, R. J., and Sheppard, B. (1985). Choosing how to intervene: Factors affecting the use of process and outcome control in third party dispute resolution. *Journal of Occupational Behavior* **6,** 49–64.

Lewicki, R. J., Sheppard, B. H., and Bazerman, M. H. (1986). *Research in negotiation in organizations,* Vol. 1. Greenwich, Conn.: JAI Press.

Lewin, K. (1947). Group decision and social change. In T. M. Newcomb and E. L. Hartley (Eds.), *Readings in social psychology.* New York: Holt, Rinehart and Winston.

Lichtenstein, S., and Fischhoff, B. (1977). Do those who know more also know more about how much they know? The calibration of probability judgments. *Organizational Behavior and Human Performance* **20,** 159–183.

Lichtenstein, S., and Fischhoff, B. (1980). Training for calibration. *Organizational Behavior and Human Performance* **26,** 149–171.

Lichtenstein, S., Fischhoff, B., and Phillips, L. D. (1982). Calibration of probabilities: State of the art to 1980. In D. Kahneman, P. Slovic, and A. Tversky (Eds.), *Judgment under uncertainty: Heuristics and biases.* New York: Cambridge University Press.

Maier, N. R. F. (1967). Group problem solving. *Psychological Review* **74,** 239–249.

March, J. G., and Simon, H. A. (1958). *Organizations.* New York: Wiley.

Mintzberg, H. (1983). *Power in and around organizations.* Englewood Cliffs, N.J.: Prentice-Hall.

Moscovici, S., and Zavalloni, M. (1969). The group as a polarism of attitudes. *Journal of Personality and Social Psychology* **12,** 125–135.

Murnighan, J. K. (1978). Models of coalition behavior: Game theoretic, social psychological, and political perspectives, *Psychological Bulletin* **85,** 1130–1153.

Murnighan, J. K. (1986). Organizational coalitions: Structural contingencies and the formation process. In R. J. Lewicki, B. H. Sheppard, and M. H. Bazerman (Eds.), *Research in negotiation in organizations,* Vol. 1, Greenwich, Conn.: JAI Press.

Nathanson, S., Brockner, J., Brenner, D., Samuelson, C., Countryman, M., Lloyd, M., and Rubin, J. Z. (1982). Toward the reduction of entrapment. *Journal of Applied Social Psychology* **12,** 193–208.

Naylor, J. C., and Wherry, R. J. (1965). The use of simulated stimuli and the "JAN" technique to capture and cluster the policies of raters. *Educational and Psychological Measurement* **25,** 896–986.

Neale, M. A., and Bazerman, M. H. (1983). The effect of perspective taking ability under alternate forms of arbitration on the negotiation process. *Industrial and Labor Relations Review* **36,** 378–388.

Neale, M. A., and Bazerman, M. H. (1985). Perspectives for understanding negotiation: Viewing negotiation as a judgmental process. *Journal of Conflict Resolution* **29,** 33–55.

Neale, M. A., Bazerman, M. H., Northcraft, G. B., and Alperson, C. A. (1986). "Choice shift" effects in group decisions: A decision bias perspective. *International Journal of Small Group Research,* in press.

Nickerson, R. S., and McGoldrick, C. C. (1965). Confidence ratings and level of performance on a judgmental task. *Perceptual and Motor Skills* **20,** 311–316.

Nisbett, R., and Ross, L. (1980). *Human inference: Strategies and shortcomings of social judgment.* Englewood Cliffs, N.J.: Prentice-Hall.

Northcraft, G. B., and Neale, M. A. (1986). Opportunity costs and the framing of resource allocation decisions. *Organizational Behavior and Human Decision Processes,* in press.

Northcraft, G. B., and Wolf, G. (1984). Dollars, sense, and sunk costs: A life cycle model of resource allocation decisions. *Academy of Management Review* **9,** 225–234.

Pennings, J., and Goodman, P. S. (1977). Towards a workable framework. In P. S. Goodman, J. M. Pennings, *et al. New perspectives on organizational effectiveness.* San Francisco: Jossey-Bass.

Perrow, C. (1984). *Normal accidents.* New York: Basic Books.

Peters, T. J., and Waterman, R. H. (1982). *In search of excellence.* New York: Harper & Row.

Pfeffer, J., and Salancik, G. R. (1978). *The external control of organizations.* New York: Harper & Row.

Pitz, G. F. (1974). Subjective probability distributions for imperfectly known quantities. In L. W. Gregg (Ed.), *Knowledge and cognition,* pp. 29–41. New York: Wiley.

Poise, W. (1969). Intergroup relations and polarization of individual and collective judgments. *Journal of Personality and Social Psychology* **12,** 136–143.

Pruitt, D. G. (1981). *Negotiation behavior.* New York: Academic Press.

Pruitt, D. G. (1983). Integrative agreements: Nature and antecedents. In M. H. Bazerman and R. J. Lewicki (Eds.), *Negotiating in organizations.* Beverly Hills, Calif.: Sage.

Pruitt, D. G., and Rubin, J. Z. (1985). *Social conflict: Escalation, impasse, and resolution.* Reading, Mass.: Addison-Wesley.

Radford, K. J. (1981). *Managerial decision making,* 2nd ed. Reston, Va.: Reston.

Raiffa, H. (1968). *Decision analysis: Introductory lectures on choices under uncertainty.* Reading, Mass.: Addison-Wesley.

Raiffa, H. (1982). *The art and science of negotiation.* Cambridge, Mass.: Harvard University Press.

Rawls, J. *A theory of justice.* (1971). Cambridge, Mass.: Harvard University Press.

Rubin, J. Z. (1980). Experimental research on third party intervention in conflict: Toward some generalizations. *Psychological Bulletin* **87,** 379–391.

Rubin, J. Z. (1983). Negotiation: An introduction to some issues and themes, *American Behavioral Scientist* **27,** 135–147.

Rubin, J. Z., and Brockner, J. (1975). Factors affecting entrapment in waiting situations: The Rosencrantz and Guildenstern effect. *Journal of Personality and Social Psychology* **31,** 1054–1063.

Rubin, J. Z., Brockner, J., Small-Weil, S., and Nathanson, S. (1980). Factors affecting entry into psychological traps. *Journal of Conflict Resolution* **24,** 405–426.

Rubin, J. Z., and Brown, B. (1975). *The social psychology of bargaining and negotiation.* New York: Academic Press.

Samuelson, W. F., and Bazerman, M. H. (1985). Negotiating under the winner's curse. In V. Smith (Ed.), *Research in experimental economics,* Vol. 3. Greenwich, Conn.: JAI Press.

Schoemaker, P. J. H., and Kunreuther, H. (1979). An experimental study of insurance decisions. *Journal of Risk and Insurance* **46,** 603–618.

Schoorman, F. D., Bazerman, M. H., and Atkin, R. S. (1981). Interlocking directorates: A strategy for the management of environmental uncertainty. *Academy of Management Review* **6,** 243–251.

Sheppard, B. H. (1983). Managers as inquisitors: Some lessons from the law. In M. H. Bazerman and R. J. Lewicki (Eds.), *Negotiating in organizations.* Beverly Hills, Calif.: Sage.

Sheppard, B. H. (1984). Third party intervention: A procedural framework. In B. M. Staw and L. L. Cummings (Eds.), *Research in Organizational Behavior,* Vol. 6. Greenwich, Conn.: JAI Press.

Shubik, M. (1971). The dollar auction game: A paradox in noncooperative behavior and escalation. *Journal of Conflict Resolution* **15,** 109–111.

Shull, F. A., Delbelq, A. L., and Cummings, L. L. (1970). *Organizational decision making.* New York: McGraw-Hill.

Siegal, S., and Fouraker, L. E. (1960). *Bargaining and group decision making: Experiments in bilateral monopoly.* New York: McGraw-Hill.

Siegal, S. (1957). Level of aspiration and decison making. *Psychological Review* **64,** 253–262.

Simon, H. A. (1957). *Models of Man.* New York: Wiley.

Slovic, P. (1972). Information processing, situation specificity, and the generality of risk-taking behavior. *Journal of Personality and Social Psychology* **22,** 128–134.

Slovic, P. (1982). Toward understanding and improving decisions. In W. C. Howell and E. A. Fleishman (Eds.), *Human performance and productivity;* Vol. 2, *Information processing and decision making.* Hillsdale, N.J.: Erlbaum.

Slovic, P., and Fischhoff, B. (1977). On the psychology of experimental surprises. *Journal of Experimental Psychology: Human Perception and Performance* **3,** 544–551.

Slovic, P., Fischhoff, B., and Lichtenstein, S. (1978). Accident probabilities and seat belt usage: A psychological perspective. *Accident Analysis and Prevention* **10,** 281–285.

Slovic, P., Fischhoff, B., and Lichtenstein, S. (1982). Response mode, framing, and information processing effects in risk assessment. In R. M. Hogarth (Ed.), *New directions for methodology of social and behavioral science: The framing of questions and the consistency of response.* San Francisco: Jossey-Bass.

Slovic, P., and Lichtenstein, S. (1971). Comparison of Bayesian and regression approaches in the study of information processing in judgment. *Organizational Behavior and Human Performance* **6,** 649–744.

Slovic, P., Lichtenstein, S., and Fischhoff, B. (1979). Images of disaster: Perception and acceptance of risks from nuclear power. In G. Goodman and W. Rowe (Eds.), *Energy risk management.* London: Academic Press.

Slovic, P., Lichtenstein, S., and Fischhoff, B. (1982). Characterizing perceived risk. In R. W. Kataes and C. Hohenemser (Eds.), *Technological hazard management.* Cambridge, Mass.: Oelgeschlager, Gunn & Hain.

Starke, F. A., and Notz, W. W. (1981). Pre- and post-intervention effects of conventional vs. final offer arbitration. *Academy of Management Journal* **24,** 832–850.

Staw, B. M. (1976). Knee-deep in the big muddy: A study of escalating commitment to a chosen course of action. *Organizational Behavior and Human Performance* **16,** 27–44.

Staw, B. M. (1980). Rationality and justification in organizational life. In B. M. Staw and L. L. Cummings (Eds.), *Research in organizational behavior,* Vol. 2. Greenwich, Conn.: JAI Press.

Staw, B. M. (1981). The escalation of commitment to a course of action. *Academy of Management Review* **6,** 577–587.

Staw, B. M., and Ross, J. (1978). Commitment to a policy decision: A multitheoretical perspective. *Administrative Science Quarterly* **23,** 40–64.

Staw, B. M., and Ross, J. (1980). Commitment in an experimenting society: An experiment on the attribution of leadership from administrative scenarios. *Journal of Applied Psychology* **65,** 249–260.

Steiner, I. D. (1972). *Group process and productivity.* New York: Academic Press.

Stoner, J. A. F. (1961). *A comparison of individual and group decisions involving risk.* Unpublished Master's thesis, Massachusetts Institute of Technology, School of Industrial Management.

Strickland, L. (1958). Surveillance and trust. *Journal of Personality* **26,** 200–215.

Stumpf, S. A., and London, M. (1981). Capturing rater policies in evaluating candidates for promotion. *Academy of Management Journal* **24,** 752–766.

Swalm, R. O. (1966). Utility theory—insights into risk taking. *Harvard Business Review* **44,** 123–136.

Taylor, R. N. (1984). *Behavioral decision making.* Glenview, Ill.: Scott Foresman.

Teger, A. I. (1980). *Too much invested to quit.* New York: Pergamon.

Thaler, R. (1980). Toward a positive theory of consumer choice. *Journal of Economic Behavior and Organization* **1,** 39–80.

Thaler, R. (1985). Using mental accounting in a theory of purchasing behavior. *Marketing Science,* 12–13.

Thibaut, J. W., and Walker, L. (1975). *Procedural justice: A psychological perspective.* Hillsdale, N.J.: Erlbaum.

Thompson, J. (1967). *Organizations in action.* New York: McGraw-Hill.

Tversky, A., and Kahneman, D. (1971). The belief in the "law of numbers." *Psychological Bulletin* **76,** 105–110.

Tversky, A., and Kahneman, D. (1973). Availability: A heuristic for judging frequency and probability. *Cognitive Psychology* **5,** 207–232.

Tversky, A., and Kahneman, D. (1974). Judgment under uncertainty: Heuristics and biases. *Science* **185,** 1124–1131.

Tversky, A., and Kahneman, D. (1981). The framing of decisions and the psychology of choice. *Science* **211,** 453–463.

Tversky, A., and Kahneman, D. (1983). Extensional versus intuitive reasoning: The conjunction fallacy in probability judgment. *Psychological Review* **90,** 293–315.

Vinoker, A. (1971) Review and theoretical analysis of the effects of group processes upon individual and group decisions involving risk. *Psychological Bulletin* **76,** 234–250.

Wall Street Journal (1981). To win a bidding war doesn't insure success of merged companies. September a, p. 1.

Wallas, G. (1926). *The art of thought.* New York: Harcourt, 1926.

Walton, R. E., and McKersie, R. B. (1965). *A behavioral theory of labor negotiations: An analysis of a social interaction system.* New York: McGraw-Hill.

Wason, P. C. (1960). On the failure to eliminate hypotheses in a conceptual task. *Quarterly Journal of Experimental Psychology* **12,** 129–140.

Wason, P. C. (1968a). Reason about a rule. *Quarterly Journal of Experimental Psychology* **20,** 273–283.

Wason, P. C. (1968b). On the failure to eliminate hypothesis . . . A second look. In P. C. Wason and P. N. Johnson-Laird (Eds.), *Thinking and reasoning.* Harmandsworth: Penguin.

Weber, M. (1949). *The methodology of the social sciences.* New York: Free Press.

Winklegren, W. A. (1974). *How to solve problems.* San Francisco: Freeman.

Wood, G. (1978). The knew-it-all-along effect. *Journal of Experimental Psychology: Human Perception and Performance* **4,** 345–353.

Zedeck, S. (1977). An information processing model and approach in the study of motivation. *Organizational Behavior and Human Performance* **18,** 47–77.

Zedeck, S., and Kafry, D. (1977). Capturing rater policies for processing evaluation data. *Organizational Behavior and Human Performance* **18,** 269–294.

INDEX